MAVERICK

For Brenda, Ivan, Linda, Shaun,
Carol, Darren, Duncan and Ryan

The Life of a Union Rebel

ERIC
HAMMOND

Weidenfeld and Nicolson
London

First published in Great Britain in 1992 by
George Weidenfeld and Nicolson Limited
91 Clapham High Street, London SW4 7TA

British Library Cataloguing-in-Publication Data
is available on request

ISBN 0 297 81200 9

Printed and bound in Great Britain by
Butler & Tanner Ltd
Frome and London

Contents

Acknowledgements

I am indebted to my friend and collaborator Christopher Leake, without whose work and constant prodding this book would not yet have been written.

Illustrations

vii

Illustrations

Norman Willis, on the record, 1988 (*Daily Record*)
Norman Willis at the EETPU Conference in 1987
Norman Willis takes it to the vote, September 1988 (*Today*)
With Norman in happier times
In joint harness with Frank Chapple
Tom Beckett, President, and Eric, then General Secretary elect, saying goodbye to Frank Chapple, General Secretary, at the 1983 EETPU Conference
On to the twenty-first century (April 1988, *Express*)
Buxted Park, the union's unique and historic country house hotel and management training and conference centre: Eric inspects the 312–acre estate for TUC infiltrators!
Eric with AEU President Bill Jordan as merger looms between EETPU and AEU
Eric and his successor, Paul Gallagher
At the EETPU Conference, 1991
Difficulties with the public address system

Unless otherwise indicated, all photographs are the author's

Abbreviations

ACAS	Advisory, Conciliation and Arbitration Service
ACTT	Association of Cinematographic & Television Technicians
AEU	Amalgamated Engineering Union (formerly AUEW)
APEX	Association of Professional, Executive & Clerical Staff
ASLEF	Association of Locomotive Engineers & Firemen
ASTMS	Association of Scientific, Technical & Managerial Staffs
AUEW	Amalgamated Union of Engineering Workers
AUEW(E)	Amalgamated Union of Engineering Workers (Engineering Section)
AUEW(C)	Amalgamated Union of Engineering Workers (Construction Section)
BALPA	British Airline Pilots Association
CEGB	Central Electricity Generating Board
CPSA	Civil and Public Services Association
EETPU	Electrical, Electronic, Telecommunication & Plumbing Union
EMA	Engineers & Managers Association
EPEA	Electrical Power Engineers Association
EPIU	Electrical & Plumbing Industries Union
ETU	Electrical Trades Union
GMBATU	General, Municipal, Boilermakers & Allied Trades Union (previously GMWU, later GMBU)
GMWU	General & Municipal Workers Union
IPCS	Institution of Professional Civil Servants
ISTC	Iron & Steel Trades Confederation
IRSA	Inland Revenue Staff Association
JIB	Joint Industry Board
MSFU	Manufacturing, Science & Finance Union
NEC	National Executive Committee
NECC	National Engineering Craftsmen's Committee

Abbreviations

NGA	National Graphical Association
NUM	National Union of Mineworkers
NUPE	National Union of Public Employees
NUR	National Union of Railwaymen
SOGAT	Society of Graphical & Allied Trades
TASS	Technical & Supervisory Section (of the AUEW)
TGWU	Transport & General Workers Union
TICA	Thermal Insulation Contractors Association
UCATT	Union of Construction, Allied Trades & Technicians
UCAW	Union of Construction & Allied Workers
UDM	Union of Democratic Mineworkers
USDAW	Union of Shop, Distribution & Allied Workers

1

From Kent to Canada:
the early years

There is no plaque over the door of 42, York Road, Northfleet, Kent, to mark the birth on 17 July 1929 of Eric Albert Barratt-Hammond – nor will there be. But humble though it was, it was my happy childhood home. I know it's *de rigueur* these days for union leaders to claim modest roots, but I really was born in a two-up, two-down complete with outside toilet and tin bath in the kitchen. My father, Arthur, was a labourer at the local Bowater's paper mill and had been gassed while serving with the East Surreys as a machine-gunner, a trench soldier in the Great War. By 1919, he had been registered as one hundred per cent disabled and suffered with debilitating lung problems and a constant cough and bronchitis for the rest of his life. Mum, Gertrude, was a local girl who had lived with her parents just round the corner in Tooley Street. Some of my earliest memories are of the tin bath on top of the kitchen table in front of a metal range and my mother sweating over the mangle on wash day. It put me off wash days, because of my mother working so hard.

I was the middle one of three children. My elder brother, Ken, was invalided out of the army in 1943 during basic training. Then he became a Regular in the RAF and did twenty-two years service as an airman. Ken saw the world, but tragically died in his early forties, not long after retiring from the RAF. He was a smart-looking bachelor with everything to live for, but in just three months he lost the power to walk or speak and aged fifty years in as many days. He had been involved in the Christmas Island nuclear experiments in the Pacific and, even though controversy about the effect on individuals continues, I am convinced he died as a direct result.

Kids have funny but rational ways of thinking. As a young boy, I used to think all grown-ups were called Arthur. That was my father's

1

name and the next-door neighbour was called Arthur, too – therefore, all adult males were Arthur. Little did I realize how much trouble a man called Arthur – Scargill, that is – was to cause me in later life, a life I will describe, not year on year but more the way I have brought influence to bear on events along its path.

Boyhood in the Thirties in working-class Britain was still lived in the shadow of the Great War. Our fathers fought in France; there were widows in abundance and legless and armless men in every street. Our games were of war, our heroes were soldiers. The virtues we admired were those of steadfastness and courage. That early influence has stayed with me all my life and, although others have described me as brave, the one thing I fear most in any situation is to be considered a coward.

My father lived until he was sixty-three – remarkable really, considering his persistent breathing difficulties, but he was a tough old soldier and lasted through a number of false alarms before the end. Three years before he died my mother called me round. He was having a bad breathing attack and it appeared he would not last the night. I stayed at my parents' home that night just in case. They had moved by then to a council house at 8, The Crescent, Northfleet, with the luxury of an inside bathroom, toilet and a garden.

Dad was so bad that I thought, I can't allow him to go through this agony. My mother had nodded off through exhaustion. A conflict of duties arose and I debated in my mind my obligation to my father: should I passively observe his pain or take action to end it? No one would have been the wiser. I felt I had to do it as a duty rather than see him suffer. In the end I did nothing and he had three more years of relative happiness. He wasn't in pain during that final period and I have often thought since, when people have put forward arguments in favour of euthanasia, that sometimes the pressure is on relatives or friends of a sick person who feel uncomfortable with themselves. There was I, thinking of myself rather than anyone else. I am relieved I decided not to play God.

My father had always been a First Aid enthusiast. Though he would never talk in detail about his time in the trenches, I am sure it came from his experiences at the front. He was a keen member of the St John's Ambulance Brigade, latterly as a divisional superintendent. Our house had the best collection of bandages, splints and creams in the area. Dad kept it all in a big medical box and would act as what the Chinese call a 'barefoot doctor', giving instant medical treatment. He treated anything from grazes to broken bones. Given different times and opportunities, he would have made a great GP.

School was St Botolph's Church of England at Northfleet. It was there I gained my lifelong love of gardening: I still relax on my allotment. The vicarage at St Botolph's had extensive gardens and the boys at the school were given plots to work. Most of us didn't have a garden of our own, so to be given seeds and a tool shed to use was bliss. But boys will be boys. More by accident than design, I was sent for a haircut one day and missed a raid my friends made on the vicar's orchard. The boys were caught by the headmaster. I felt rather deprived on the Monday morning when each of the miscreants was lined up for a thrashing: I thought I should be part of it. But my turn would soon come for a caning. It was administered by a teacher called 'Dolly' Allen, who was anything but a dolly. She was very free with the cane and seemed to enjoy using it. We had graduated by the time we were eight from pencil to pen and ink, using the old-fashioned inkwells, and I kept getting large inkblots on my work. I received six of the best on each hand. I was baffled by the blots until I realized they were being flicked there by the boy next to me, Wally Peck. He was getting rid of his surplus ink by flicking it on to my book. I couldn't snitch on Wally, but I made it clear he was not going to put any more ink in my direction.

Even at that tender age, I realized that security came from teaming up with the smartest and the strongest – collective action. It was the best way of containing the bullies in the outfit. In later life, it became a necessity against some of the more extreme elements in the trade union movement who are not averse to physical intimidation if other forms of persuasion fail.

My early boyhood was spent as a member of one of the many gangs who fought mock wars in the abandoned chalk pits around North-fleet. The pits had been dug since the nineteenth century in order to make cement, but had now grown over with trees and blackberries. They had become a wilderness. Acres of unspoilt countryside made up these pits – tunnels and caves hewn from the chalk – where our gangs used to fight with catapults and bows and arrows. After seeing Buck Jones cowboy films on Saturday afternoons, we would mount raids on the chalk trains and be chased away by the men running them. One of the pits was flooded, and we learned to swim there and build rafts. It was a freewheeling childhood: parents now would not let their children play in such an untamed area.

3

When the Second World War broke out, our school only had teachers for two half-days each week. I took the selection exam for the Eleven-Plus and passed, and I waltzed through the Gravesend Grammar School entry exam, too. The problem came when I took the oral test. Although it was seen by some as a 'social screening' test, I could not complain for I blew it before the headmaster. Headmasters had terrified me since I was asked to take a message at the age of seven to the head at my old school. I forgot to take off my cap, and received a belt on the side of the ear which sent me spinning into the corner of his room. Thereafter, I had a fear of headmasters, which still leaves me with a residual wariness when I deal with them. So when I was asked by the grammar school head what was wrong with a series of multiple choice pictures, I stared rigidly ahead ignoring the pictures and said, 'Nothing, sir.' I was not selected for the grammar school. The irony is that I am now a governor there.

But for the war, I would have gone to a secondary modern; instead, my father asked me if I wanted to be evacuated to Newfoundland. Bowater's, with whom my father was now head timekeeper, had factories at Northfleet, Sittingbourne and Merseyside. The company had also built what amounted to a paper mill town in Newfoundland, and the people there offered to look after the firm's British children for the duration of the war. Volunteers were sought to sail to Canada on the Bowater paper ships, which had limited passenger accommodation. From all the hundreds eligible, I was the only child from Northfleet who said yes.

I was gardening with my father when he asked me. It was early 1940 and I was ten. My mind was full of storybooks like the *Wizard*, the *Rover* and *Hotspur*. There were characters like Strang the Terrible and a special agent called Wolf of Kabul. There were tales of Mounties, canoes, cowboys and Indians. The other world which boys inhabit was made of such stories which we acted out in our chalk-pit playgrounds, so when I got the chance of a real-life adventure, the joyous response was, 'Yes, please, Dad.' It took him back a bit. He was a quiet man and I think he was surprised at my enthusiasm.

I ran to the house to tell my mother and dashed into the kitchen shouting, 'Mum, I'm going to Canada.' The effect on her was dramatic. She literally went white-haired in a matter of weeks with the worry of me going so far away. I can only understand the anguish felt by my parents since I have become a parent myself. Here they were with England on the verge of an invasion, or so they thought at the time, with Hitler overrunning Europe like a juggernaut. My elder brother was fourteen and itching to join up the moment he could and my sister was too young to leave home, so I suppose my parents must have thought it better one of us was safe across the Atlantic than none at all. As I have told friends jokingly since, I was chosen to be evacuated by Churchill as Britain's best – the seedcorn – just in case things went wrong and he needed to call us back to start all over again.

Accordingly on 10 August 1940 I boarded a train from London, Euston to Liverpool, at the start of my great wartime adventure. It was lucky I went that day, because had I been taking the usual route to school on my trusty metal scooter, I could well have been blown to bits during a particularly violent daytime air raid. The Germans strafed a road called Waterdales with machine-gun fire. You can still see the bullet holes on the walls to this day. Instead, my father took me up to Euston where he handed me over to Nurse Hogarth, a formidable but kind Australian lady who took charge of me and a dozen children from Bowater's Sittingbourne plant. Nurse Hogarth sailed with us all the way to Newfoundland.

We had to wait in Liverpool for three days on the *SS Corner Brook* before we embarked on what was to be a month-long voyage. There were air raids on Liverpool before we left and a number of ships in our convoy were torpedoed as we sailed to our new homes across the Atlantic. The crew treated us royally. At home, we always had something to eat, if only bread and jam, but because of our circumstances, it wasn't always enough to satisfy a growing lad's appetite. To be presented with the amount and quality of food we got on board was like entering an Aladdin's cave of delights. You could have more if you wanted, and there was bacon every morning for breakfast. At home, it was only birthdays and Christmas when you might get a whiff of that.

The last thing my mother had pressed into my hand as I left home was a packet of home-made ham sandwiches wrapped in greaseproof paper. I had seldom had ham in my life. The old working-class attitude was that the breadwinner was fed as well as could be, so my father was normally the only one to get such things. Everything was rationed, so my mother must have given up God knows how many points to get the ham, but as soon as we boarded the train at Euston, everything was provided. Two days later, at anchor in Merseyside, I realized I still had the sandwiches in my bag; they were stale if not moving by then and I threw the packet into the water. I can't eat a ham sandwich now without a twinge of guilt remembering my gentle mother's unspoken fears and pain.

The sailors had a couple of puppies, so that took our minds off everything. We spent hours tickling them and running around, forgetting most of the time we could fall victim to a German torpedo at any moment. I shared a cabin with Len Holloway. He was fourteen and we got on pretty well. Len stayed in Newfoundland after the war. Even though the tradition there was that everyone volunteered for the Forces when they were eighteen, Len didn't bother. He was away from Britain, so avoided conscription. He worked in Newfoundland instead and has since retired there. In the narrow, black-and-white world of the young, I judged him pretty harshly for failing to volunteer.

I was the only child who was not sick during the voyage. This was a great advantage, because it meant I could eat my fellow evacuees' food as well. I was a very slim lad when I left Liverpool, but had acquired a few pounds by the time we got to the other side.

When we reached Halifax, Nova Scotia, we were fêted by the local people. They took us for a motor boat ride on a lake: it was like a wonderland. We were each given five dollars, which, at the rate of exchange then prevailing, was worth about a pound! For one dollar and sixty cents, I bought my first camera – a Baby Brownie using 127 film. Thus began a love of photography that stays with me still.

Our reception in Nova Scotia prepared us for our wartime adoption by local families in Corner Brook, West Newfoundland. Of course, we children were apprehensive and fearful – would we be chosen? Working-class children weren't full of confidence, and I was basically shy and reserved. But the homes we were to go to had been determined well in advance, and I couldn't have been luckier. Elsie Nichols, a matronly lady, gave me a warm smile as I was introduced, and I knew immediately all was well. Her husband, Warren, was to become my hero. He went fishing, shooting and hunting. He was one of those people who could have done almost anything had he set his mind to it. We decided that I should call them Auntie Elsie and Uncle Warren, rather than Mum and Dad. They had five children: Gladys, who was married; Joyce, who lived at home and worked locally; Duncan, seventeen, who joined the Canadian Army a year later; Kitty, thirteen, and Bert, eight. And there was Edna Hanson, Joyce's Norwegian friend, who was like another big sister to me, and part of the family.

Edna and I still send Christmas cards to each other as do all the surviving brothers and sisters. Edna and Joyce bought Bert and me the best presents we could have hoped for the first Christmas I was out there – Daisy air rifles, known as BB guns. We had campaigned with a ruthlessness known only to boys and hardly deserved the kindness of our big sisters.

Although Duncan was away for most of my stay in Newfoundland, he was also very much a heroic figure to me. He came over to England with the Canadian Army and spent some of his leaves with my family. He survived the invasion of Europe and the subsequent campaign through France. Everyone I met in Corner Brook and Nicholsville had good words for Duncan. He was a model whose step and shadow were hard to match. Duncan had been named after his uncle, Warren's brother, who had been killed in France in the Great War serving with the Newfoundland Regiment. In all the terrible carnage of famous regiments at the Battle of the Somme, the Newfound-landers suffered the highest number of casualties. The day after the battle opened on 1 July 1916, only a handful of survivors answered their names at roll-call. The population then of Newfoundland could not have been more than 200,000 and practically every family was in mourning. In the light of this widespread suffering in such a small community, the island's regiment was subsequently made an artillery unit.

In 1990, fifty years on, I wrote to the West Newfoundland newspaper, *The Western Star*, to thank the local community for the shelter they had given me in those hazardous years. I wrote:

Fifty years ago, a group of English children left Merseyside to cross the Atlantic on the *SS Corner Brook*. I was one of those children.

Our families in Southern England had experienced the beginning of Hitler's Blitz; indeed, Liverpool was bombed while we waited to depart. Parents, worried by what was to come, including the prospect of invasion, decided to accept the generous invitation of Corner Brook families. That invitation from Bowater employees in Corner Brook to Bowater United Kingdom employees assured them that English children would be safe in Newfoundland in their care.

I spent five years with Warren Nichols' family – happy and proud years – never more so than when Duncan introduced me as his brother! I owe the family more than I can say. But my purpose in writing this letter is not to publicly acknowledge that fact but rather, through your publication, to recall that tiny fragment of World War II.

War brings tragedy and loss to many people and there are few redeeming features. But here and there the decency and kindness shine through the shadows of conflict. The warm welcome we were given, not only by our 'new' families but by the whole West Newfoundland community, must surely count on the side of man's humanity to man amongst all that inhumanity.

I have never forgotten the people of Corner Brook, Nicholsville and Deer Lake. Across those fifty years, I remember that frightened boy of ten who lost his fears among you. On his behalf, I salute and thank you.

My wife, Brenda, and I have visited Duncan and his wife, Mabel, several times in Nicholsville where they now live. For me it is always like coming home, but their warmth and hospitality quickly won Brenda to share my love of the Nichols and of Newfoundland.

I immediately took to their schooling system and did very well. Every Christmas, Easter and the end of the school year in June, there were written exams in every subject. If you failed to pass at the end of the year, you were kept down until next time. It meant that each grade included children who could be three years older than others in the same class.

The Nichols' home was a large wooden detached house with substantial gardens – a far cry from York Road, Northfleet. Uncle Warren was superintendent of the Woods Department in West Newfoundland, and the foremost authority on the regional environment. His grandfather was one of the original settlers who came over from Nova Scotia to cut pinewood for shipbuilding. The settlement he founded thirty miles up the Humber River was called Nicholsville, where Uncle Warren had a second home and farm beside the river.

A recent history described the area thus:

. . . untouched wilderness; an abundance of wildlife and huge stretches of pine that today's loggers would call paradise. In the late nineteenth century, this was the view pioneers had of the Humber River area just above Deer Lake. It was inevitable that someone would brave the elements and try to settle this untamed region. George Aaron Nichols was the first to take advantage of the wealth the area had to offer. He was a pioneer in the true sense of the word.

He arrived in Newfoundland with his wife Harriet, née Widdon, a trained nurse by profession, and their two sons – George Aaron junior and John.

They spent their first winter at Humbermouth and in the spring of 1868 travelled up river about thirty miles to what is now called Nicholsville. Initially, Mr Nichols came to cut the huge pine in the area but soon realized the vast potential of this place and decided to take squatters' rights on the land. He set up permanent residence on the north side of the river and in 1870, received a grant for his land from the government. The place provided everything essential a newcomer could need. The soil was rich and fertile which made excellent farmland, an abundance of pine and other trees provided wood, both for sale and for building materials. The vast wilderness provided a seemingly endless supply of wildlife, food and furs as well as a large variety of wild berries. The Humber river was teeming with fish and provided a transportation route for both the settled areas and the remainder of the hinterland.

The Nichols family made use of all these resources and, coupled with their own instinctive capabilities, became as self-sufficient as any family or group could ever hope to be. They made their own soap, butter and clothing; they raised some domestic animals for meat, wool and eggs; they collected berries, trapped game for fur, fished, hunted for any extra meat needed. The numerous caribou in the area provided any additional meat needed, along with rabbit, partridges and other small game. Mr Nichols made his living by combining several of his talents. He cut the huge pine in the area to sell at the mill at Corner Brook. He trapped small game during the winter months for their furs and, with his vast knowledge of the area, he served as a guide for many a tourist.

His talent for guiding carried over to his sons and grandsons. In the tradition of George Airon senior, they continued to take tourists on fishing and hunting excursions for many years. The expedition sometimes included well-known people such as United States President, Franklin D. Roosevelt.

After leading a rich life filled with hard, honest work, George Aaron Nichols died tragically when a tree fell on him in 1911. Part of his obituary, written by the Rev J. M. Allen, said:

Mr Nichols was no ordinary man; a born pioneer, tall, lithe, alert with a long black beard and moustache; an eye denoting unlimited pluck and energy, though none who'd ever enjoyed – how many have – his company and his hospitable home, will ever forget the kindly twinkle in his eye.

It was a lovely Sunday afternoon as we laid him to rest in the sweet plot where some of his children already lie. There was quite a gathering from along the lake and river to pay their respects to one who all liked and all feel they shall not see the like again.

Warren Nichols was very much in the mould of his grandfather.

We spent weekends and most of the summer at Nicholsville. I loved it. Berry picking, tending the vegetables, haymaking, fishing and swimming filled our days. On the home farm was Warren's mother, 'Grammie' Nichols, two younger brothers, John and George, and sisters Eva and Dorothy. Grammie was a wonderful lady who was expected to have, and usually did have, the answer to everyone's problems – a true matriarch, leading that little community. In August, a host of grandchildren, including myself, helped John and George 'make' the hay. If you worked especially hard, Grammie would invite you into her lounge at the rear of the house to listen to her battery-powered radio; if you were really consistently diligent, she would knit you a sweater. Such accolades . . . such recognition . . . meant more to us boys than medals.

John and George were like elder brothers to us, though I have said since that if we boys could have elected a father, John would have come top of the poll. With them we learnt the ways of the woods, as we looked for the cows, that had wandered miles up the river, to milk in the evening. When autumn came we put out snares to catch rabbits. Uncle Warren would go off to hunt moose, which would end up in a locker hired in a large communal deep-freeze. He would keep a couple of pigs in summer and slaughter them.

I fished for trout with a worm on the end of a hook, with a line tied to a stick cut from the nearest alder bush. My first salmon was a twelve-pounder that I jigged as it passed when I was fishing for trout: the hook caught it by the tail. The great salmon could not use its strength, otherwise it would have surely broken the line. When I landed the salmon, it wriggled around so much I couldn't control it. Bert, who was three years younger than me, whacked it over the head, and we had salmon for supper. To me, this life was like paradise.

We went regularly as a family to the United Church of Canada, which includes the Methodists amongst others. It was surprising how quickly we 'Limeys' were accepted by the locals, who were soon hearing how we had endured German bombing raids we had, in fact, never been through. I joined the Scouts and became a patrol leader. It was a great area to go hiking and camping. I was a bit of a swot at school: I always came first in class exams. In one exam, I got four one hundred per cent marks in Arithmetic, Algebra, Geometry and Physics. I liked sport, but never excelled at it. I was keen on ice hockey, but not being an accomplished skater, I ended up in goal having to deal with that hard puck. I decided to set my mind to learning!

I had a very lucky war. I was taken into a family who treated me as one of their own and I was thousands of miles away from the bombing raids which pounded the Home Counties. But, like all boys, I wasn't perfect. One wet day, a few of us wrestled on the front lawn, which was Uncle Warren's pride and joy. By the time we had finished, it was torn to pieces and churned up like a ploughed field. Warren didn't say a word to me, but Auntie Elsie made me feel considerable remorse. She told me, 'If you were his son, he would have given you a good hiding.' I felt that cruelly and would have preferred the 'hiding'.

Warren Nichols knew all there was to know about the great outdoors. I remember once he took a canoe up river to hunt for moose. He had an old Lee Enfield 303 army rifle and took just two bullets. There was confidence for you. Naturally, he came back with a moose, which he butchered on the spot ready for the freezer. Nothing was wasted. Uncle Warren skinned the moose as well. A moose-skin rug was the first thing I stepped on when I got out of bed.

This idyll could not last for ever: the war in Europe ended in May 1945. I remember running down the road singing that I was going home without realizing what that meant. Newfoundland had become my home and my family. I had kept in touch with my parents by letter, but I have always been poor at corresponding and it was only pressure from the Nichols family which kept the letters intermittently flowing. By then, I was sixteen having left Kent at ten. I was doing well at school and looking forward to going on to college when, suddenly, my life was turned upside down once more.

It was just before that summer's High School exams and I had gone to the Nichols' farm at Nicholsville to do a bit of studying. One day the telephone rang with news that I had to go to St John's across country

11

the next day. Uncle Warren was due to go to St John's that morning anyway, so we went together. I had less than a day to say goodbye and thank everyone for five years of my life. I thought at one stage of taking to the woods and hiding so the call to return home would somehow disappear. I had become a different person, with a new family and friends, so it was with a heavy heart that I boarded a cargo ship at St John's and shook hands with Uncle Warren.

On board was a DEMS (Defensively Equipped Merchant Ship) unit made up of Royal Artillery and Royal Navy gunners. They took me under their wing, gave me an army uniform and let me shoot at mines. As we docked at Sheerness, I was shinning up a rope ladder from our mess when one of the gunners shouted, 'Eric, your dad's here.' My dad wasn't a very big man, only about five foot six inches tall, so he looked astounded when he saw this strapping six-footer coming towards him. He said, 'God, you've grown.' My father looked a lot older; his ill health and the war had combined to age both my parents.

I was back home, back to a different reality. Warren Nichols wrote to my father soon after, requesting my return in order to continue my education. Much as I wanted to go, I could not face the pain it would give my mother. Instead, I followed my father into Bowater's and became an apprentice electrical fitter. My union career was about to begin.

2

The fools of Treasure Island

If ever Mrs Thatcher had needed a reason to impose restrictive legislation on trade unions, then the Isle of Grain laggers' dispute provided all the ammunition she needed. Twenty-seven grossly overpaid semi-skilled laggers, who insulated pipes and boilers, held a £580-million project to ransom, caused one of the biggest splits in the British trade union movement and shamed the TUC with sickening picket-line violence.

I knew the massive Isle of Grain refinery more than twenty-five years before the laggers' dispute erupted in August 1979. The North Kent site on the Thames estuary was known as Treasure Island because of the high wages paid there. All the worst examples of trade union abuse were rife, so I suppose it was inevitable these shameful practices could not go on for ever.

My first job in the construction industry was at the Isle of Grain, building the BP oil refinery. I was one of 8,000 construction workers. Even in the early 1950s, the money was good and it was not long before these lucrative earnings enabled me to marry my wife, Brenda. After our honeymoon in Bournemouth, I returned to work at the site. At the tender age of twenty-three I was immediately elected shop steward.

I became a steward almost by default. While I was honeymooning on the south coast, a row about a wage claim led to an overtime ban. The management of George Wimpey said they were not having it, and they persuaded our union officials to lift the ban with the permission of the shop stewards. But our union rule book says you cannot change a decision of the shop or section without having another meeting of that shop. The members are supposed to decide, not the officials or the shop stewards, so, on the very Monday morning I came back in

13

October 1954, the previous shop steward was removed. The members were divided and I was the only one 'clean' of the overtime issue. I replaced the shop steward and found myself in charge of 500 'sparks' as a full-time shop steward. I never looked back after that. Later, I was to become convener of the whole site, the Norman Willis of the Isle of Grain – but not quite as substantial as Norman. I was a very spare lad in those days.

The place was pulsating with walkouts, strikes, leapfrogging wage claims – the ultimate recipe for disaster. The Communist Party was so well organized there that it had an Isle of Grain branch. The one unorganized group was McAlpine's. The Transport and General Workers' Union tried to organize them. The Communist Party attempted to 'educate' this largely Irish workforce. Strangely, McAlpine's used a Roman Catholic priest as their welfare officer in lieu of shop stewards. The rest of us could not get a look in.

One day, the Communist Party decided to have a bread, wages and Socialism type of meeting in the canteen for the McAlpine men. The Irishmen packed the hall. In the front row was the priest. Beside him were his most stalwart parishioners – with hurley sticks! The Communists, many of them members of the EETPU, were brave men indeed for they continued with the meeting unabashed. Immediately they started, the priest jumped up and said, 'What about Cardinal Mindszenty?' This was the Hungarian Primate who was being persecuted by Eastern-bloc Communists at the time. There was uproar. The cry was taken up by the audience, then a crowd of club-swinging Irishmen rushed the platform. The Paddies were furious at the Communists trying to lecture them while this hero of a priest was being persecuted in Hungary. The Commies weren't hanging around for a beating so they jumped on to a jeep and shot off the Isle of Grain at high speed. To their credit, they were back in the canteen the next day, selling the *Daily Worker*.

Shortly afterwards, Danny Cremen, a Transport and General Workers' Union shop steward, who was a good friend of mine, brought an Irish newspaper on to the site. Describing the lucky escape of the Communists from the Grain, the banner headline read, 'IRISH CHASE REDS OFF BRITISH ISLAND'. This was at the time of the Korean War. It made the story even more topical and hilarious, because it sounded like a military engagement.

The most powerful Communist at the Isle of Grain in the early days was Jack Fraser, a member of the EETPU National Executive and a senior steward on site. Jack was a hard man. It was tough guys like him who were responsible for the ETU difficulties that came later. In the early Fifties, redundancies were declared. These were partly aimed at Jack and his trouble-making activities. The men challenged the job cuts with a seventeen-week dispute, which ended in defeat. Jack was not re-elected steward, but he still had presence even without power. When the foreman and the chief engineer came along and said, 'You're sacked,' Jack looked them menacingly in the eye and asked, 'Which one of you is sacking me?' The two gulped and walked away to think about their answer.

They came back one week later and repeated the performance. Jack asked again who was sacking him, and the foreman said, 'I am.' Jack said that was all he wanted to know, picked up his tools and went. But he had won himself a week's extra money because these people were so scared of him.

One of the consequences the electricians suffered as a result of this strike was that they were no longer provided with tools. All other skilled craftsmen were. Until then, all of us on Treasure Island had been equipped, at management expense, with the most up-to-date, sparkling set of new tools when we started on a job. Once I became a shop steward, I decided to use my charms on management to have this perk reinstated. I told them they were making us provide our own tools, but they employed a number of thieves. Other trades were nicking our people's equipment and such attractive items as pliers and screwdrivers had gone missing. I suggested they replaced those tools which my members were having stolen. As relationships improved, they finally gave way: I would provide a list of what had been stolen every month and, believe it or not, the personnel manager or his assistant would go into Chatham, buy the tools, and I would distribute them.

This system became a bit irksome after a while, so I said, 'Let's put a price on the tools, with so much for a screwdriver, so much for a wrench.' There was now a price list for the tools we didn't have. Whole toolkits were falling off the jetty, and because 'sparks' have a wicked sense of humour, I had to start exercising an official quota and cut the list down before I put it in. It reached a state of farce: when familiar faces came along, I had to tell them, 'You were here last month. I can't have another claim from you.' The cheques were flying out like confetti to pay for lost tools. It was costing the company far more than buying the damn things and eventually the inevitable happened: the 'sparks' were provided with tools once again. Persistence wears away stone in the end. This was just one example amongst scores of ingenious negotiations that I learnt at the grassroots.

Another duty which I and my colleagues refined to an art form was claiming 'compo' – compensation. Like all construction sites, Treasure Island had large numbers of accidents, but what has always appalled me with the system of compensation in Britain is that it has nothing to do with the damage a worker has suffered. It is all to do with what blame can be attached to an employer. I have always believed that we should move towards a system where it is the degree of injury sustained which determines the level of compensation paid from a national fund. Even in my early period as a steward, I always tried to spin the best yarn in order to exact the largest payment for injured members from their employers.

Electricians do lark about, and one of the most glaring cases I put forward was on behalf of an old electrician's mate who broke a leg in a cable way out near the jetty. Some of the lads had been throwing stones at each other, one stone went astray and this old chap took it full on the shin. It broke his leg. There was no way by telling that story that he was going to get any compensation, and he was going to be laid off for some time. I told him he had reached over to get into the cable way, it was wet on top of the coping, his hands were unable to grip and he had slipped to the bottom, breaking his leg.

'Is that right, lads?' I asked.

'That's right, Eric,' they said.

The result: £700 compensation, more than enough to tide the fellow over while he recovered. It was quite illegal, I suppose, but it was only short-story writing, really. I gained a bit of a reputation for striking a hard bargain with employers and men would ask me to come to other construction sites and get them a better deal. It was rather like having a clan, or fan club, who wanted to be led by the chief of the tribe.

Years later on the power station site, the laggers belonging to the General and Municipal Workers (GMWU), led by the tall, gangling David Basnett, owed no such allegiance – not to their union, their workmates, just to their own selfish greed. Their dispute began officially in August 1979, three months after Mrs Thatcher began her first term as Prime Minister, but the origins of the débâcle dated back to 1976. It was then that the entire Grain project was shut down for six months in a dispute over protective clothing for the laggers. At the heart of the matter was the fact that this relatively minor group of blackmailers called the tune when it came to commissioning a power station, for these were the 'finishers'. Without the laggers, who were glorified plasterers slapping a covering on pipes and boilers, the plant could not operate. Not a penny's profit could be made on the hundreds of millions already spent. That is how they were able to hold managements and, as it turned out, the entire TUC to ransom.

Laggers at the Grain were being paid £11 an hour, or £440 a week, while my skilled members got £2 an hour. At the Monsanto chemical plant in the North East, laggers used their clout to earn a weekly £1,200 or £30 an hour. The Grain dispute came to a head when the Central Electricity Generating Board finally snapped and refused to allow the pay explosion to continue. It audited the operation of the laggers' bonus scheme by their sub-contracted employer Cape, Darlington and Newall (CDN) and discovered productivity levels nowhere near justified the pay levels. The CEGB told CDN the laggers could not have more and that they would have to come in line with the rest of the 2,000 workers on the power generation project. The laggers, true to form, threatened to strike, but before they could, a strike by scaffolders over their bonus payments hit the site. Although only four laggers faced being laid off, the whole lot refused to work. Two weeks later, after the scaffolders' dispute was settled, the laggers refused to go back unless there was work for all of them immediately. This was an impossible demand, and they knew it.

Their dispute was to last more than a year and tarnish the trade union movement at a time when it was under unrelenting attack from a Conservative government, some members of which seemed committed to ensuring our extinction. Every day of delay caused by this pointless game of anarchy cost the CEGB £50,000, but the truth was that the laggers had complete control over their destiny and the GMWU lost control over them. The laggers, or the bandits, as I preferred to call them, appeared not to care that they were likely to put 2,000 others out of work, for the CEGB was at last of a mind to shut the whole site for good rather than kowtow to any union. The project to build Europe's biggest power station was already four years behind schedule.

In April 1980, 600 men were made redundant because the CEGB postponed completion of two of the five planned power generation units. I went down to the site with my colleagues from other unions. The workers agreed that they were not going to allow

17

the laggers to destroy their jobs. We found out that even though the laggers were maintaining a minimal picket line at the Grain, most of them had found jobs elsewhere, some in Germany, others in the Middle East. They were all right, thank you very much: they were working, but they weren't going to let others work.

The crunch came when the EETPU, backed by the Amalgamated Engineering Union, led by Terry Duffy, and the construction workers, headed by Johnny Baldwin, announced we would supply trainees to do the lagging work for another employer, the main contractors, GEC and Babcock's. This is what brought on the pain of the Grain, and the GMWU mounted a massive picket. Complaints were made to the TUC by David Basnett of the GMWU that we were trying to take their members' jobs, even though it was clear the laggers had found alternative employment and that the dispute would lose jobs for thousands of other men at the Grain. It was bizarre.

One of my closest allies at this time was Johnny Baldwin, the courageous leader of the construction workers. We had been shop stewards together on the Grain and at Tilbury power station. Johnny had been a front-turret naval gunner in the Battle of the River Plate, and there were few braver than this tough little fighter, so when he telephoned me at my hotel in Scarborough during the EETPU's Industrial Conference in the summer of 1980, I was surprised to hear him suggest that we join CEGB Executives flying into the picketed Grain site by helicopter.

I said, 'No way, Johnny. This is the big one, mate.' The GMWU was planning to mount a massive picket to stop our people going in the next week. I told Johnny, 'Look, if we're going to ask our people to go through those picket lines, we have got to be right up front, right up there in the first coach.' I added wryly, 'Anyway, we're both up for re-election, so it won't do either of us any harm.' John quickly saw the point and readily agreed, and early on the morning of 27 May 1980, Johnny and I clambered aboard the first coach.

It was a journey into a hail of flints and staves, spears and stones, which rained down on the coaches, smashing windows, gashing heads and jarring nerves as we ran the gauntlet of baying yobbos. Thirty coaches carrying 1,200 union members wanting to work got through the screaming mob of 400 pickets, helped by the police, who made 36 arrests. Later, behind the safety of the wire perimeter fence, I was photographed holding a great chunk of Kent flint. It had been used as a missile, smashed through the coach window and gashed open a foreman's head. I had spoken over the years at TUC and other conferences about energy, industrial democracy and nuclear power and not raised a hiss or a boo, but the picture of me holding that enormous piece of flint did more for me than a dozen learned speeches. It was a stark symbol of the violence which had penetrated a movement dedicated at its birth to protecting the ordinary man.

What depths we reached that day at the Isle of Grain over a group of people who did not even deserve to be in our ranks! The pictures on the television that night exposed the thuggery in our midst. David Basnett's behaviour during the whole affair was eccentric, to say the least, and the violence and savagery brought discredit and dishonour upon his union and the entire movement. Kent's Assistant Chief Constable, Michael Gibson, made it clear after the riot that the police had tried on numerous occasions to discover from the GMWU what would happen that day. There had been no response. Mr Gibson said, 'I do not think one could say this was intended to be peaceful picketing. It was intended to forcefully prevent people going to work. The union never contacted us and its officials never told us what they were doing. That is why I think they behaved with unbelievable irresponsibility – and I shall say so in my report to my Chief Constable.'

Not for the last time did I have to combat this violent streak in the trade union movement. It was a change in the way people argued and dealt with each other. The problem became more and more intense with violent lobbies at conferences by the Socialist Workers' Party, reaching its peak at the time of the miners' strike and the Wapping dispute. It was only by standing up to such violence that we have prevented the thugs from being successful. I do not regret a single action I took or statement I made at that time, for my members returned me to the EETPU Executive with a record vote exceeding 10,000. Controversy and activity never harm you in the trade union movement. The members may not agree with all you say and do; so long as you are acting for them, they will support you.

Despite the fact that he was clearly in the wrong, David Basnett was very upset that he could not get his own way, so he took his case to the TUC and, as usual, this resulted in a hotch-potch of shabby compromises, half-truths and pathetic bartering. There were interminable meetings going on night after night into the autumn of 1980 in the run-up to the TUC Conference at Brighton. We had to appear before the TUC General Council on 20 August to account for our sins along with our 'co-accused' in the Amalgamated Engineering Union (formerly AUEW). I was defiant as usual: I know no other way. I hadn't exactly helped myself by threatening in advance to sue the TUC in the High Court if it tried to expel us.

In a challenging style that was to be repeated in following years, I said:

> The problems of the Isle of Grain are a microcosm of the problems of large sites in Britain. The project is four years behind schedule. It was to have cost £209 million; it will now cost £580 million. These costs will be paid by all of us as consumers and by industry as we are less able to construct plant of any kind in this country. However, that is the background to the crisis at the Isle of Grain.
>
> The present dispute extends back to August 1979. The laggers' dispute with their then employer, CDN Installation Limited, sprang from the effects of a scaffolders' strike – not from dissatisfaction over their own bonus. It is true that CDN had given notice, in July, as was their right, to terminate their existing bonus scheme, but that could have been dealt with through their own machinery without dispute.
>
> In August 1979, the scaffolders' dispute forced CDN to lay off some laggers. The laggers' response was all or none – so all were laid off. When the scaffolders returned to work in September on the instruction of their union, CDN notified the laggers that a phased return to work could begin. The laggers' response was, again, all or none. The dispute drifted on. In October, CDN informed the laggers that they were deemed to have terminated their own employment. On 22 October, the notice that CDN had given in July to terminate the bonus scheme expired.
>
> At a meeting between the GMWU and CDN on 31 October, the company finally offered – (1) complete reinstatement of the workforce, without loss of continuity, on 5 November; (2) a payment of £550; (3) payment of August Bank Holiday; (4) minimum earnings level to be paid whilst discussions on a new bonus scheme took place.
>
> Up till this time, the laggers had received massive financial support amounting to thousands of pounds from other workers on the site, even though many laggers involved had found employment elsewhere, leaving only a token picket of four.

The CEGB made it clear that unless they had an assured lagging capability, then the future of the site and 2,000 jobs were in jeopardy.

The laggers' branch was unmoved by the looming unemployment of those who had supported them. For that branch, solidarity was a one-way affair – the site supported them, but they accepted no obligation to maintain the employment of the other 2,000 workers. The laggers' branch turned down the offer of compensation and reinstatement, an offer which was regarded by the GMWU officials and by other shop stewards as a reasonable and honourable basis for ending the dispute. The decision was not taken by the laggers on Grain, certainly not by the thirty labourers attached to them on the site, but by the branch in Essex. This same branch had previously consistently refused to provide sufficient laggers to complete the job on time.

Despite the 'go-it-alone' policy pursued then by the laggers and GMWU, the other unions still persisted in trying to help them, mainly through their influence on the CEGB. Further meetings took place between CDN and GMWU. An improved settlement was reached, recommended by the GMWU officials and again rejected by the laggers' branch on 19 December 1979. The CEGB had by then terminated CDN's contract and sought an alternative lagging contractor. Finally, agreement was reached with a new contractor, Cape Contracts, and the GMWU. The CEGB awarded the contract to the new contractor, the national officials of the GMWU recommended acceptance and the lagging branch again said, *'No.'*

The CEGB stopped all work on 4 and 5 units, resulting in 600 redundancies. They announced that without a resumption of lagging work they would close the whole site in June 1980. *We took then, as we have throughout the discussions, the protection of jobs as our priority* – not the preservation of unwarranted earnings for the minority.

We pressed the CEGB to put the lagging work out to tender. They did and contracts were awarded to GEC and Babcock's. We insisted they take on GMWU laggers – they agreed, but the GMWU refused to supply labour. Only then did we support the training of new laggers to save the project.

The GMWU failed to make a settlement of the dispute. Three times they recommended one, but were rejected by the lagging branch. They terminated the dispute and advised their members to seek work elsewhere; many have done so, some as far away as Saudi Arabia. They were offered the work by

GEC and Babcock's, but refused. The laggers could only have intended the closure of Grain as an awful lesson to any other client who resisted their demands for earnings higher than craftsmen. It has been rightly said that the Isle of Grain had been hijacked by twenty-seven bandits.

Our actions to maintain employment were met with a mass picket to stop the project. The GMWU officials were unable to control that picket and many of you will have seen, through television, the violence and savagery that so discredited the GMWU. That picket failed in its objective – to stop the station – but we are still faced with an often-postponed threat to call all laggers out on strike and picket all power stations – operational and those under construction.

Our actions have also now faced us, along with the AUEW (Amalgamated Union of Engineering Workers), with the threat of expulsion from the TUC. All this because we have throughout put the preservation of jobs as our primary principle.

We support the TUC's attempt at deriving a formula to resolve the dispute, but question the practicability of the actual formula produced.

They fail to take into account the various offers, settlements, etc, which could have resolved the dispute in an honourable manner, and compensated the laggers for their losses due to the scaffolders' strike.

If these then are the reasons for the formula's failure, in what way exactly does it fail? Basically, it fails because it is not acceptable to all the parties concerned. And, in this way, it goes against the TUC General Council's own report which states that ' . . . Securing these arrangements requires agreement by all the parties involved with large sites – clients, employers and Unions . . . '

The formula is unacceptable to:

1 the client,
2 the employers,
3 the overwhelming majority of the trade-unionists on the site,
4 AUEW(E); AUEW(C) and the EETPU who represent seventy per cent of the workers on site.

It is unacceptable to all involved other than the 3GMWU for the following reasons:

The TUC, or rather the Finance and General Purposes Committee, and at most relevant times that has meant Len Murray and Tom Jackson, have tried to find an acceptable formula – so far without success. Their first attempt was to advise (under TUC rules this means instruct) all unions involved that:

– lagging work on the Grain should be done by GMWU laggers employed by a TICA contractor;
– they should be able to earn more than £4.60 an hour;
– other workers on site should not use laggers' earnings to improve their own.

In other words, an open-ended earnings situation for laggers – a freeze for all others. Needless to say, the GMWU found it acceptable and the rest rejected it. Many more meetings have taken place to find a formula acceptable to all parties. Up till now they suffer from being unacceptable to the CEGB, to some unions involved and to the Joint Shop Stewards Committee. As our only motive throughout the piece has been to preserve employment, we cannot support any formula which will bring us into conflict with the CEGB and so jeopardize that employment.

What has to be remembered is that all the laggers involved in the original dispute could start work on Babcock's or GEC tomorrow and earn as much as any skilled craftsman on those firms.

Other unions who have 'accepted' the TUC's advice at national level have either not attempted to secure agreement at local level, or have been rejected by their members when they have done so. Some have cynically 'accepted' on the grounds that the formula is unworkable anyway.

We could easily provide a worthless piece of paper saying we accept the General Council's advice, but how can we, in all honesty, do that when we know we could not secure the agreement of our members? We told the Finance and General Purposes Committee this, and the fact that we would be unable to take any industrial action to secure the implementation of the advice. We were told by the acting Chairman that no action was required from us, only our agreement. It seems sincerity is not what is required, only empty gestures.

If we disagree with the TUC's formula, for the reasons given, we certainly would not quarrel with most of the objectives which it is supposed to attain. These objectives can be outlined as follows:

1 To keep the site open, to preserve employment and to create

conditions in which work in numbers 4 and 5 units could proceed. We unreservedly support this objective and would point out most strongly that without the 'new' laggers, the site would be closed and this objective impossible.

2 To secure the harmonization of bonus earnings among the crafts.

Again, we support and have, together with fellow unions, put a great deal of work into securing support for a 'site understanding'. Our members employed by the main electrical contractor have already worked out with their employer their place in that 'understanding'.

3 To restore the lagging work to properly qualified laggers in membership of the GMWU.

Our support for this object is qualified. Lagging work is and has been available to GMWU laggers at Grain and we have insisted that should be so. However, the words of the objective imply that only GMWU laggers are entitled to do lagging work. No other union involved in construction will agree that. An insulating firm, a subsidiary of Cape's, has been for some time insulating, cladding, lagging the interior of the building – under civil engineering rates and conditions and employing T & GWU members – they will not recognize a GMWU monopoly.

4 To make satisfactory alternative arrangements for those workers currently employed on lagging duties.

We agree with the objective but find no practical way to implement it.

5 To promote a common approach by the trade unions and the TUC to a commitment to agree comprehensive arrangements for the conduct of industrial relations on large engineering construction sites.

We are pleased that the TUC have joined us in this fundamental objective. The NECC 'unions have laboured towards' this end for a decade.

Yet, for merely challenging the ability of the formula to obtain these objectives, we are faced with the threat of suspension from the TUC.

We cannot accept that by giving highest priority to the preservation of employment that we are acting in a manner detrimental to the interests of the Trade Union Movement, nor that by giving an empty undertaking, for that is all it could be, to accept the General Council's advice, can we be seen to be acting in any but a dishonest and insincere way.

The General Council verdict delivered at Congress House was that we had to cease doing this lagging work. After the TUC knuckleheads had passed judgement, I was furious at their stupidity. I went out past Frank Chapple, who was on the General Council and sitting there with the ludicrous task of watching the clowns judge his own union. As I swept past Communist Ken Gill, General Secretary of the white-collar union, TASS (Technical, Administrative and Supervisory Staff Union), he was right there under my mouth.

I said, 'You bunch of fools.' They did not like that remark, but it was true.

Frank said later, 'They'll never forgive you for that.' They never did.

What I meant by that remark was that the Left and its allies through habit or intimidation were determined to secure conformity to their decisions. Their obsession was elevated above all else. In Britain, they used abuse, even physical assault, together with suspension and expulsion – in Stalin's Russia the same people would have had us shot. Throughout the world, their spiteful creed allowed no possibility that they might be wrong.

The Congress saw TUC General Secretary Len Murray bustling between Executive meetings of the AEU and ourselves. Ultimatums and deadlines came and went.

Proof that the laggers' dispute, like every other industrial confrontation, was fair game for the extremists came during TUC week at Brighton. Frank Chapple, Terry Duffy and Johnny Baldwin were forced to run a gauntlet of abuse from militant pickets organized by the Socialist Workers' Party. The dozen or so pickets claiming to be laggers sacked at the Isle of Grain were accompanied by John Deason, an executive member of the SWP and organizer of the 'Right to Work' marches in the 1970s. Beer was spilled on the carpet in the foyer of the Old Ship Hotel on Brighton seafront as Frank stormed past the jeering mob who were shouting their familiar war cry of 'scab'. He quite rightly described them later as 'scum'.

Still the future membership of the EETPU and the AEU hung in the balance. Basnett wanted his pound of flesh. Labour Leader Jim Callaghan even offered to mediate as the TUC headed like a charging rhinoceros towards a 14 October deadline date for us to give in. We finally accepted a compromise, agreeing to hand back the lagging jobs to the GMWU, but with the G & M committed to a joint agreement with other construction unions.

I and my Executive colleague Eric Clayton voted against. I said, 'I don't accept. Let the bastards throw us out.'

Frank told me, 'We got most of what we wanted.'

In fact, the TUC formula was not agreed by the CEGB and employers. It was all finally settled by the unions concerned on terms far worse than were available to the laggers eighteen months before. The laggers would no longer enjoy a separate agreement from the rest of us; they would be part of an entirely new national engineering and construction industry agreement. And, to be fair, they have been part of and have honoured that agreement ever since.

In fact, this had been a goal I had been concerned with since 1970 as a member of a National Economic Development Council working party on negotiations at large sites like the Isle of Grain. This new deal halted the constant leapfrogging on wages not only between sites but within sites themselves. These problems were the reason our construction industry had lost its competitive edge. Contracts were not being completed on time or for the original price. The Isle of Grain was the most lurid example of that wage league yo-yo. We were the worst builders in the world for reliability. Now, all that has been transformed.

Of course, the Left were gunning for me at our next major Conference. They put up a motion saying, 'This Conference believes that EETPU members should not cross picket lines when in dispute. Above all else, one trade or group should not do the work of another trade involved in a dispute.'

I met it head on and said:

Let me begin by saying that we always seek to assist other unions engaged in legitimate action, but we give no one a blank cheque. We do not abandon our critical faculties when faced with a picket line. The absolute terms of the motion are breathtaking – no union picket lines to be crossed. It does not say 'official picket lines'. Are we then to stop short of any picket line, even when the strikers have a disreputable cause? Are we to accept that a minority can, simply by involving the holy inviolate picket, involve the majority? What nonsense.

Let me exaggerate to make my point. Suppose that in a large establishment a department goes into dispute because coloured workers or women are to be employed for the first time. That is not inconceivable. Is it really being argued that the majority should honour a picket line for that purpose? Are there no memories in this hall that stretch back to the Chrysler dispute, where our electricians were locked in battle with a multi-national to secure the implementation of an agreement already signed? Do you not remember that, despite the impeccable justification our members had, no one heeded their picket lines and ASTMS (Association of Scientific, Technical and Managerial Staffs) supervisors did their work? Some of you are the philanthropists of the trade union movement. You bear every ill we suffer. Every injustice is heaped upon our union without complaint. But immediately we have a difference with another union, never mind the justification, their cause is your cause. Well, we are not going to bear that. We will defend the legitimate interests of our members wherever that leads us, and whatever the consequences.

After recounting the Isle of Grain story, I ended with:

The motion says we were wrong to engage in the battle to save jobs. By all means, pass pious resolutions at the TUC and at conferences of this kind on unemployment. But when faced with the reality of securing work, then back off. Remember that not only were construction jobs at stake, but jobs in the threatened power engineering industry and in electricity supply. The motion would have us placate every greedy minority and, in the case of the Grain, would allow the project to be destroyed and 2,000 men sacked.

We did not back down and much of the credit for it must go to those of us, particularly John Baldwin, who took that firm stand at the Isle of Grain – realists on an island of dreamers.

3
Signpost to the future

I was the hope of the hard Left when I joined the union Executive in 1964. But not for long. Backed by a gaggle of Communists, Trotskyists and fellow travellers, my election victory over Frank Chapple and his ally Les Tuck for the South East and Kent National Executive seat was heralded in the *Daily Worker* as 'a significant victory, and a shock for the Right-wing establishment' of the Electrical Trades Union (ETU).

Though later events would lead to me being dubbed a Right-wing maverick, Eric Albert Barratt-Hammond was a bit of a Leftie in his youth. I spoke my mind, perhaps too often. Within months of being elected to the National Executive, I was denied permission by the General Secretary, Jock Byrne, to write a letter to the *Daily Worker*, urging the union leadership to drop its proposed ban on Communist Party members. It seemed to me then, and still does, that to ban any section of opinion from full membership negated the basic tenet of trade unionism – that workers in common employment should unite together to defend and advance their legitimate interests. *All* workers, not all except those with a particular view. My banned letter argued that the union would have a better chance of improving its members' lot if it ignored the 'Goldwaters' and the 'Maos' in its midst. I failed to persuade Jock or the Executive, and the ban went ahead after an overwhelming ballot vote of all the members. I had learnt a lesson; it made me more determined than ever in future to use the views of the members as a trump card rather than those of committees unrepresentative of the grassroots.

I warned my Left-wing colleagues at a series of meetings after I joined the National Executive that it would take twenty years of hard slog, of listening to the members, before they could again assume power. They paid no heed and, as a result, ended up in the wilderness. All they did was to snipe and criticize and physically punch and kick those who were trying to consult the membership. If anybody is responsible for my being erroneously regarded as a rabid Right-winger, it is those reactionary Red Lefties. Historically, the Left were always those who wanted to give more power to more people, to take it from the kings, the barons, the industrialists. In recent years, it has been the reverse. The Left in both the Labour Party and the trade union movement is prone to say, 'We know best. It's the people on the committee who know best.' As a result it has been left to us on the so-called Right, in fact those who would not accept such elitism, to push for one member, one vote in the Labour Party and give trade union members the right to re-elect their officials. The terms Left and Right, therefore, have been turned on their heads.

The biggest shock for the Left was that, within less than two years, I was to become one of Frank Chapple's greatest allies and switch my radicalism to the other side of the political spectrum. The immediate reason for the change was my determination to win national minimum wages and conditions in the industrial wastelands of the electrical contracting industry. In my time as a worker and later shop steward in the special contracting section of the London Electricity Board at West Thurrock power station, I had seen the crying need for action. But after the High Court victory over the Communist ballot-riggers by Frank Chapple and the new General Secretary, Jock Byrne, progress was the last thing the Party wanted, particularly if it meant a reduction in the numbers of low-paid. They were, after all, the Party's most fertile recruiting ground.

I had become a Labour councillor at Gravesend plus a vocal and active participant in the union's delegate conferences, but joining the Executive was like winning promotion to a different league. I felt all the daggers were pointing at me, that I was treated with suspicion and circumspection. They didn't damn well trust me. In fact, Frank Chapple, who was by now the obvious pretender to the Byrne throne, realized that what I wanted was to work. I've always been a fair grafter and he just piled me up with duties, which I set about with gusto. Much of that work was allocated to me by the late Mark Young, a national officer who was later to become General Secretary of the British Airline Pilots' Association. Mark handed me a massive portfolio of everything from flour milling to paper. He became a friend and I was grateful to him for providing me with this early opportunity to shine.

One day at Heathrow, however, I realized that trade unions were no better than the City or big business when it came to conniving, back-biting and double-dealing. Mark turned to me and said, 'You know, if we work together, we can turn over Chapple and Cannon.' Here was a member of the most Right-wing group on the Executive saying they could make common cause with the soft Left and get rid of the President and Assistant General Secretary.

I told Mark to forget it. I said, 'We've been through enough in this union. If Chapple and Cannon make sense with their proposals, I'm going to support them. I think it's in the interests of the members and the union.'

The real turning point which set my former Left-wing colleagues firmly against me was when I lined up with Frank Chapple and others to bring the troubled electrical contracting industry into the modern world. I had spent my formative years working in it, and it had been a buccaneering sort of existence. We went on each job and fought for conditions and improvements and facilities, only to have to start again at square one on the next site. It really needed some continuity and national standards applied to it. There simply weren't any. Despite vehement and sometimes violent opposition from the Left, our union and the 3,000 and more employers of 40,000 men formed a Joint Industry Board. It comprised half union and half employers' representatives with an independent chairman to deal with productivity, training and discipline within the industry, in fact to run it. This was my first revolution, a signpost to the future.

Extracts from a paper I wrote then for Frank Chapple to give to an employers' conference in 1966 read pretty well today. The sadness is that the problems identified are still without remedy in many sectors of industry. Under the title 'The effective use of manpower', I wrote:

> . . . The implication in the subject matter of this paper is that effective use has not and is not being made of manpower in the Electrical Contracting Industry. Indeed, if this were not so there would be little point in discussing the matter. We will find, therefore, that the most fruitful area of discussion is that of the shortcomings of present techniques and practices. From such a discussion some pointers at least should emerge to the more effective use of our manpower.
>
> It is relevant to examine the continual manpower drain from our Industry. Why is there such a loss? Obviously because workers

would sooner be employed elsewhere. The main reason for this is the relative insecurity of employment and lack of opportunity in the Industry. Of course, working conditions can, and must, be improved and they are an important element in the identification of the worker with the Industry, with something he can be proud of, not something he comes to with distaste, endures with protest and leaves with pleasure. But central to changed attitudes, basic to stability, is security. The casual nature of employment in the Industry must go. In the place of insecurity we must put opportunity. Opportunity not only in relation to earnings, but above all in regard to status. The skilled manual worker, the technicians and supervisors who come from their ranks, must be given the reward and position in industrial society in keeping with their growing importance. I am aware that in discussing our own Industry vis-à-vis the rest of the Construction Industry, a parallel argument could, and needs, to be advanced to obtain recognition of the proper importance of our collective work. There is little gain for us and the nation if we use our manpower more effectively only to quietly cover the shortcomings of information and planning of the main contractor and customer. If we are to claim and gain the rightful status for our skilled men then we must jointly see that the Industry's status is established with contractor, client and government.

The rates of pay we have agreed for the next three years should help us to retain labour formerly attracted by higher rates in other industries, but wages are only one factor as to whether a man will stay in the Industry. Given reasonable rates of pay and success in achieving stability and improved status, which of our present practices are inconsistent with maximum efficiency?

The continuance of the grade of mate is probably the first that springs to mind. The existence of this category, of electricians' assistants, is itself an obstacle to the efficient use of manpower in this grade. Its agreed removal must surely be seen as a considerable token of the Union's intention to make the Industry more efficient. The use of those experienced and capable as electricians will ease the shortage of skilled labour.

The basic objective of our new agreement is to raise the levels of skill of workers in the Industry and thereby increase productivity, not by our members working harder but by their working in a more effective way. I sometimes feel that engraved on the hearts of some

31

members of the Association is the Biblical text: 'In the sweat of thy face thou shalt eat bread.' Not that they make my members sweat, but they are convinced that the solution to our problems is that operatives should work harder, longer and generally expend a great deal more effort.

We see no merit in manhandling cable drums hundreds of yards when they can be delivered closer to the job. If working harder is the solution, then throw away your power-assisted tools and go back to the hammer and rawlplug tool. If effort is the answer then ban bending machines and make them use a block. Hard work, effort and longer hours are not the way forward. The continual application of intelligence and skill is the only way to increase real production.

The financial incentive for workers to improve their skill is provided, but if we are to realize our objective then a radical look is needed at the opportunities provided for adult training. It will not be enough for us to send our respective representatives to the Industrial Training Board or to take comfort from the existence of the Government Training Centres. We must look at our work requirements, engage experts to look at their techniques and train selected workers in the revised techniques resulting from such examinations. These trained groups could then instruct their fellow workers. Possibly the JIBs (Joint Industry Boards) we are to set up under this new agreement could see that such technicians are trained and made available to employers as a whole. Parallel with this, and in a similar way, the levels of management and super-visory skills must be examined, improved and the rewards com-mensurably increased. The need for improvement amongst this section of the Industry's workers is probably the most critical. The effects of the shortcomings of an incompetent electrician are fairly localized. When a site supervisor in charge of a couple of hundred men is not up to the mark, the result can be disastrous for the firm and the two hundred.

In any discussion about our affairs, it must be kept in mind that competition, believed to be the source of efficiency, is so intense in Electrical Contracting that it often produces the opposite effect. The fact is that electrical contractors are rarely, if ever, contracting to the client who has requisitioned a building project, but are nearly always sub-contractors and subject to all the weaknesses of such a relationship.

When my Union reviewed the position of Electrical Contracting in the light of the rates of pay and conditions of our members, we were forced to the conclusion that only the closest cooperation between the Union and your Association could produce the circumstances required that would make possible on the one hand greater efficiency and on the other the wages and conditions we desired.

We would, however, be burying our heads in the sand if we did not take full account of the existing state of affairs and say very, very clearly that we cannot have the effective use of manpower or improvements in efficiency if the existing competitiveness continues and the Industry is treated, as often it is, as of secondary importance in the planning of the building project, for we cannot effectively use manpower in circumstances in which the building plans have rapid changes made in them and the electrical contractor, anxious not to offend his client, has to conceal such problems with what often amounts to a Dickensian approach to his labour force. It must be recognized that this is the twentieth century in which the idea that the worker has not the right to reason why is not only out of date but fails to take advantage of the burning desire of all thinking people to be creatively involved in society in some form or other; that there is a serious shortage of skilled labour and the idea of completing a job with larger and larger squads of poorly paid and badly trained operatives is certainly not in keeping with modern thinking, nor does it recognize the serious shortage of all types of labour and is, indeed, responsible for the labour-cost pressures which are bound to crucify a labour-intensive industry which, if continued in circumstances such as exist today, would probably lead to unforeseen changes in both the organization and methods of the Industry.

Taking these considerations into account, how is it possible then to use manpower more effectively? Greater use must be made of business efficiency and method study in order to bring a degree of planning into the price that is tendered for the job. Simple costing of labour and materials plus five per cent will not do. In such costs, planning, conditions of work, and the supply of tools, equipment and protective clothing must undergo a radical, if not a revolutionary, change; provision must be made for consultative committees drawn from all sections of men employed for the purpose of examining any weaknesses in planning which show themselves from day to day.

Workmen will always respect a decision when it is based on efficiency and organization. This is especially true where human relations are good and built into the decision. If men have the feeling that they are part of a team, and that the particular task they perform is essential to the success of the team, then they are much more likely to give of their best and involve themselves in doing what has to be done.

It is primarily the task of management to create this common bond. It is not only necessary that management should organize the technical elements of production efficiently, it is also as essential that they have a positive attitude to human relations.

Good communications are a tool for achieving success. It is essential that every participant should be informed of not only what is to be done, but how and why. This is just as necessary to success. A dialogue skilfully conducted will not only carry the commands and instructions from above, but will give management a clear picture of the responses from below. The cardinal feature of good communications is to tackle problems before they have resulted in criticism or conflict and not to wait until the conflict has broken out.

Untrained and inefficient management cannot get the best results from the capital they use or the labour force whose efforts it is their duty to coordinate. The wages and conditions of the workers suffer, as a result.

Where the skills of a worker are not properly or fully utilized, then productive effort is wasted; no matter what agreements the trade unions come to with employers about payment, these agreements cannot fully compensate the worker for his skills which are badly used. The worker has a stake in ensuring that his skill is used to the greatest effect. It is not only a question of his skill in which the worker has an interest, there is also his labour time. Time spent waiting for work is unproductive. Although the trade unions negotiate agreements to compensate the worker for this unproductive time, in practice the unproductive time depletes the total wealth available for redistribution.

Both sides of the Industry must understand at all levels the cost of failing in our task. At best it will mean that we will need a greater supply of less-skilled immigrant labour to supply the increasing labour-intensiveness of the Industry. It goes without saying, if such circumstances as this apply throughout British industry there will be increasing social problems from such circumstances. At worst it could mean a break-down in the improved relationship that has taken place in the last three years which could result in a considerable slowing down and increase in the cost of power stations and industrial projects as well as a delay in building schools and hospitals. The snowball effect this could have upon our economy could not be foreseen, but it would certainly not be the way to lift Britain into twentieth-century industrial efficiency and certainly no way of protecting and improving the standards of living of us all.

The paper's themes of skill, training, involvement and partnership have been my guiding light throughout my union career and were the foundation of our agreement for electrical installation. The deal we were about to strike with the electrical contractors would form the basis of the now controversial single-union agreements favoured by Japanese electronics companies investing heavily in Britain and Europe. No matter how many threats were made, and a good many were, I was not going to allow the Left to pull my strings, so we parted company after they told me if I didn't stop supporting this new deal in the industry, then they would not support me in the elections. I said, 'So be it,' and with one brief phrase, I was free.

The Left's clear threat to ditch me was made by a former friend of mine, Fred Morphew, a slight and spare little man who used to be an RAF flight sergeant in bombers in the Second World War. Fred, Secretary of our Dartford branch, said the Left was removing me from its 'slate' after I launched the contracting deal with my first major speech at our National Industrial Conference on 26 May 1966. Taking me to one side at the Pier Pavilion in Colwyn Bay, Fred said, 'If you continue to support this deal, you're out.' The result was rather different. I went on to beat off a Left-wing challenge convincingly when I came up for re-election to the Executive. Fred, like so many of the Left, ended up in our Fleet Street branch, which for the next twenty years was safe haven for the hard-liners.

There was no way, in all honesty, I could reject the contracting deal. It was the biggest advance in the industry since 1919, a full decade before I was born. Over the next three years, it lifted the hourly rate by an average of half-a-crown to ten shillings per hour. The increase – a shilling the first year, followed by two ninepences – amounted to a rise of 33.3 per cent. This was in an industry which, long before Arthur Scargill reared his ugly head, invented the term 'guerrilla strike' by organizing walkouts at a succession of sites and created a chaotic nightmare of wage leapfrogging for employers.

The new deal was radical. It provided for the grading of electricians, recognizing that all of them weren't equal, that we should de-casualize the industry so that we had an employment pool in order to allocate people to different firms in different regions. There was a new means of discipline for employees and employers.

The Left feared the worst. They said they would all be put in the lowest grade, sent hundreds of miles away from home and if they refused face disciplinary action. It worked out quite differently. Most electricians are in a higher grade, the employment pool has helped them to gain employment and there has been only one employee disciplined in twenty-five years, but there have been many employers disciplined for breaking the agreement and fined as a result. This was an advance of union control and involvement, the biggest for many years.

As soon as news of the deal broke in the Press, we were marched on at our Bromley headquarters by a 300-strong demonstration. A garbled account of the agreement had been produced in the *News Chronicle*, highlighting the apprehensions of the members. The mob demanded to see Frank Chapple and me. It was just before lunch, and the only place we could accommodate them was our canteen, which we needed to feed the staff. So Frank agreed to see them at two o'clock that afternoon. It turned out to be a major mistake. They went down to the local hostelry and tanked up on drink. The television cameras were at the Hayes Court headquarters by now. When we went into the canteen we were met with a wall of noise. You couldn't hear yourself speak.

After about five to ten minutes of this, I said to Frank, 'We'd better go. We're not doing any good here. They're not going to listen to us.' As we turned to go, about thirty of them pounced on us and beat us up quite badly in the corner. I'm an easygoing fellow and I don't lose my temper very quickly, but what I cannot stand is anybody laying a hand on me. So I drew back to hit the nearest fellow, only to feel a hand on my arm. It was Frank, who had the reputation of having a tempestuous personality. He was as cool as a cucumber, and he advised me, 'For Christ's sake, don't retaliate. That will only make it worse.'

We were saved by a bearded police sergeant, who was among a group of policemen called in by our staff outside the mêlée. Afterwards, when we were being debriefed by police, I asked the sergeant, 'How on earth did you get that fellow off Frank's back so quickly?'

He said, 'Easy. I just squeezed his balls.'

The whole thing had been a real shaker. I was young, fit and thirty-eight, and I shrugged it off, but Frank was off work for three months as a result. He was bruised and shaken up, and he had been working non-stop for years, so it hit him hard.

For the next six months, I addressed branch meetings all over the country almost every evening to make sure the members understood the deal they were being offered. This was my blooding, literally, as an Executive councillor. By the time our Industrial Conference took place at Scarborough in the summer of 1968, the Left were still trying to fill the agenda with critical resolutions attacking the contracting deal, but the experience of the members was that they were sitting pretty. They liked the deal. They had been given a wage increase way beyond the levels obtained by other workers. Even better was the fact that few were in the basic grade, most were at the 'approved' level and some were technician electricians. All of these were regarded as honourable estates.

The Left, and the Communist Party in particular, had lost a great prize: control of the union with perhaps the greatest power of all, the power to switch off the lights. It was like a magnet to the far Left, and that is why they paid so much attention to it in the post-war years. Having had this prize snatched away from them, they became almost irrational, so they did not view anything that the new Executive did in a reasonable way. They simply said, 'If they say today is Tuesday, then we'll say it's Wednesday. If they say black, we'll say white.' It was an obsession: they were not capable of agreeing with any initiative we made, no matter how desirable it was. That was their downfall, because the members would find something was desirable and vote for it.

We had a duty to lead, a duty to sign these radical agreements, but we only did so after the members had decided for themselves. This left the Communists and their cohorts marooned on their own elitist island, where the members counted for nothing. Meanwhile, the new radicals, including me, were returned at election time with ever increasing majorities. After all, the Left had lost the leadership of people like myself and Roy Sanderson, later to become leader of our white-collar section. Without us, they were in the wilderness.

You could not take away that 1966 contractors' deal with dynamite from the electricians now. It gave them such a move forward in the building and construction industry that, even today, wage claims from the Union of Construction, Allied Trades and Technicians seek to obtain what we won a quarter of a century ago. It permeated many other industries and became the model for several others. But it all very nearly went awry thanks to, of all things, a Labour government under Harold Wilson.

The Prices and Incomes Board, chaired by the former Tory MP Aubrey Jones, objected to parts of the deal. Here we were, having taken an industry by the scruff of the neck and given it its biggest ever shake-up, being told we had done wrong. We were forced to delay implementation of part of the deal which had transformed electrical contracting from a cockpit of industrial strife into one breaking new frontiers of industrial relations. However, in their second report on the agreement a couple of years later, they were better disposed. It read:

> We have gone into all those aspects of the Agreement (setting up the Joint Industry Board) in some detail not only because they are fundamental to understanding it, but also because there are certain features which seem to us to be exemplary. Although we have reservations on individual features of the Agreement, taking it as a whole we think that it represents a notable achievement in industrial relations, training and employment policies over a remarkably short period. In particular we would commend for consideration elsewhere the concept underlying the JIB of a permanent body of experts at the service of an industry and under joint management-union control, which is almost unique in the private sector of British industry.

It all went through in the end. But not until after a rather disturbing experience. At an early meeting of the National Joint Industry Board, I objected to our people on site being referred to as 'JIB (Joint Industry Board) job/shop representatives'. I wanted them simply to be called EETPU (Electrical, Electronic, Telecommunications and Plumbing Union) representatives. Despite my protests at the meeting, and a good deal of lobbying during the lunchtime recess, the Chairman, Tom Daniels, former Chairman of the North West Electricity Board, insisted when the vote was taken that he had the two-thirds majority required for a rule change.

Just before the vote was taken, I had the bizarre experience of trying to awaken one of my 'troops', Jimmy O'Neill, from the South West. He had a habit of falling asleep during long meetings. This was no exception. No amount of coughing, shouting or table thumping could bring him round. Despite this setback, I worked out that, in fact, Mr Daniels was just 0.5 per cent short of his target, and I challenged the ruling. Later, at our next Executive meeting, I was backed by the union President, Les Cannon. Two days later, Mr Daniels dropped dead from a sudden heart attack. I felt uneasy about his demise, but I won the point. Since then, I have become rather wary about challenging elderly gents who chair meetings I attend. It can be fatal.

Jim Houston took over as the JIB's Chairman a few months afterwards in January 1969, and has guided this partnership ever since and become the firm friend of both union and employer representatives. I learnt a great deal from him. A persuasive and rational man, he applied his abilities without stint when the parties (the union and employers) clashed. His logical and sometimes caustic tongue has brought us both back to the path of partnership when we've strayed.

The Joint Industry Board has been of benefit to both employees and employers, providing the one with wage rates and conditions beyond those enjoyed by other construction trades and the other with a highly skilled workforce prepared to accept more effective methods of working. The country, the general community and industry have benefited. High productivity has, in the main, meant lower prices. The industry is so competitive, with more than 3,000 employers, that any advance in efficiency is usually used to undercut another contractor's price. Hence the need for a strong union to ensure that cooperation and skill are properly regarded and employers all operate from a level playing field so far as labour costs are concerned.

We have also served the country well with our training programme. The industry has always had a high ratio of apprentices to skilled workers, but in 1982 the intake fell from the previous 3,000 to 200. This caused great concern for three main reasons. Firstly, a low intake of apprentices would inevitably create a skill shortage in years to come. This shortage would itself become more critical with higher economic growth, thus creating the sort of bottleneck industry has found itself in before, and which it is impossible to overcome quickly because the implementation of the necessary training programme takes time.

Secondly, the organization supporting a training scheme capable of handling large numbers cannot be created overnight. It requires the involvement of hundreds of colleges and instructors, as well as considerable material resources. In electrical contracting, we were getting to the point where this machine was beginning to break up because of dwindling recruitment of apprentices. If this had continued, it would have taken years to rebuild.

Thirdly, and most importantly, the plight of young unemployed people could not be ignored. I felt very strongly that my union should stop paying lip service to their problems and do something positive to help.

It is against this background, then, that along with the electrical contracting employers, we established in 1983 a radically new training programme. It is not based on arbitrary periods of time, but on standards. Training is completed when a nationally applied standard of practical competence, along with academic success, is reached. During the training, wages are also linked to the achievement of measured standards and not to birthdays, or the anniversary date of the start of the training period. The scheme also removes the age restriction usually applied to apprenticeship training, making it possible for apprenticeships to commence at any age. It also provides for the movement of apprentices between employers, thus ensuring they receive training in the complete range of skills they require. It is important to understand that a truly standards-based training scheme such as this proves not only the competence of the individual trainees, but also the quality of the training they receive. A bad performance by a group of trainees in a particular region of the country will probably indicate the existence of a bad training programme.

The effect of the new scheme was dramatic. Although not a Youth Training Scheme, we were able to persuade the government to support it with YTS funds. In 1982, there were 200 apprentices; the next year, 2,500 which increased every year; in 1989, we recruited more than 5,000 young men and women. They are all guaranteed not just one or even two years, but training until completion of apprenticeships. If the engineering industry had done the same, they would have an intake of 50,000 apprentices each year, instead of fewer than 5,000 and we would be making up some ground lost to our competitors in the skills league.

None of this would have been achieved without the will and determination of the union's Executive. The training scheme entailed a significant contribution on the part of government and the electrical employers. The union had to contribute something to secure the participation of the other two parties. We reduced the wage rates, particularly in the first year, to bring them in line with the YTS allowance. It brought upon my head another shower of criticism and abuse, but we stood our ground and I can look in the mirror each morning without flinching when I recall that more than 20,000 young men and women are either skilled with satisfying jobs or on their way up to such jobs. All that would have been denied them without our resolution and the relationship we had built within the JIB.

4

The miners – lions led by donkeys

I gave miners' leader Arthur Scargill the chance to win the year-long pit strike just three months into the dispute. My offer was simple and straightforward, but proved impossible for the National Union of Mineworkers' Marxist President to accept. I told the NUM in a confidential letter to its General Secretary Peter Heathfield on 24 May 1984 that if the miners' union staged and won a secret national ballot in favour of strike action to save pits and jobs, our union, in turn, would use its ultimate weapon – calling out the power workers.

No government, not even Margaret Thatcher's with its inbuilt will to smash the unions, could have resisted that threat to daily life. The strike would have continued for days rather than twelve months. With the lights out, electricity supplies cut and troops maintaining basic services, public pressure would have forced Mrs Thatcher to make the biggest political U-turn Britain had ever seen. Miners and their families would have been saved the disgrace of defeat, months of hardship and misery, and been given the chance to rebuild their communities, their union and their pride.

Instead, the massed ranks of Arthur Scargill's flying pickets reduced a once great union to ashes and halved its membership at a stroke. The deep divisions caused a lasting split with the brave working miners who united under the banner of the breakaway Union of Democratic Mineworkers, led by the plain-speaking, burly Nottinghamshire official, Roy Lynk, later to become my close friend and ally.

The strike had begun, without a ballot, on 6 March 1984 over the closure by British Coal of the Cortonwood colliery in South Yorkshire.

This was then used to support claims by Mr Scargill that, nationally, 20 pits and 20,000 jobs were to be axed by British Coal Board chairman, Ian MacGregor, whom he described as the 'American butcher' brought in by Mrs Thatcher to destroy the mining industry.

Right from the outset, the pit strike was a bitter and violent affair. As a trade union which believed in ballots and the rule of law, we were against violence, particularly after some of the experiences the EETPU leadership, including myself, had endured. But, perhaps most of all, we had a conviction embedded in our political souls that elected governments could only be removed by a fully democratic vote. I had to make our attitude clear to the members and the world outside, and so I went for Scargill's jugular. Using the phrase for the first and certainly not the last time, I told our union's Industrial Conference at Scarborough in North Yorkshire that the miners were 'lions led by donkeys'. The description encapsulated the brave solidarity of ordinary miners and the stupidity of those who led them.

I was to use the insult to even greater effect, and be howled down by the loony Lefties, at the 1985 Labour Party Conference when the NUM was speeding towards certain defeat. I borrowed the phrase from the German First World War general, von Hindenburg, who used it when describing the fine fighting qualities of the British soldiers in the trenches on the Somme while criticizing the ineptitude of their military commanders. My father had been a Great War trench soldier, so I said the words with feeling. There were mining regiments on the Somme, so I thought this description was not only apt, but would hit home where it hurt. The miners were no more defeated by their own inability than were their gallant forebears.

We in the EETPU could have been cowards and walked on the other side, letting Scargill get on with it, but that is not my way. We had to explain to our Conference and our members why we opposed Scargill. The NUM leadership was ignoring the basic right to vote, and their blatant refusal to allow the individual miner a say as to his own fate stuck out like a jagged rock. My Scarborough speech was the one upon which I was to base a series of bitter attacks on Scargill, baiting him to condemn the violence and allow miners a vote.

I began by stressing that a dispute in another industry was none of our business, but interference in the steel industry by the NUM should concern us, and a picket on power stations certainly did. I expressed my sadness that Scargill had now turned his back on the cohesive TUC energy policy thrashed out with the NUM when it was

43

led by his predecessors, Joe Gormley and Laurence Daly. The 'Plan for Coal' had given the coal industry the stable framework which would allow it to expand to the end of the century. But, as I told Conference, under Scargill the NUM actively campaigned against TUC policy and cast doubt on the competence and strength of other energy industry unions to serve the interests of their members. Speaking as the recently elected TUC Energy Committee Chairman, I saw it as my duty to bridge this difference.

Then I came to what was really behind the miners' strike – an attempt through extra-parliamentary action to overthrow a democratically elected government. As I told the delegates at Scarborough: 'The other component of this dispute which concerns us is the attempt to widen the action to embrace other industries and to effectively bring about a general strike, which can only have the political objective of over-throwing the government. It is only the Notts miners with their proper and honourable insistence on a national ballot that stand in the way.'

Driving my message home, I quoted Arthur Scargill, who wrote in the Communist *Morning Star* newspaper on 28 March 1984: 'Every sinew in every factory, office, dole queue, docks, railway, plant and mill will need to be strained to the maximum. Waiting in the wings are four million unemployed whose numbers could swell the picket line at any time. What is urgently needed is the rapid and total mobilization of the trade union and labour movements to take positive advantage of a unique opportunity to defend our class and roll back the machinery of oppression, exploitation and deep-seated human misery . . .'

What twaddle, what hypocrisy, I mused. This nonsense could have been written by a committee of Stalinists in the Kremlin. Maybe it was. But that revolutionary rhetoric was moderate compared with a pamphlet I then quoted headed: 'Support the Miners with a General Strike'. It said: 'Such a General Strike, waged by the whole of the working class and its middle class allies, will involve the revolutionary struggle for power. Its outcome must be the overthrow of the historically outmoded capitalist system, the smashing of the state machine and the establishment of a Workers' Revolutionary Govern-ment.' That quote said it all and revealed the motive behind the madness of the miners' strike.

As I declared to our Conference: 'It is not the prospect of victory for such policies that frightens me. It is the inevitability of their defeat. A defeat which will not only do great harm to the NUM, but to the whole trade union movement.' I made it clear then as I have since that our union was not prepared to bring down elected governments. Rejection of an arbitrary law might be justified in Poland, Russia, South Africa or Chile, where citizens were denied a democratic vote, but not in Great Britain.

I am setting out these arguments in some detail, because what I said then provided a valuable insight into the nightmare that would have ensued had Scargill won. In view of later events, my comments turned out to be an ominous prophecy. Putting my personal stamp of authority on our stance towards the NUM leadership, I declared, 'Who do these nursery revolutionaries think they are kidding? Abandon our support for law and parliamentary democracy, and trade unions are defenceless. There are other powers exerting their will in the balance of society – some of them command disciplined men with guns in their hands. If we remove – if we provide the justification for removing – the muzzle of law from these hounds, we will not quickly be forgiven. What army, what police force, both Conservative institutions, will properly serve a future Labour government if we prove that the electorate, the ballot box, is not supreme?

'All of us who have spent our lives in this movement have been raised with a respect for miners, for their loyalty and steadfastness. Their security and rewards should be beyond doubt, and differences over the continuation of particular pits can surely be determined by agreed criteria or even an independent commission. The ingredients of an industrial victory for the miners are there if only their leaders would move to secure them and, in the process, they would gain the support of the whole movement. As it is, I am reminded of the German general von Hindenburg's description of the British Army of the Great War, considering the fighting qualities of the British soldier and their generals. He said they were "lions led by donkeys". The miners *are* lions. I'm not sure our members could be so described, but neither are we here on the Executive donkeys.'

Early in the miners' strike, NUM Vice-President, the hard-drinking craggy Scot, Mick McGahey, had coined the term 'domino effect' to describe how industrial action had spread from one pit to another. I firmly told our Scarborough delegates, 'We will not allow our union to become another domino. We will not placidly accept the escalation from one day of action to another resulting in a nationwide strike. The Executive will not support such a serious extension without the consent of all trade unions involved through a ballot vote, and even then our recommendation would be to vote "No".

45

'The work of our members in the electricity supply industry is of great value to the whole community. Indeed, without it, civilized life would cease. It may well be that the coming months will test all of us in the way we bear that responsibility. I hope you understand from what I have said that we will act in the indivisible interests of our members and our country.'

Despite the fact that the miners' dispute was escalating rapidly, with horrific scenes of violence on the nation's television screens each night as miner was set against miner, family against family, it was not even being discussed by the TUC General Council. This was due to the quaint traditions of the TUC carthorse – nicknamed thus because of its lack of speed. Because Arthur had not asked for help, we could not even talk about it. At the May 1984 council meeting, John Lyons, the General Secretary of the Electrical Power Engineers' Association, tried to raise the issue. But he was told by the gaunt and grey Len Murray, who was about to hand over the TUC reins to Norman Willis, that this was not a matter for discussion.

What a ridiculous tradition, I thought, as I drove back to our Bromley offices from the TUC's Bloomsbury headquarters. It had reached the point where I was convinced that the miners were in for a hiding. I switched on the car radio to hear that the latest attempt to get negotiations going between the NUM and the Coal Board had foundered. It was then that I wrote to Heathfield, believing somewhat mistakenly that he was more rational and more prepared to listen to reason than was the NUM *Führer*, Scargill. I offered Heathfield support, but only if they had a ballot, if they renounced the violence on the picket lines and if they renounced the political objectives in the strike to bring down the government. If they did those things, I would have a ballot and urge our power station members to stop work in their support. Heathfield knocked me back on all three demands.

I kept quiet about that exchange of correspondence. I could have damaged the miners then. It was only when I was getting hammered at the TUC Conference at Brighton in September 1984 that I referred to it, though not in great detail. I let out the real significance of the letters when I had to justify myself to my own Conference at Blackpool in July 1985. In my letter to Heathfield on 24 May 1984, I told him I had been moved to write on a personal basis 'because of my growing concern that your present dispute could result in a considerable setback for the NUM – a setback that can only adversely affect the rest of the movement'.

I told Heathfield my union was 'absolutely opposed' to law-breaking and the political use of strikes to bring down elected governments, adding, 'The overlaying of this dispute with political rhetoric and objectives is an obstacle to our support.' Then, I sank the knife deep into Scargill by suggesting the rest of the NUM leaders abandon him and seek their own peace deal. I wrote, 'The other main difficulty is the division in your own ranks. To put it bluntly and privately, could the NUM disavow the overt political objectives of some spokesmen – maybe in the form of making it clear that their sole objective is securing the future of the industry through an honourable negotiated settlement? Could they even at this stage unite their union with a national ballot?' Even though I was seeking the impossible from such a vehement political ideologue as Scargill, I felt there was a faint chance of Heathfield realizing the NUM was staring defeat in the face.

I added, 'I ask these questions because if you did, then I would do all in my power and influence to bring real assistance to the NUM. I mean by that I would recommend to our Executive that we ballot all our members in coal-fired power stations to stop work in your support. Frankly, without the moves from the NUM that I have indicated, such a recommendation would not have a chance and I certainly would not initiate it.'

Heathfield's reply on 1 June was a desperate disappointment. As I sat in my office at Hayes Court reading it, I felt like picking up the telephone and telling him he was a hypocrite. The letter may as well have been dictated by Scargill, for it lacked any positive comment. Had Arthur written Heathfield's script? According to Heathfield, it was all the government's and MacGregor's fault. The NUM was to blame for nothing. There would be no national ballot, and the law would be ignored if necessary.

Heathfield wrote, 'My own view on the breakdown (last week) of discussions is that MacGregor's intransigence, in particular his unwillingness to negotiate at all, has led to the dispute. He simply issues ultimatums and expects everyone to respond. Senior members of the NCB (National Coal Board) are personally horrified by his style of management. I consider the rest of the movement will be seriously affected if the NUM loses this dispute. Many of our members, and other trade unionists, consider the NUM to be the last line of resistance to the present government attack on the Labour Movement. I acknowledge that you may not necessarily share that point of view.

'The NUM has consistently recognized that legislation designed to weaken the trade union movement may have to be ignored. Indeed, had not our predecessors chosen to ignore laws which prevented them from combining together, we would not be exchanging correspondence.'

Heathfield claimed that miners in pits immediately threatened with closure had 'responded spontaneously'. 'In other areas least affected,' he added, 'local ballots have shown overwhelming opposition. In the latter, calls were made for a national ballot,' Heathfield admitted. But he went on, with the surly arrogance which gives we trade union leaders such a bad name, 'I do not consider a ballot in such circumstances can be part of the democratic process. In reality, it is an attempt to apply a veto and prevent men from defending their jobs. I do not consider miners in the least-affected East Midlands should have the right to say to miners in the acutely affected North East, "You can't defend your jobs." It has also been recognized that a national ballot would not change the situation, ie Notts would continue to work if the ballot result was positive. If negative, Yorkshire, Scotland, Wales, North East would continue to strike.' With that kind of bewildering ability to stand logic on its head, no wonder the NUM were not just beaten, but beaten to a pulp.

The NUM could have had help from us which I think would have been decisive and the dispute could have been over by the middle of 1984. Instead of that, it dragged on and on, bringing shame on our movement, which will find it hard, if not impossible, ever to recover. The government would not even have attempted to take on the power workers and the miners at the same time. So, although we were seen as the hammer of the miners throughout that dispute, we did offer them an honourable and dignified way out if they really wanted a resolution of the matter on industrial terms and in a way which their own members would have supported – that is, by having a ballot. They would have avoided a split and snatched victory from the jaws of defeat. Arthur has a lot to answer for.

By August 1984, on the eve of the Trades Union Congress at Brighton, the NUM had asked for TUC support. It already had certain Left-wing union leaders handing over suitcases full of cash to NUM officials, who were not paying a penny in strike pay to men locked out of the pits, but, of course, cash was paid out to flying pickets. By contrast, our union paid out a total of £39,000 in strike pay to our handful of men in the industry. Scargill wanted to take the rest of the movement with him on his crusade to rid Britain of Maggie Thatcher without a ballot and by any means possible, including a violent revolution to overthrow the state.

The TUC General Council produced a statement on the miners' dispute it wanted Congress to support. It gave Arthur a blank cheque. The statement backed the NUM objectives of saving pits, jobs and mining communities; supported a concerted campaign to alleviate hardship in the coalfields and maintain the union financially; and agreed to harden up the dispute by not moving coal, coke, or oil substituted for it, across NUM official picket lines. It was a statement I went on to describe at the Conference as 'dishonest and deficient'.

It was also a sad end to Len Murray's tenure. It would have been nice to see old Len go out on a high. Instead, he looked older and more worried by the minute. When, later that week, he handed over the General Secretary's chair to Norman Willis, until then the unofficial TUC clown prince and joke-teller, things went from bad to worse.

That week at Brighton was Hammond against a wall of noise and ignorance. Only my old ally John Lyons and a chap from the Iron and Steel Trades Confederation backed me. The rest fell over in Scargill's wake. I came under tremendous pressure to keep my mouth shut that Monday afternoon at Brighton. The evening before and even that morning, I was approached by various TUC grandees and asked not to rock the boat, but it was too late for that. I would not be silenced.

Even in the Brighton Centre where the Conference was staged, David Basnett of the General and Municipal Workers' Union, a man considered to be the ultimate fixer of TUC events, failed in his attempt to work out a shabby compromise. He said, 'Come on, Eric. You're not going to cause a fuss, are you? Let's muck it about a bit. Put your hand up for this and that to get us through the week. The lads in the power stations won't walk out anyway.' I wondered if I was the only man on the planet with the view that Scargill was a menace who must be stopped. I looked up at the tall, gangling figure of Basnett and declared, 'If I'm the only one here with the guts to tell Scargill his fortune, I'm having my say.'

There was a formidable array of trade union opinion against me, some of it vociferous, some of it in sorrow. Even John Lyons asked me to 'keep my head down' and not repeat in public what I said at the General Council. When I refused to bend the knee to Arthur, John decided to say his piece, too. It was quite outrageous. I don't know what we were there for if not to speak what we thought was our members' minds, and to vote in that way. Surely, we were not there to confuse things so much that our own members did not know where they stood? The rest of the General Council must have been deaf, the lot of them. If anybody was a friend, a candid friend, it was us as far as the miners were concerned.

Len Murray told Congress the TUC stood 'shoulder to shoulder' with Arthur. I winced at the thought of how those thousands of miners were being made empty promises which neither Len, nor anyone else at the TUC, could keep. Union members were asked by Len to 'dig deep in their pockets' for the miners. More recent NUM inquiries into the alleged misuse of millions of pounds of the union's funds during the strike give those appeals an even more bizarre look.

Scargill would have won his standing ovation if he had simply sneezed that year. Everything he did or said was Holy Writ. He got raucous applause for a speech in which he slammed MacGregor, Thatcher and unions like mine which had not handed over their bank balance and their open-ended support. Scargill also made a threat. He said if the TUC rejected the motion backing the NUM, the movement would be 'stained until the end of time'.

I had a last check over my notes as railwaymen's leader Jimmy Knapp, white-haired beyond his years, went over the top to tell delegates how his union would not walk past a cow if it crossed a field with 'NUM picket line' written on it. Even Gavin Laird, a man I respect and leader of the engineers, made a speech supporting the miners. It is not one about which he cares to be reminded.

When ASLEF (Associated Society of Locomotive Engineers and Firemen) train drivers' leader Ray Buckton, the TUC Chairman, beckoned me to the rostrum, I knew I was in for a hard time as a howl went up from the Left. The second time I was unable to continue because of the barrage of abuse, I used a barb I had prepared in my hotel bedroom the night before. Ray Buckton shouted above the din of the farce, 'Let him finish, and then shout if you wish.' It won a pause and I was ready for it. Through clenched teeth, I snarled, 'Hitler would have been proud of you lot.' As I had hoped, that made them even angrier. I savoured that one.

It seemed a spontaneous, heated response, but it wasn't. It seemed to me that the Left's determination to suppress any voice opposed to them was no different in principle to the Nazi tactics as they fought for power in the early Thirties. I told Congress that members of the General Council had voted in favour of the statement expecting that the threatened strangling of the power stations would be ineffective. But I warned, 'My union is not going to stop electricity as a result of this statement or ten thousand like it.'

Men I thought had guts sat on their hands and did nothing to back me as I added, 'It is hard to say to tens of thousands of decent miners who have been out for six months that their leaders have misled them, that they cannot win Scargill's sort of victory. However, there is another reason for some leaders holding back which is less honourable. It is fear. Not just fear of the NUM zealots, but fear of being politically attacked by the 57 varieties of political extremist who have attached themselves to the miners' cause, or fear of being branded Right-wing or fear of being put under pressure in their own union. What is outrageous is that all this flinching bears no relationship to the views of their members. They are appalled by the violence and they want no part of it. The General Council has spoken in this statement. Today Congress will speak. But, I tell you, brothers, your members have yet to be heard. In their name, I oppose the statement and the motion.'

I lost, of course, by a massive majority. But history will show I was right and they were wrong. We were the only union to test the water with a ballot. I put my statement, Len Murray's and the TUC's to our members. They backed me by 5–1. Members of the EETPU and many other unions wrote in in their shoals saying they were glad somebody had stood up and told the truth. They belonged to the Transport and General Workers, General and Municipal, the whole lot. I firmly believe that we kept trade-unionism alive in the electricity supply industry that winter, because without that sort of trade union voice that they could relate to, I think many would have walked away from trade unions altogether. Hundreds wanted to join us from other unions, but we did the decent thing and did not take them in, even though with hindsight perhaps we were a little naive and idealistic at the time. If I had known then what I know now, I would not have hesitated. I'd have welcomed the lot of them with open arms. But at least we were trying to play the game.

That evening, after the debate, Arthur Scargill, myself and David Basnett were asked on BBC2's *Newsnight* for a round-table discussion with Peter Snow. We were going over the dispute and our views. Unbeknown to us, they were relaying this to MacGregor at a studio in London. Later the *Newsnight* people were very apologetic and claimed there had been a mistake: MacGregor had been listening to what we were saying and commenting on it, while we were unable to comment on what he was saying. I thought it was rather sharp practice, and it was one of the few times Scargill, Basnett and myself were united in our condemnation of the media.

At the end of the programme, David Basnett made another appeal to me, this time in front of millions of television viewers, to unite behind the TUC. I said, 'We'll have a ballot vote of our members, you have one of yours, and I'll abide by their decision.' Of course, he never did have a ballot vote. Neither did Arthur.

The misery for the miners and their families continued unabated through the winter of 1984. One month later, the Scargill strike bandwagon was up in Blackpool selling its elixir of job losses and false hope at the Labour Party Conference. Tory newspaper proprietors must have been rubbing their hands with glee at the prospect of seeing Labour Leader Neil Kinnock suck up to a monster like Scargill who was losing him votes by the minute as the public were alienated by the rantings from the picket line.

As my driver, former policeman Les Hill, took me to our usual hotel, the Norbreck Castle – nicknamed Colditz because of its bleak appearance – I swallowed with my usual dry throat. I tend to suffer with it, particularly when I do a lot of speaking. So when I was trying to attract the attention of Eric Heffer, the burly Left-winger in the chair at the Conference in Blackpool's Winter Gardens, I was sucking a lozenge. I wasn't going to strain my voice by shouting. I wanted to save it to tell a few fortunes. With Heffer in the chair, I didn't have much prospect of being called. So I turned to my EETPU Executive colleague Eric Clayton, who had a powerful stentorian voice and said, 'Eric, you've got to get me in here.' Heffer had not seen me amongst the forest of hands. He certainly didn't want to. So Eric bellowed out, 'What about taking somebody against?' They were all in favour of the miners, so Heffer said, 'I've been asked to take somebody against. How am I to know who's against?' Then Heffer nodded at me with a wry smile and said, 'Eric Hammond.' I was still sucking the sweet, but I was so surprised to get to the rostrum that I didn't take it out and I made the entire speech with the lozenge in my mouth.

It was one of the speeches which pleased me most, because I led them right into a trap at the end. Rising above the constant heckling, I quoted from a previous conference report which stated, 'We should not be passing resolutions and looking with confidence to elections two or three years hence. But we should realize the vital struggle of the age is upon us here and now, and we should sit down to the hard concrete work of devising measures for taking part in the struggle and driving the government from office and from power.' I added, 'It sounds familiar: is it Scargill, is it Skinner (Dennis Skinner), is it Benn (Tony Benn)? No. It wasn't written this year – it was taken from the 1926 Conference report, and the speaker was Oswald Mosley. I oppose the statement and the motion. Beware the road you tread.'

Earlier I had castigated Labour's National Executive Committee for failing to call on the NUM to observe the TUC picketing code, or to demand an end to the violence and hooliganism on the picket line. As I told them that they were making a complete climbdown to Scargill, I was faced with a barrage of yelling.

Heffer, of all people, came to my rescue. My main concern was that he would stop the clock and not dock me any time for my allotted period. He said, 'Order, order, order. Comrades, this is a Labour Party Conference, not a rabble outside. Whilst I am in the chair, no matter how much I or anyone else may disagree with the person speaking, they will have a proper hearing in this conference. I know passions are running high, but there is a tradition of this movement, which is basic tolerance. Continue, Eric.'

I didn't let that one go. I told the baying hounds of the far Left, 'It seems some of the comrades are in favour of free speech everywhere else in the world except this conference.' I warned them they would live to regret the charade they were enacting at the next election. The British electorate, I told them, did not trust appeasers at home or abroad. And in a further prediction which, sadly, proved true, I declared, 'The cult of the personality, the cult of violence, has been created and will haunt this movement for many years to come.'

The real losers were the dedicated people in the NUM and other unions who were misused by Arthur Scargill. There really wasn't a better way to destroy that union. If a group of CIA plotters had sat down in 1983 and said, 'How can we wreck this union?', they couldn't have gone about it more effectively than Arthur did.

As we faced that winter of 1984, more and more people in the movement were coming to the view for which they had shouted me down. The miners were on to a hiding to nothing. They were basing the dispute on sand because they had not had a proper ballot. NUM members were going back to work.

The Union of Democratic Mineworkers was formed on the basis of

Scargill's denial of members' rights. They saw that he was going to intrude even further into their rights. Once the UDM was formed, I had a number of private meetings with Roy Lynk, and we staged a meeting of the two union Executives at our Cudham Hall training college in Kent – well away from the glare of the television arc lights. We decided that we had much in common and ought to work as closely as we could together. But the Press got hold of it and, as a result, Norman Willis wrote to me saying he was concerned to have read reports that we intended to form a breakaway union which could form the nucleus for an alternative and more Moderate TUC.

At the same time, I was embroiled in the difficulties of Wapping. I could not fight on every front. So I sent Norman a copy of a statement we had made, saying we were friends of the UDM. I assured Norman this fully conveyed our view. We had no formal alliance with the UDM, but we sought to be friends as we do with all democratic unions. We were unable to develop our relationship then, but I very much hope that both myself and my successor will make strides towards a full merger with Roy Lynk and his fine band of trade unionists. I think we can and will do that.

At the EETPU's Biennial Delegate Conference at Blackpool in July 1985, the Left in our union, or at least the rump of it that remained, was determined to have a go at me. The NUM had lost the strike in March and had returned to work with their tails between their legs. The motion condemning our Executive for saying the NUM was wrong was the only one on the agenda which referred to the miners' strike. It came from that noted mining area of Milton Keynes and was heavily defeated on a show of hands. This was not before I had pointed out that the real mining areas knew that we alone had given men who were dual members of both the EETPU and the NUM regular strike pay amounting to a total of £921 each. Those involved were grateful for the material support we gave. They didn't get a penny from Scargill unless they acted as his picket-line storm troops. None of our people did.

I read out a letter from a member in Barnsley, right in Scargill's native Yorkshire heartland. He wrote, 'Thank you for the final cheque, amounting to £201.60, in payment to the account in respect of the NUM dispute. I should like to thank you once again for this money which, in the circumstances, was more than welcome, having received no remuneration and even food parcels from the NUM.' We looked after our people. Scargill didn't.

Eric's father, Arthur Hammond

Below Eric on the beach at Ramsgate, 1934

Eric, aged 10, in 1940

Above left With fellow evacuees on board SS Cornerbrook en route to Newfoundland

Above In Newfoundland: Eric (centre) with the Nichols children, Duncan, Kitty and Bert

Right Skating on Newfoundland ice

Above Eric (on the left, back row) in the Suez Canal Zone, 1951

Married to Brenda, Gravesend, 1953

Ivan, the first born, with proud parents

Isle of Grain, 1953. Eric did Frank Spencer impressions before Michael Crawford!

Addressing a strike meeting at Tilbury Power Station, 1957

Cocky local politician, 1956

New Executive Councillor honouring union veterans, 1964

In China, 1979, with Eric Varley, Secretary of State for Industry

Hammond catches 'em young in China!

October 1990: the EETPU donate a mini-bus, printing press and office equipment to the Soviet Independent Miners' Union

Planting a cherry tree at Hitachi's south Wales factory, 1985

Left Ron Todd

Right Les Cannon

Left Ron Todd

Brenda Dean

Tony Dubbins

Norman Willis was choked off by the whole affair. The TUC had made valiant efforts to find a solution, but that man Scargill always got in the way. He would never keep to one position. He was like a blessed eel. Arthur was at it again when the TUC trooped up to Blackpool once more in September 1985. You would have thought Arthur had won the strike the way he strutted about. It was a black Monday for the trade union movement as, by a majority of just 64,000, Scargill won the right to a complete review by the next Labour government of all cases of miners jailed as a result of the strike, reinstatement of sacked miners, reimbursement of the NUM and all other unions for all money confiscated by fines, receivership and sequestration, plus the ending of all pit closures, other than by exhaustion. What Scargill was after, really, was that he should be made immune from the effects of the law and the effects of the strike.

The Left, surprise, surprise, led by such notables as Lou Adams of ASLEF and Alan Sapper of ACTT, the television technicians' union, all bowled in with their support for Arthur. Then there was Norman, who made a real mess of it in a bumbling speech in which he actually accepted most of the demands, bar one, the call for reimbursement. There was nobody against.

Norman told Congress there was a 'profound unease' about substantial parts of the demands set out in the motion. The Left gave the hapless and hopeless Norman plenty of stick as he said many had told him of their unease. Norman's lone voice was not enough to swing it, and he went down to Scargill by 4,585,000 votes to 4,649,000. I held fire, and everybody else did, too. I thought I would get everybody's backs up, but it was a mistake not to speak.

I didn't make the same mistake a month later at the Labour Party Conference at Bournemouth. I hit the headlines by once more describing the miners as 'lions led by donkeys'. It did not stop Scargill winning again, this time by 3,542,000 votes to 2,912,000. We had put forward an almost identical motion to the one at the TUC. Labour's NEC opposed retrospective reimbursement. Even Kinnock could not swing it by asking Arthur to remit his motion. No amount of arm-twisting would persuade Scargill. But the public take little notice of Labour Conference decisions. What they do notice is when an angry old hound like me rears up and snaps at my tormentors.

Ron Todd backed Scargill. He did not much care for my donkeys simile and said, 'I have heard references this morning to lions being led by donkeys. Well, I am an animal lover. I tell you something. I prefer donkeys to jackals.' More importantly, Gavin Laird of the engineers and the GMWU's David Basnett came out of their shells and went against Scargill.

To deafening boos and catcalling, I bated the Conference with the remark 'Who wants the headline "Kinnock Defeated, Scargill Reigns Supreme"? Is it our friends, or is it Thatcher and (David) Owen who desperately want you to support this motion? This time use your head and deny them.' I didn't have long, so I shouted against the tide of bleating Lefties to warn that even though trade union leaders were important people, none of us was above the law: 'If we convince the British people and British trade-unionists that we are prepared to allow trade union bosses to operate without penalty from the law, they will rightly reject us.'

My concluding remarks earned me the expected boos, but also some applause. I said, 'The miners did not choose to strike. The triumvirate (Scargill, Heathfield and McGahey) did and they were defeated. They were defeated because they did not trust the miners, because they refused to make the necessary industrial alliances. The miners were no more defeated than were their gallant forebears on the Somme. Lions led by donkeys. They should spend the rest of their lives atoning for that fault, not hawking their defeat from conference to conference.'

Shortly after the Conference, the Energy Secretary, Peter Walker, told me at his office at Millbank, Westminster, that Mrs Thatcher had said to him, 'I wish I had thought of that donkeys quote first.' I always liked Walker because he was a man of independent mind. People looked on him, I suppose, as someone who was poised there waiting for the sack from Thatcher because he was of a different Tory school. But he would not accommodate her in order to hold office, so she had to put up with him.

As for Scargill, he was a sad figure in the end; a very sincere man, but completely wrong-headed about the way he was to go about protecting the miners. There never was the protection for the miners that he envisaged: that is, that pits would stay open even beyond their economic life. The government and the Coal Board had made up their minds that they were going to have to have a fight, so it would seem from all the circumstances that they set up Scargill, and prepared themselves for a battle royal. Then, it was only a matter of time before their pursuit of a policy that they were not going to have pits go beyond their economic life meant a clash was inevitable. The government was well prepared. It had massive stockpiles of coal. Peter Walker had consulted me about oil-fired power stations, so they kept on extra sets at the Isle of Grain in Kent which were burning round the clock throughout the dispute ten per cent beyond their stated capacity.

Had Scargill, the donkey who led those valiant miners, taken up my call for a proper ballot in May 1984, he could have saved himself from the ignominy which followed. But it is his men and their families we should pity the most. They lost what is most important to every human being – their pride.

During this period of the miners' dispute, Norman Willis and I took up office – immediately after the September 1984 Trades Union Congress. Even though neither of us was actually in post, we were both beset by the crisis created by the strike. Despite his years as a TUC backroom boy and before that as researcher to Jack Jones, the veteran former leader of the Transport and General Workers Union, Norman was ill-prepared for the period ahead, which was to see the trade union movement divided and diminished as Mrs Thatcher's industrial relations reforms cut a swathe through the TUC's beliefs and traditions.

He is a poet and would probably be happier in just that capacity – going around reading bits of poetry to other poets. He was not equipped, either by experience or by temperament, to be the man whom the trade union movement needed in this difficult period. Norman wasn't the man for managing, controlling and directing a change which was necessary. His predecessor Len Murray didn't get on with him. He gave Norman no substantial duties to perform. Len basically gave Norman the job of going around kissing babies' heads at Labour clubs throughout the country at trade union meetings. This did not equip Norman to deal with the problems facing British industry or trade unions. It did, however, qualify him to be elected to the TUC's top job, because he became a very popular gladhander, a hail-fellow-well-met. In the end, that counts for a great deal in the sort of trade union leadership circles which finally decide who is to be General Secretary of the TUC.

Norman was a safe bet, because he was voted in by union leaders who did not have to bother asking the members whether their choice should become leader of that unrepresentative group. He had been challenged by David Lea, head of the TUC's Economic Department. At the time he was looking for support, he bumped into a group of us

EETPU fellows at Scarborough where we were staging our industrial conferences in 1984. Norman was attending a conference in the same seaside town organized by a rather obscure body called the General Federation of Trade Unions. This was a group of small unions affiliated to the TUC. As usual, when there are electricians about, there is plenty of jesting and joshing. We asked Norman what it was worth for us to support Lea. Norman, knowing our reputation amongst the brethren, declared, 'Do anything, but don't support me.' So I always claimed to him afterwards that since we backed David Lea, we were responsible for his success.

However, when we got into our difficulties over taking government ballot money, I did suggest to him an alternative way of becoming General Secretary of the TUC. I argued that the TUC was, indeed, a union and therefore there was an obligation under the new Tory laws that the General Secretary should be elected not by the people who come together to form the Trades Union Congress every September, but rather by the general membership of trade unions. At that time, it amounted to almost ten million people. I said that nobody else in the country would have such a constituency, such influence arising from the vote of so many people. It would be well beyond the vote gained by a Prime Minister, any MP or Cabinet Minister. This was obviously impressing Norman until suddenly the penny dropped and he said, 'Yes, but who else would be on the ballot paper?' I assured him I hadn't thought of the matter until he mentioned it, because he seemed rather anxious that I should not be a competitor.

Would I have won? I reckon I had a good chance. Looking at the few measures that have been taken of genuine opinion, those polls show our union to be more in touch with the members than any other leadership. Even when they threw us out of the TUC, a number of polls taken then showed more rank-and-file members backed us. The mass of trade-unionists thought the TUC was in the wrong: that always gave me great heart for the fight that was to come. So, who knows, maybe Norman could have become a full-time poet after all had he been prepared to accept the risks of the real election world.

During our regular meetings at TUC headquarters, Norman would invariably uncork a bottle of his favourite tipple, the Mouton Cadet *blanc*. There were always a number of get-togethers in Norman's office after a committee or General Council meeting. The wine was nearly always open. I have left Norman after sharing a bottle or two feeling quite at ease with the world, only to go to his outer office and see two others waiting to see him. They would be treated as hospitably as I was. This largesse has never caused any major problems or embarrassment, but old Norman believes that his poems, his jokes and his singing are more acceptable amongst his audience than really is the case. Another glass of wine convinces him that he must sing another song. He once did it at an American Embassy party, and the wife of the Ambassador, Charles H. Price II, politely but firmly asked him to leave the stage he was sharing with a Dixieland band. But I have never known Norman to be nasty to anyone – in or out of drink. He may get upset, but that's as far as it goes. In fact, in the summer of 1991 Norman took the pledge and, as a result, lost three stone in weight.

Norman was basically a peg which didn't fit into the right hole. He is typical of the trade union movement, which is full of people who just want to get along from one meeting to the next. They have little purpose, other than filling seats. They don't give the impression of wanting to change anything. That's what makes committed Left-wingers like Ken Gill and Arthur Scargill so effective. They can take a bunch of chickens at the rush, who will all go along with an idea because most have hawks back in their own Executive committees. They are not going to cross the big hawks at the General Council only to have it reported back to their little committee, who would take them to task. So there's almost a system of blackmail and re-cycling of what goes on at the General Council and that, in turn, is batted to and fro between the TUC and the individual union Executive. It gets quite removed from what the ordinary Joe feels or wants.

My view is that most of the so-called trade union barons are just nice people wanting an easy life, muddling along to the next committee meeting. One exception is Rodney Bickerstaffe, General Secretary of the National Union of Public Employees. He is ambitious not just for his Left-wing policies, but for himself, too. Rodney, a close ally of Arthur Scargill during the 1978–9 Winter of Discontent, made his big advance in the TUC's councils when he became Chairman of the Economic Committee. The previous Chairman had been David, later Lord, Basnett, leader of the General and Municipal Workers Union. His retirement in 1986 meant that the chairmanship of this most powerful committee, next to the Finance and General Purposes Committee, was up for grabs. The election was to take place at the May Economic Committee meeting. It was going to be a close thing.

At the time, we were at our Conference in Scarborough. The

Moderates, including us, were supporting Tony Christopher, General Secretary of the Inland Revenue Staff Federation. What better choice than a man whose members dealt with tax affairs at the heart of the economy? Tony was seen as a quiet, but able man who did his homework. We were keen to get Tony elected, so I promised to do an early morning dash down to London, attend the Economic Committee and vote for him.

There was plenty of time, but as always with British Rail, never enough when things are going wrong. Trains were cancelled and, frustratingly, there was nothing I could do. I finally arrived half an hour after the meeting started – choked to see Rodney Bickerstaffe in the chair and believing it was all because of my inability to get there on time. Rodney had won by just one vote. I didn't feel quite so badly about it afterwards when I discovered that Gerry Russell, a member of the AEU Executive, who was also supporting Christopher, had got to the meeting five minutes late. Otherwise, things would have been different.

During the meeting, National Union of Railwaymen's leader, Jimmy Knapp, mentioned the case of a passenger who was suing British Rail for its failure to get him to a crucial appointment. This had cost a great deal of money in lost business. Looking Bickerstaffe right in the eye, I said, 'Chairman, perhaps Jimmy Knapp can advise me how I can get some recompense from British Rail for the disaster they have visited not just on me personally, but on this country by seeing to it that you have been made Chairman of the Economic Committee by virtue of not getting me here on time.' There was a chuckle all round and Bickerstaffe had the grace to laugh. But I wasn't laughing when I said it, I really meant it.

Unfortunately, Tony Christopher would not stand again when the next election came around. Such was the power of the status quo vote in the TUC corridors of power.

5
Thatcher's ballot bonus

For decades, those fearful of members' power in the trade union movement argued that postal ballots were too expensive. To stage them would automatically force a rise in membership subscriptions. They got away with an undemocratic and unrepresentative system of voting through badly attended branch meetings, or by simply appointing leaders through small committees of activists. This denial of the basic democratic rights of union members reached its height in the post-war years as the unions, or at least their leaders, grew in strength and power. But it was all to end in the radical Thatcher years, when it was open season on the union bosses, whose privileged positions were placed under the Tory spotlight. In one fell swoop, Maggie Thatcher swept away years of abuse. Though I was never her greatest fan, the one decision she did get right was to underpin the value of secret postal ballots and let the union members, not their leaders, decide. Thatcher did a favour to everyone who believes in fair play and union democracy.

In 1985, my union was to stand united with our friends in Terry Duffy's Amalgamated Engineering Union as we faced expulsion from the TUC for claiming government funds for our ballots. It ended with a miserable TUC climbdown as ostrich-like union leaders were forced to pull their heads from the sand and join the rest of us in the twentieth century, but, more than anything, it was a crucial test of whether the unions were prepared to accept the rule of law by a democratically elected government. The Left twisted and turned and more than flirted with the idea of breaking the law. Within days of Jim Prior, the ruddy-faced Secretary of State for Employment, setting up a scheme to make payments from public funds towards the costs of secret ballots, the TUC made it an offence to accept. Many general councillors and general secretaries felt their days would be numbered when each of their members had a postal vote. TUC minutes from that period state clearly that transgressors would face disciplinary action if they applied for funds without a specific decision of Congress. Nevertheless, the mood of outright opposition was reinforced by a special Wembley conference of union Executives in April 1982.

At that time, I was still just an EETPU Executive Councillor, but Frank Chapple gave me the chance to say my piece. I did not tell the TUC what it wanted to hear. I suggested that the opposition to taking public money from some sections of the movement masked their fear of the changes that would come in the wake of members' power, and I pointed out the double standards of the TUC taking £1.6 million a year from the government for education purposes and nothing for ballots. Political parties, including Labour, took money, too. They received substantial public funds at election times, including free post. Norman Tebbit, the aptly nicknamed 'Chingford Skinhead', who had become Employment Secretary after Prior, must have been dancing around his Westminster office with glee as speaker after speaker made it clear they did not like the idea, as Terry Duffy put it, of 'taking orders from the bottom'.

I asked the conference: 'Does anyone here really believe that the Tories have produced this (employment) bill to improve industrial relations? No. They calculate that if they are seen to be union-bashing, then they will gain electoral advantage. Are they wrong? Does not every measure of public – indeed, trade union members' – opinion show that we have only minority support?'

The pace of the ballot money wrangle hotted up at the end of 1984 when Tom King, the latest Tory Employment Secretary, set a February deadline for ballot money claims. Any retrospective claims made after that would be invalid. I was a new boy and had been General Secretary for only a couple of months, but I wasn't going to allow our union to turn down Maggie's offer and lose this money owed to our members. In any case, they had helped provide, through taxation, the very public monies we were claiming. It's not every day somebody offers something for nothing. Those of us who held regular ballots always believed that, one day, the trade union movement would come round to a more reasonable frame of mind.

There had been no pressing need for unions like ours and the AEU to claim and, as far as we were concerned, it was money in the bank. But when the government moved the goalposts, the need to claim was more pressing. We were owed £250,000. The AEU was due to collect more than £1 million. Once our Executive had decided to apply for the money, I notified Gavin Laird, the AEU General Secretary. He told me, 'If you're going for it, so will we.' Gavin secured the same decision from his Executive. It was then that the full weight of the TUC's bull-headed adherence to the past was brought to bear.

The Employment, Policy and Organization Committee, with responsibility for these matters, interpreted the 1982 Wembley conference decision as meaning that it was not claiming the government ballot money which constituted an offence. The real crime was receiving the money and having it in your pocket. We were not anxious, and never have been, to be put outside the TUC, but I needed to secure the monies due to us for past ballots. We did not, however, do it in a very efficient manner. We deliberately failed to fill out forms in a thorough way and thus invited further questions from the government; in other words, we put sand in the machinery deliberately to slow down the whole process, so things went back and forth and we did not get the money immediately.

Gavin at the AEU was having to run the union solo because the terrible lung disease emphysema had struck down Terry Duffy and forced him to work from home. We were in a healthy financial position, but financial matters for the AEU were more pressing and the £1 million they had claimed was needed to help them out of their difficulties. Gavin pressed ahead at full speed to get the money and the AEU received it by the middle of the year.

The miners' strike had just ended, leaving the Left without a cause to fight. Then, along came the ballot money issue, providing them with a ready-made favourite target – the AEU and the EETPU. Norman Willis, who was in his first year as TUC General Secretary, was not in a hurry to go to battle stations. The movement had been tarnished sufficiently by the pit strike. But the Left are never as happy as when they have something to beat, something to decry rather than to build. They are not builders. They are destroyers. They thought they were going to humiliate the AEU and ourselves by having us climb down. They badly misjudged the enemy in Terry Duffy, Gavin Laird and myself. I am convinced that if it had come to it, the AEU would have taken the same road as us: respected the views of their members, taken the money and left the TUC.

I kept a note of my words to the July General Council. I said:

I will not repeat in detail the arguments used previously here and at various meetings of the Employment, Policy and Organization Committee. They are all still valid:

– that the Wembley recommendation on ballot money was advisory and not mandatory.
– that an undertaking had been given that no disciplinary action would be taken unless expressly so decided by Congress.
– that recommendation 2, 'unions shall not hold or participate in secret ballots on union Membership Agreements', has been breached by all major unions apart from the NUM.
– that major policy decisions have been widely ignored and broken over the years without disciplinary action.

Bill Keys will remember how his SOGAT (Society of Graphical and Allied Trades) London Central Branch violated TUC Equal Opportunities policy and that prohibition of ballot money does not sit well with the eagerness with which you all seek government money for educational purposes.

I thought that, by arraying such arguments of merit and balance and logic in January, you would be persuaded. I was wrong! I have made it clear that my Executive cannot surrender the authority given to them by our members, reinforced by our Conference, to the General Council. I have asked you if any other union would do otherwise.

Again, I was wrong to make such an argument, for it's not about policy! It's not about power/authority of the General Council! It's about members! I'm obliged to Ken Gill for putting me right. I quote from the *Morning Star*, 18 July: 'After yesterday's meeting, engineering staff and craft union TASS General Secretary Ken Gill said he was confident that the AUEW would be expelled. As expulsion would remove the protection that TUC-affiliated unions enjoy against recruitment of their members by other unions, Mr Gill added: "I would be surprised if they had half their membership after a year outside the TUC."'

Also in the *Morning Star*: 'Engineering staff and craft union General Secretary Ken Gill said that the remarks attributed to him in yesterday's *Morning Star* "unfortunately appeared right out of context and totally misrepresent my position. My views are similar to almost all trade union leaders. If the AUEW were expelled from Congress, it would be an unmitigated tragedy".'

Now the *Morning Star* Industrial Correspondent and former Industrial Organizer of the Communist Party, Mick Costello, is very careful about putting any General Secretary in quotes. He would be doubly so given his special relationship with Ken, Chairman of his paper, political comrade and Chairman Designate of the TUC. But what mouth-watering prospects! The *Morning Star* went on, 'It is understood that many AUEW members in the car industry in the Midlands would be happy to join the more progressively led Transport and General Workers' Union. Craft members of the AUEW would also be attracted to other unions.'

How naive of me not to see the 'real politic' within this matter. So let me respond in like manner. I speak only on behalf of the EETPU, but let me put our position beyond doubt. Suspend us – put us outside the TUC, declare open season on our membership and we will not lie quiescent waiting to be carved up. We will do what is necessary to survive; unthinkable pacts, amalgamations, membership free-for-all. Can you soberly look at the political and industrial scene and believe that in such a battle you will gain more from us than we will attract from you! The net winner would probably be non-trade-unionism. The main casualty – the prospect of a Labour government.

I fear – I am convinced – that if you start this process it will inexorably lead to such an end. I beg you to draw back. I do not ask for a U-turn on policy, nor any special treatment. Only the same forbearance shown to others in breach. By all means express your displeasure, your censure, but don't destroy our unique historical structural unity. We will never have political and doctrinal unity, and attempts to impose it will end with structural division.

Some may feel that they can support an investigation today and look forward to a 'fudge' somewhere along the line. Don't delude yourselves. Set this wagon rolling and we are full speed for collision. For our part, although we will do what little we can to stop its momentum, we must act as if the worst will happen.

During the major debate on industrial relations which dominated the TUC Conference at Blackpool in September 1985, only I bothered to mention that in direct breach of the Wembley recommendations three years earlier, more than sixty ballots on union membership, or closed-shop agreements, had been held. None of the big-name unions like the Transport and General Workers and the General and

Municipal were in the dock for this. The AEU's head was on the chopping block, because they had actually taken the money.

We were under growing pressure from our own activists to secure our ballot money. Acting on my words to the General Council in July 'as if the worst will happen' and convinced that we would be next in line for the chop, I had already started talks with Rupert Murdoch about setting up a new printing plant for News International at Wapping, East London. I was convinced that, because of the ballot money issue, it would not be long before we were forced outside the TUC, possibly setting up an alternative and more Moderate member-based umbrella trade union grouping with unions like the AEU and the Union of Democratic Mineworkers. What better start, I thought, than striking at the heart of the Left and giving one of its favourite safe havens, the print unions, a bloody nose?

At a meeting of our National Executive on the eve of Congress at the Norbreck Castle Hotel in Blackpool, we decided that if the AEU was put out of Congress we would walk out immediately behind them, even though we were not under immediate threat of expulsion at that time. I told both Gavin and Norman Willis of our unanimous decision, so I suppose that concentrated minds. Throwing out one major affiliate would be a calamity; getting rid of two would be not only the start of a new movement, but a disaster.

During that week, Gavin was running on overload as the pressure mounted on the AEU to come to heel. He had two major difficulties. First and foremost, Terry Duffy, a former army boxing champion and even greater fighter for reason had, tragically, been too unwell to travel to Blackpool because of his worsening condition. But, like the tough operator he was, Terry was issuing tactical advice down the telephone even though he was hardly able to catch his breath and had to speak in between gasps of oxygen. The second problem was that Gavin was not on the TUC General Council, so had to depend upon his representatives Gerry Russell, Gina Morgan and Ed Scrivens not to wobble or waver. Gerry Russell, a cheery Scouser, was often a bit of a maverick, but on this issue he remained absolutely stable. Ed Scrivens, who was seen as the weak link by the TUC machine, was having his arm twisted left, right and centre, but I thought, it's no good me twisting his other arm or he really will be in pain. So I left the AEU deliberately alone and did not urge them to do one thing or the other.

You don't get many letters of appreciation from Gavin Laird, but at the end of that nightmarish week for the AEU, I had a very pleasant letter recording the fact that we had not laid a hand on them, but had been thoroughly supportive throughout.

The industrial relations debate resulted in the TUC retreating into its thick shell of rigidity. Every call, including mine, for a review of the now outdated Wembley decisions of 1982 was rejected. I was at my most moderate and statesmanlike in the view of one commentator, as I spoke that Monday afternoon at the Winter Gardens. Against all the odds, I tried to warn the brethren they were jumping into a pit dug for them by Thatcher and her PR men. I said that the purpose of our motion was to keep the TUC together. 'Unless we are successful,' I added, 'we shall all be diminished; the advances that are called for in the agenda will wither and a Labour government will fade in prospect.'

The TUC had allowed the government to claim it was they who stood for the rights of the individual union member. I said, 'The public perceive us as apparently hostile to individual balloting, especially postal balloting. We appear to them to be more concerned with preserving antiquated systems of electing governing bodies so that a handful of people can determine the votes of thousands. We appear to be more concerned to avoid upsetting activists than to give members a proper strike vote. The public see us as more concerned to dragoon workers into union membership than to win them positively for our brotherhood.'

I attacked the way in which the Wembley recommendations had now become mandatory decisions, adding, 'That is the strange and metamorphic way that the General Council has with words. Words mean what the Council says they mean.' I knew I was swimming against a tide of ignorance and rule-book illogicality, but I hit home. 'The TUC is an alliance of free and independent organizations,' I declared. 'Rigid discipline and adherence to rules will inevitably destroy it. I find it ironic that those who call for action or absolute fidelity to TUC rules and policies are the same people who claim that the laws of the land can properly be defied.'

I asked Congress to ' . . . examine every word and nuance of the law in advancing our position . . . ' I repeated the example I had put to the General Council when we debated support for the GCHQ unions: 'I suggested that we should have a ballot on the call for a "Day of Action". I said that all ten million of us should have a ballot on the issue every month, that it should be a postal ballot and that we should all claim the costs from the government under their scheme. That would have imposed a £3-million trade union fine on the government every month . . . Of course, that would have meant using our heads and not the much vaunted heart that was set in concrete in 1982 . . . '

Ron Todd could not resist; he responded with: 'Eric Hammond says we should consider the politics of the head and not the heart . . . Yes, colleagues, much of what I feel does come from the heart. How stupid of me! I really believe that for trade-unionists and Socialists that is where most of it is born – from the heart.'

After the inevitable applause for Ron had died down, I was given the right to reply. I did not know, but ought to have guessed that he had suffered all his life from the inevitable nickname. So he more than understood my unfriendly intent when I opened with: 'I am more sad than angry at the opposition to our call for review (of the outdated and wrong Wembley decisions). I am familiar enough with the work of the power brokers that "Sweeney" Todd has willingly joined . . . ' Leaning over the rostrum and looking Brother Todd directly in the eye, I drawled, 'Ron, I understand dinosaurs had big hearts, too . . . !'

But I had a less lighthearted warning for Ron and any others who fancied their chances by trying to steal our members if we were expelled from the TUC. I repeated and enhanced my private July words to the General Council and I warned, 'Put us outside the TUC, declare open season on our membership, and we will not lie quiescent waiting to be carved up. We will do what is necessary to survive; unthinkable pacts, amalgamations, membership free-for-all . . . You ain't seen nothing yet!' I pleaded with them to draw back from a decision they would regret, one that would diminish the prospects of a future Labour government. It was a waste of time: the hearts won.

The next morning, I had a strange exchange with Ron just before the General Council meeting at the plush Imperial Hotel on Blackpool seafront. I had not had time to get to know Ron, being a novice on the Council, but that day I discovered three things about him. Ron is a very accomplished pianist, the Liberace of the trade union movement one might say. He plays light classical music with a keen ear. Secondly, and this is not intended as a jibe, he knows a lot about dinosaurs. He has a house full of dinosaur bones and fossils, so many they have overflowed to his garage. Thirdly, Ron hates to be thought ill of.

Just before the meeting that day, Ron had finished tinkling the ivories, and he came over to try and explain himself, almost as if the previous day's debate was still going on. He wanted to set the record straight even with an arch opponent like me.

Ron said, 'You were wrong, Eric . . . about the dinosaurs.'

I said, 'Well, Ron, I often am wrong.'

Ron went on, 'Dinosaurs didn't have big hearts.'

I thought he was joking, so I said, 'It was just a way of speaking, of making a good point, using poetic licence.'

But Ron was insistent. He said, 'Dinosaurs didn't have very big brains. In fact, they had two brains – one in their cranium and another in their rear which controlled their locomotion.'

I turned to him and said, 'Ron, if only you'd told me about this before the debate, I could have polished that up into a real riposte to you, and said dinosaurs used their arses for brains, as did our opponents.' He laughed.

It was a lighthearted moment in an otherwise gloomy week for the trade union movement. We had tried in vain to make the TUC progress to a more rational frame of mind. After a series of seemingly endless discussions behind closed doors between the AEU's Gavin Laird, Norman Willis, Ron Todd, David Basnett of the General and Municipal Workers' Union and Bill Keys of the Society of Graphical and Allied Trades, a classic TUC fudge was served up for Congress dessert. The main ingredients were that the AEU would not apply for further government funds until after a ballot of their membership. The AEU also agreed to insert a statement with the ballot forms stating that the union acknowledged the authority of Congress and accepted that a 'Yes' vote to continue taking the money would mean suspension from the TUC.

Although relieved that an immediate crisis was avoided, I was disappointed that we were unable to action one contingency plan. The electricians employed in the conference centre at Blackpool decided (by secret postal ballot!) to switch off the lights and silence the microphones if we left Congress. I intended my last words to be: 'In the interests of safety, leave this hall, because in ten minutes, you're going to be more in the dark than ever!'

It had not been a bad Congress for the EETPU. After winning the argument (but not the vote) on a review of union attitudes to the new employment laws, we were ready to press other worthy causes. I pledged our support to GCHQ (Government Communications Head-quarters) – a pledge we fully honoured. Roy Sanderson vigorously defended our strike-free deals, arousing the mob by rejecting NUPE's criticism, saying it was that union, in 1979, who almost single-handed got Mrs Thatcher elected in the first place. Paul Gallagher attacked moves to get closer to the Communist World Federation of Trade Unions; Barry Davis drew attention to the attacks on free trade unions by the Left-wing government of Nicaragua; Alf McLuckie spoke up for the environment.

It was exciting. I told Norman Willis I felt like a general launching my cavalry colonels, one after the other, against the enemy's weak spots. I chided him that the Chairman, Jack Eccles, refused to call our speakers on Poland, defence and the Middle East. He said he had had enough from the EETPU and told the President to refuse any more speakers from our union.

At the end of this farcical week, Edward Pearce wrote an amusing piece in the *Daily Telegraph* – 'An evil smile among the TUC's straight faces':

What I like best about Eric Hammond is his evil smile. It flickered on and off all morning in the aftermath of the General Council's issue, a little after midnight, of the first-ever ballot paper with a Health Warning.

It is felt in Blackpool that the retreating Council has put the Grand Old Duke of York into the ranks of the world's great strategists, and that the only decent thing left to do is to keep a straight face, hence Mr Hammond's evil grin . . . The acting General Secretary of the AUEW chose Mr Scargill's hour for his own quite wonderful intervention.

Gavin Laird, who had quite inappropriately retired after the midnight negotiations at the Imperial Hotel to the Louis XVI Room, has a taste for irony. It works on the mutual invalidation principle. After a routine invocation of unity, reconciliation, democracy, and other Hegelian propositions, he spoke of 'friends like the TGWU' and 'good colleagues like GMBATU' (General, Municipal, Boilermakers and Allied Trade Union). Even with Mr Laird's command of a Buster Keaton straight face, such a description of the loving colleagues he had detached from his carotid artery would have lacked plausibility. But when he referred to 'the electricians with their magnificent history and tradition of militancy', a ginger kitten leapt delightedly out of its container!

Mr Hammond, who devotes most of his militancy to fighting the TUC, rocked on the platform in quiet, contained hysteria.

With friends like the TGWU, good colleagues like GMBATU (which insists on sounding like a port in West Africa) and militants like the electricians, the TUC will need every one of the next twelve soothing, conference-free months.

We had already decided to have a vote of our members on the ballot money issue. They voted by an overwhelming 9–1 to see off the TUC and call its bluff. The AEU vote was almost 8–1 in favour of taking more state cash. It was the second time in twelve months that AEU members had backed their leaders. Each time, they were able to reclaim the postal and other costs. Immediately the second vote went through, Gavin applied for a further £300,000 to cover ballots in the previous six months. These magnificent ballot results forced the TUC to come to terms. They staged an embarrassing special conference at Congress House in London of senior union officials in February 1986, which ended the ballot money ban. No action was taken against either our union or the AEU, and soon afterwards they were all jumping on the ballot cash bandwagon – even Ron Todd and the Transport Union dinosaurs.

Norman Willis wrote to all general secretaries on 13 March confirming what was by then a foregone conclusion: that accepting government funds for ballots was no longer a crime in the eyes of the TUC. In typical TUC doublespeak, the massive climbdown read, 'In the light of the conference, the General Council agreed that the acceptance by affiliated unions of public funds for ballots should no longer be a disciplinary issue, and that the Employment, Policy and Organization Committee should consider the policy implications of this, including whether it is practical or desirable to give advice to unions which might decide to apply for such funds under the present ballot funds scheme.'

Norman's letter amounted to a coach and horses being driven through one of the TUC's major policies and smashing it to pieces like plywood. As Ron Todd said at Congress, 'I am telling you we had eight points at Wembley and if you throw them away, you throw away the future of the British trade union movement.' Just five months before, it was *the* issue. Now, it was in tatters. Yet again, albeit belatedly, the TUC had caught up with the 'sparks'.

In 1982, NUM President Arthur Scargill had said the only thing to do with bad law was to break it. He claimed that was the only way we would make progress. According to his misguided view of life, without this law-breaking, the suffragettes would not have gained their right to vote. But the TUC's decision to keep within the law made nonsense of his remarks. There was to be no opting in and out of obeying the law as the mood took us. Some unions on the Left were openly hostile to observing the laws of the land, but they paid the price. The National Graphical Association lost more than £600,000 during the *Messenger* dispute with Eddie Shah. The process was repeated with the NUM and the vast fines and seizure of funds imposed upon it during the miners' strike. The fines stood and they never got that money back. Those bloody noses were enough to change anybody's mind about obeying the law.

I sensed throughout the ballot money battle that members of the AEU executive were being propped up by telephone calls from their dying President Terry Duffy. He literally dragged himself to the phone to tell them they mustn't give way. I remember the headlines on the eve of Conference quoting Terry saying, 'No surrender'. If credit is due to any one man in changing the direction of the trade union movement at that crucial turning point, it goes to Terry Duffy. He kept the AEU, who were not noted for their solidarity, on track. Terry, like me, had taken the trouble to ask the members if they thought we should take the government money. Our members regarded the question as irrelevant and thought we would be mad to refuse it. There was no one outside a small circle of politicos who had any doubt that it was sensible to take the money. But the TUC is rarely sensible.

Often, the only thing people like Ron Todd and his dinosaurs understand is a stunning blow to the head. It certainly took a few blows before the common sense of taking the ballot money sunk into their thick skulls.

6

Wapping, point of no return

Wapping was a dispute waiting to happen. Many years before Australian-born media baron Rupert Murdoch became the *bête noire* of the newspaper industry, the print unions had begun to seal their own fate – and that of their members. Like lemmings sprinting to jump over the precipice, the print unions, aided and abetted by weak newspaper managements, had featherbedded their members and lulled them into a sense of false security.

In the Sixties and early Seventies, forty per cent of Fleet Street printers were over the age of sixty-five. If they managed actually to work two days out of the five they were rostered it was a miracle. The rest of the time they were driving taxis, running newsagents or, in many cases, working aptly named 'casual' shifts on other titles. Hundreds of these men, the foremost beneficiaries of trade union restrictive practice, were in their eighties. Some were unable to climb the stairs to reach the wages department so sent their sons, cousins or nephews in large printing 'families' to collect the money instead. The octogenarians had been forced to stay on that long because short-sighted print union barons had failed to negotiate a pension scheme.

This omission was typical of the nineteenth-century attitude print unions took when they bargained with newspaper managers. Those managers, in turn, looked no further than that day's paper and surrender to that day's pressures. Once you got a job in the print, it was a job for life. Work was handed down from father to son and grandson. A type of industrial Mafia operated which meant the unions, not the employers, decided who would do which job. The union was the employment agency. If the man who was sent was too old to climb the stairs, could not spell or was just plain lazy, employers had to like it or lump it. Strikes were almost a daily event. Unbeknown to readers who were unable to buy their paper on the newsstands, the peace deal thrashed out over fish and chips and bottles of Scotch usually allowed print workers payment for the period they had been on strike plus a wage rise to avoid it happening again.

By the late Seventies and early Eighties, it became clear this could not, and would not, go on. My union, partly by being in the right place at the right time, was to act as a catalyst – a bridgehead – in an industrial revolution which was to change the face of British industry forever. In my view, Wapping, even more than the 1984–5 miners' strike, gave employers and unions the chance of a fresh start, an end to the old ways and the opportunity to make pacts which would help workers and management seek a future free of the 'them and us' attitude which had bedevilled British industrial life for half a century.

It all started in 1982. The EETPU's 1200-strong London Press Branch had always been in the camp of the hard Left. After we had beaten Communists and other irreconcilables in other parts of industry with both elections and arguments, their leaders retreated into the arms of their comrades in Fleet Street. The 'cess pit of the EETPU Left' is how one of my colleagues described the Press Branch. It was, for us, both a convenience and a danger. Frank Chapple rationalized by saying that the Press Branch and management in Fleet Street deserved each other.

By 1982, the Press Branch was dominated by Communists and a group of fellow travellers led by the Branch Secretary, Sean Geraghty, a *Daily Mirror* electrician. Geraghty, a short, bald-headed, barrel-shaped Irishman, had often boasted in bars such as the King and Keys next to the *Daily Telegraph* that his men could stop the Fleet Street presses at the flick of a switch. This they had done on many occasions, and, in the days when ballots were a luxury the unions did without, the power was switched off at regular intervals. Even though the Fleet Street 'sparks' had been a thorn in the national leadership's side for too long, Frank Chapple told me, 'Let's keep the buggers in the union where we can keep an eye on them.'

They were not, even in the leadership of the Press Branch, all of the same mind. At the end of 1982, on a momentous day for me, at the count of votes in my first election as General Secretary, my opponent, Communist-supported John Aitken, told me of the plot to take the EETPU Press Branch into SOGAT. I had an inner smile at his treachery to his comrades who had fully supported him for the post of General Secretary. I reported back to the Executive Council. They decided that employment should be taken from the Press Branch and handled by the area office. The control of employment was the basis of the Left's power in Fleet Street. They also decided to set up a Committee of Inquiry into the Press Branch, consisting of Frank Chapman and Paul Gallagher with Tom Rice as Secretary.

Tom, who was to loom large during the whole Wapping saga, was an able, intelligent and tough officer. He ran our white-collar section which had grown under his leadership. He was also a good friend who had virtually been my campaign manager during the General Secretary election. That inquiry exposed the conspiracy of SOGAT, its General Secretary Bill Keys and its London Machine Branch, to put the EETPU out of Fleet Street. Later, on 26 August 1983, the TUC had no option but to find against SOGAT.

I revealed the depth of the plot to our Conference by simply reading SOGAT's debate at theirs. These are some extracts:

The London Machine Branch delegate said: 'The London Machine Branch, as a committee, was the instrument used by the Executive Council and the General Secretary to bring the electricians into this union. We acted on the advice and guidance of the General Secretary.'

Another delegate said: 'A meeting took place at a hotel near Gatwick between the General Secretary, national officers and representatives of the Fleet Street branch of the EETPU.'

In fact, these representatives were not only representatives of the Press Branch, but EETPU Communists who were not officers. The delegate went on to say: 'During the course of that meeting, broad agreement was reached that it would be a practical advantage to this union to take the Press Branch of the EETPU into membership and let matters progress from there. As I said earlier, we as a branch were approached by the General Secretary and on his advice and guidance we took these people into membership.'

Of course, at the TUC, the General Secretary of SOGAT denied such involvement, loading it all upon the London branch. We did not then, at that time, have the information to contradict him.

It was with some satisfaction that I sat alongside Frank Chapple and Tom Rice as David Basnett, General Secretary of the General and Municipal Workers' Union, read out the award of the Disputes Committee he had chaired. SOGAT, despite its protestations of innocence, was ordered to return to the EETPU every member it had recruited and not to take on any more. The Communists had been beaten and prevented from stealing our branch. Their hostility to the

EETPU increased and, for our part, we still had a score to settle with the print unions.

They did not give in easily and their refusal initially to implement the award brought them before the General Council. The Left, particularly Ken Gill and Ken Cameron, sought to come to Bill Keys' and SOGAT's aid and argued that there was some case for the award not to be pressed. I said that I had not intended to enter the debate, being a very interested party, but that I was indifferent as to whether they pressed SOGAT to implement the award or not. In fact, I preferred them not to, but I had to make it clear that if the General Council condoned SOGAT's behaviour, then the rules were changed and every member of every union had the right to join the union of his choice. For my part, I would run up the 'Jolly Roger' and raid all their memberships. The two Red Kens rapidly withdrew their support for SOGAT.

Another factor in our approach to Wapping was not widely known. We had been engaged for more than two decades in an ongoing battle with the hard Left. Internally, at the TUC, within the Labour Party, we found that our enemies were supported with money from Fleet Street. The treasury of the hard Left was maintained by the less than voluntary contributions exacted from print workers. The decline of the hard Left's power within the Labour movement stems directly from the smashing of their financial base – post-Wapping, Neil Kinnock and every other rational Labour leader owes us a great deal.

Of course, there were matters of direct interest to the union that also motivated us. The accelerating changes of technology within industry meant not only that our members were taking on more training and becoming more skilled, they were also confronted with a new challenge. The maintenance role had moved into direct operational and production areas. As I saw it, we had to 'follow the electron' AND TREAD ON SOME TOES. I wasn't going to shed tears because this was now the day of the electrical and electronic worker!

Oddly enough, I have never been inside the Wapping plant, even though the violence and intimidation which emanated from our involvement with it will haunt me for the rest of my life. Murdoch bought the East London site in 1978. Six years later, he had invested more than £100 million in Wapping and another satellite plant at Kinning Park, Glasgow, but both lay idle, because Murdoch's men were unable to negotiate with, or buy off, the print unions. That's where we came in.

Many have assumed, quite wrongly, that our union talked to Rupert Murdoch because we had already made deals with Eddie Shah to bring out the new *Today* newspaper using electronic page make-up with EETPU members instead of the traditional print unions. The fact is that there were many more forces at work which helped bring myself and Murdoch together – and it was before we met Shah. The long series of highly secret meetings which led to Wapping began on 31 January 1985.

The talks had been set up through Woodrow, now Lord, Wyatt, who had acted as Murdoch's intermediary. That first meeting was attended by myself, Murdoch, Tom Rice and Bruce Matthews, Managing Director of News International. A lot of fencing went on, the union and the company each sizing up the other. But the result of that meeting was that Tom and I found ourselves on 19 February at the Bedford Square offices of Murdoch's News International Group at 3 pm.

Speaking quietly, but with firm intent, Murdoch, who was again accompanied by Bruce Matthews, a no-nonsense likeable Aussie, said he was looking for ways of 'utilizing' his Wapping plant. Resistance by the print unions to any deal which would end their restrictive practices meant the venture was in danger of turning into a white elephant. Having set out the scenario, Murdoch, whose American newspaper empire had shed thousands of staff as new technology had been introduced, made it clear he wanted to do the same in the UK. What could we do to help, Murdoch asked impassively. Could our members set up the machinery?

'Not only that,' I told him, 'but they could operate it as well.' There was an almost audible click as Rupert suddenly realized that here was an opportunity to end print union power once and for all. He turned to me and said, 'Eric, I think we might be able to do a deal.'

We never did formally sign any document and I was able throughout to deny we had an agreement with News International. Even as I write this in 1991, Rupert has continued to resist my demands for a deal which would give our union formal recognition for the risks it and its members and their families took on his behalf. Murdoch, however, immediately saw, because he is a great opportunist, that he had a lever. And a lever is what we were: without it being agreed, that's the way we saw ourselves. There was an opportunity, if things went right, that we could establish a bridgehead within the newspaper industry: this is what we sought at Wapping. In the course of time, we hoped things might settle down and, even inside the TUC, we would have that foothold and be raising a flag for the acceptance of technology, a modern partnership in the industry which would be irresistible to the whole of the print and paper empire.

This was not an unreasonable basis upon which to work – that is, if it all went right. At the very least, it would provide the means by which to lever the print unions into a more reasonable attitude. That's how Murdoch saw it. They would then make a deal with him and allow the operation of Wapping to go ahead. His means of bringing all that about was to say, as he did, that he was going to print a new paper at Wapping, the *London Post*, and he would also say to them, 'If you don't make an agreement with me on modern terms, then I'm going to print it using somebody else. Take your pick.' One can never enter the recesses of Murdoch's mind to know whether he really intended to print the new paper, or whether he was using the idea as an excuse to shift the rest of the UK operation to Wapping, but Bruce Matthews, his right-hand man, was convinced there was going to be a new paper.

For the print unions, there was to be a brutal choice offered by Murdoch. In effect, he would tell them, 'Either come to Wapping and work on these modern terms, or I have these dogs here, in other words EETPU members, who will be unleashed not only to install the equipment but operate it as well.' As it turned out, the print unions, SOGAT and the NGA, walked right into Murdoch's mouth and he gobbled them up without mercy, because, although he could have printed just the *London Post* at Wapping, Murdoch made the calculation that he could also print all his other titles at Wapping as well. And what he wanted the print unions to do was to abandon those titles in the dispute over the *London Post*. That is exactly what they did.

The NGA and SOGAT had this phoney claim that they wanted jobs for life. They wanted all 6,000 of their members guaranteed jobs – what you might call everlasting life and just about as attainable. Of course, Murdoch would not grant that. He told them what would happen if there was a dispute. It was not as if there was a secret hole or a net for them to fall into; he signalled it. This was a trap, there were big arrows pointing at it. Tom Rice warned them; Norman Willis warned then, but they walked right into it.

I must say that we had not allowed for that. We thought they were more sensible. Our argument was that, yes, we were being used to get the print unions into a more acceptable frame of mind to use new technology, but in doing so, our union was doing them a favour, because that was the only way they were going to survive in News International. We didn't take into account the fact that their leadership was incapable of exercising the proper authority to say, 'Look, lads, you're going to lose. You're on a hiding to nothing, and therefore you should back off and we should make terms.'

The terms were that they would have had a manning level of about 1,000 down at Wapping; they would have had 2,000 left in Fleet Street. The people who were over sixty-five certainly would have gone, and some others, with Fleet Street terms. That was the least they could have expected and Murdoch gave them six months notice within which to negotiate. So, even with hindsight and attributing to us the worst motives, that we were trying to grab a chunk of Fleet Street, the *London Post*, which indeed we were if that situation presented itself, they could have remained and gained. But they didn't take the opportunity that was there. They really did all the worst things in terms of their own members and their own organizations that they possibly could have done.

I try not to look back and wish matters had been different, nor to complain at News International's duplicity – after all, we were using Murdoch as much as he was using us. But, for the time being, events have gone his way rather than ours. He has shown no spark of gratitude, even though he couldn't have succeeded without us, and without the support of our people at Wapping. Despite that, I find him personally an acceptable sort of fellow. I can relate to him. A very polite man, and polite to subordinates and the little people. You don't always get that with newspaper magnates! Nevertheless, it all went sour in the end. Murdoch would say it went sour between us because we wouldn't spit in the face of the TUC and say, 'To hell with you. We're representing these people at Wapping and we'll make an agreement with Murdoch.' But Murdoch *would* say that with hindsight.

We had foreseen the prospect of the TUC coming down heavily on us if he started producing even the *London Post* at Wapping. We saw that our union, diverse as it was with 370,000 members spread over every industry, was hardly likely to put into jeopardy its membership of the TUC over a handful of people at Wapping, so we were going to have to contain the TUC's strictures on us. This was something we anticipated and we told Murdoch that. We had to draw a line and not have our relationship with him develop too far. But, in the course of time, the situation would move on and we may well have been able to pick up the threads. For the time being, he would just have to have a relationship with our members and not formally with the union.

Murdoch would say it went wrong because we didn't make the agreement with him there and then. His view was that, had we turned our backs on the TUC, everything would have worked out. But we told him, and he knew, that this was not a practical possibility and that, if the TUC found against us, we would have to conform. The fact is that Murdoch was not bold enough. His relationship with us could have been a model, not just for the newspaper, but the whole of British industry. Murdoch was too cautious and not man enough to take on the challenge offered by my union. Murdoch's way of going about things has resulted in a workforce at Wapping with little pride and considerable fear of its management. I feel pity for the timid Mr Murdoch. Had he grasped the hand we offered, things could have worked out well for News International and the EETPU.

I am only able to recall the many meetings, lunches and breakfasts because of the foresight of my secretary, Sylvia Hill, in storing my diaries from that period. Of necessity the notes were cryptic, the venues discreet. When you're planning a revolution, you don't meet up where you could be spotted by your enemies. So, when we met, it was usually fixed through Bruce Matthews' personal secretary, Sheila Hardcastle, whose telephone number is dotted liberally around the appointments we made.

The meetings were held at various places depending upon their importance. If it was a planning meeting with Bruce Matthews, it might just be with Tom Rice in the executive dining room at the old offices of the *Sun* and *News of the World* at 30 Bouverie Street, off Fleet Street. Various other meetings took place in the plush Mikado Room at the Savoy or the Bachelor Room at Dukes Hotel at 35 St James's Place, but the crucial meetings took place just a few doors away from there at 25 St James's Place – Murdoch's luxurious London apartment overlooking the park. It was a splendid place, tastefully furnished and decorated. One wall was all glass and overlooked Green Park. Because the flat was split level, you walked upstairs to the dining room where servants came with the food. Murdoch doesn't drink much, so if you got wine with your meal, you knew your presence mattered. He was dressed in a suit and tie, spoke quietly and had always done his homework.

By the time I met Murdoch along with Tom Rice and Bruce

Matthews at the flat for lunch on 9 July 1985, his determination to go ahead with Wapping had gathered pace. He made it abundantly clear that Wapping was going to happen – with or without the print unions. 'We cannot afford for this grief to go on any longer,' he told us.

In April, Tom had flown to the USA to inspect the American way of producing newspapers. He was impressed, not only by the efficiency of the operations, but by the great opportunity it gave our union to roll back yet another frontier – I increasingly saw our union as a set of individualists, pioneers if you like. By now, the die was cast. We were preparing for war. In less than a year as General Secretary, I had raised the hackles of the Left, first by my opposition to Scargill and then with my defence of the union's decision to accept government cash for ballots. Now, I faced a harder test which would force me to use hefty bodyguards and have police panic alarms fitted in my home. My wife Brenda would receive disgusting and abusive phone calls, and I would fear for my safety on a number of occasions.

In February 1985, Murdoch had met his top team of executives in New York. One month later, the *London Post* project was formally announced. TNT, the worldwide delivery combine, in which Murdoch had a major stake, was drafted in to distribute papers from Wapping in case the rail unions, who had traditionally done the work, cut up rough. Christopher Pole-Carew, who earned notoriety as an anti-union manager while Managing Director of T. Bailey Forman Ltd, publishers of the *Nottingham Evening Post*, was brought in on 13 May to set up the computer operation at Wapping through his company, Computer Print Consultants. As far as I understood it, Pole-Carew, a macho manager I had little contact with, was pretty well in charge of what became known as Project X – the nitty-gritty organization by the American Atex Corporation and others of the computer systems to be installed at Wapping.

Before Wapping developed fully, however, we had a preliminary skirmish with the print unions. On 1 April 1985, we met *Today* publisher, Eddie Shah, for breakfast at the Grosvenor House Hotel in London. I was there with Tom Rice, John Grant, the former Labour Employment Minister and SDP convert who had joined the EETPU as Head of Communications, and Lord Harris of Greenwich, who had acted as a 'fixer'. One month later, we shook hands at a further meeting with Shah at the Berkeley Hotel at Witton Place, Knightsbridge. The 'sparks' would become printers on computer. We had broken the mould. By the time details leaked out in July, it was too late for the print unions to do anything about it. My confidence had increased with my experience as General Secretary. I had a growing conviction in the correctness of my union's commonsense policies and its right to achieve its own destiny, unimpeded by the latter-day Luddites who inhabited certain trade union headquarters.

Murdoch could buy all the fancy computers and printing equipment he liked, but without the skilled labour to install and operate it, his whole project was sunk and he would be stuck for years with a workforce living in the past. That's where our Southampton Area 22 office came into play. For years, the office had kept a detailed record of our unemployed electricians in the area. It dealt with requests for labour without reference to Head Office so I was unaware when another employer or agency was requiring labour. It was way outside London and thus acted as the perfect base for Wapping recruitment. By the time the print unions discovered what was afoot, it was too late. Through the EETPU local Secretary, Mick Scanlon, and his assistant Vivian Seaman, members were sent for interviews with the Charles Paterson jobs agency in London, in the same way as they would be sent to other applying employers. The same agency arranged interviews on a similar basis in Glasgow to recruit for Murdoch's new plant at Kinning Park.

The print unions had begun to foster suspicions. They loved conspiracies so, naturally, thought we were involved in one, but there was nothing I could do to stop the ball rolling. I know of no words or person, certainly not me, who could have stopped those men taking Murdoch's jobs or his money. Once he had them down there at Wapping, he had powerful cards in his hand. There was nobody going to beat that hand. The most important fellow to Murdoch was not a man who belonged to a union or anything else. It was the man who kept his machines going and was able to maintain them. That's the message that's seeping through industry now. It's changed the whole pattern of working. Gone are the days of the maintenance men emerging from their little cubbyholes just on the occasions when things go wrong. But lack of flexibility had gone on for so long in the print industry that instead of change just evolving, it was a massive revolution that took place all at once at Wapping.

The print unions had believed they were invincible. All they had had to do for decades was to say 'Boo', and managements and other unions would come to heel. They had no other experience than that of winning industrial disputes. They failed to see this situation was different. Neither Murdoch nor my union was prepared to roll over. To understand that Murdoch was serious was beyond the print unions, even though Tony Dubbins of the NGA and Brenda Dean, the pleasant lady at the helm of SOGAT, understood it; but while they did many things to try to avoid the consequences, they didn't have the standing amongst their members to lead or convince them. The real responsibiltiy for Wapping, then, lies firmly at the door of the leadership, or rather the lack of it, of the print unions. For it was they who were guilty of gross incompetence, weak leadership and a negation of duty to their members. It may be unkind to spell it out, but it's true.

As I have explained elsewhere, our relationships on other matters with the TUC were not good. Indeed, they were at crisis point. I and my colleagues on the EETPU Executive Council were convinced that, at the Trades Union Congress at Blackpool early that September, both our union and the Amalgamated Engineering Union (AEU), led by my good friend Terry Duffy, would be suspended or even expelled for accepting government money for ballots, before the end of '85. How better could we have met that event than by seizing the initiative in the newspaper industry – the heartland of our opponents? In the event, of course, the TUC backed off. That threw us a little off balance – the momentum of our planned retaliation pushed us forward. Instead of Wapping breaking at the time that we were being expelled from the TUC, we were to begin a long drawn-out and bitter battle to maintain our TUC membership. I did not think then that it was a waste of time, but the events of the next two years were to prove that this was so.

On 30 September 1985, at a meeting at the Inn on the Park Hotel in London, Murdoch formally told the print unions and our officials, including Tom Rice, that he planned to bring out the *London Post* at Wapping the following spring. Other titles could follow if talks proved fruitful. Negotiations had to be concluded by Christmas, a joint statement after the meeting declared. The previous day, at the Winterbourne Hotel, Bournemouth, our union Executive had agreed that any requests from employers for labour from our Southampton area office should, in future, be referred to the EETPU headquarters in Bromley. This decision was relayed to the unions at the talks with Murdoch the next day by Tom Rice, who insisted Southampton usually had only fifty casual workers on its books, not the hundreds it was claimed were being bussed into Wapping every day. The fact is that the Wapping recruits were drawn from a far wider area. And there was little we could do to stop people intent on finding employment. Why should we, anyway?

By now, the strain on the print unions was beginning to tell. Splits were emerging as their leaders began to realize the game was up. The Fleet Street gravy train had hit the buffers. SOGAT national officer, Bill Miles, let the cat out of the bag on 20 November when he said on a Diverse Production programme on Channel 4 television that, if necessary, his members would cross NGA picket lines to retain jobs. Miles stated: 'If, after failure to reach an accommodation with the company about new technology, the NGA, or any union, was putting at risk the long-term employment possibilities for our members, in other words, they were, in fact, closing the titles down for ever and a day, then we would have to think seriously about crossing their picket lines and getting the newspaper back on the street.'

It was with some pleasure that I watched the reply from a stunned NGA General Secretary, Tony Dubbins. He obviously could not believe it and said he would be interested to see Bill's comments on film.

Murdoch was piling on the pressure now. Wapping had become a fortress, surrounded by barbed wire – the most secure factory in the world. There was nothing like that to protect us. The print unions, like a dying dragon, were turning very nasty as they realized their days of power and influence were numbered.

Under pressure from the SOGAT National Executive, Brenda Dean wrote me a four-page letter on 3 December, asking whether my union planned to reach single-union agreements with Murdoch at Wapping and Glasgow. It was a subtle and cleverly worded letter designed, I believe, to maximize our apprehensions. But implicit in it was the threat that unless we satisfied the SOGAT hard men, they would report us – 'snitch' to the TUC 'head boy', Norman Willis. I shall come to Norman later, but, suffice to say, he failed in time to convince the print unions of the reality that he understood. Brenda's letter stated, 'the voice making an official complaint to the TUC on the Shah situation and on the News Group (Murdoch) situation is now getting louder and is more and more and more, in the absence of an alternative constructive report, being listened to'.

'Bull,' I thought as I put the letter down on my desk. 'You're scared witless, Brenda.'

Tom Rice replied on my behalf. He pointed out that negotiations with News Group had been conducted at branch/chapel level. No reference to national level had been made. He cheekily reminded Brenda of the EETPU's support for single-union deals, reinforced at that summer's policy-making conference. Tom also disputed Brenda's claim that it was not SOGAT policy to 'exclude any union from their rightful place in the industry'. Whilst accepting Brenda would not, personally, want to exclude the EETPU, Tom said this had not always been the view taken by her National Executive Council.

The manoeuvering at the TUC continued apace. The 9 December meeting of the TUC Printing Industries Committee pushed us to agree a joint union approach to Murdoch in order to secure a draft agreement for Wapping. The next day, my Executive instructed Tom Rice to tell both the TUC and Murdoch that the EETPU did not rule out legally binding agreements, voluntarily made; that it recognized the right of management to manage, subject to satisfactory workforce consultation and involvement; it was prepared to negotiate agreements which made industrial action unnecessary, and that the union left the issue of closed shops to local ballots. This was not what the TUC brethren wanted to hear.

Their gloom must have been reinforced on 10 December when Murdoch stated no one would go to Wapping without legally binding agreements. 'I've had seventeen years of hell,' said Murdoch. He wasn't having any more. Norman Willis tried to act as honest broker between my union and the print die-hards, but to no avail. He called me in on 12 December and we got nowhere. With the print unions wriggling like worms on a fish hook, I was not about to be bludgeoned into a corner by a bunch of gangsters. I told Norman it wasn't on. But I knew these words were wasted on SOGAT and the NGA who, by now, were after my blood – literally in some cases.

The first hint of a long strike over Wapping came in Norman's letter to me on 17 December. It said that in the light of our response, that we could not agree a joint approach to Murdoch, SOGAT would stage a ballot of their members for strike action at the *Sun*, *News of the World*, *Times* and *Sunday Times*. SOGAT said it did not intend to allow the EETPU to undermine the traditional print union organization in national newspapers by coming to a single-union agreement with News International. The NGA, of course, was not to be left out. It told Norman it wished to protest about our actions under the TUC's rules and disputes 'principles' – something which struck me as ironic at the time as, in my view, principles were something they had discarded long ago.

To Murdoch, all this was just like a feather blowing in the wind. On 19 December, a Thursday, Murdoch extended the Christmas deadline for a deal just for our union. A day later, manning talks with the NGA, SOGAT, AEU and the National Union of Journalists collapsed in failure.

Bill O'Neill, probably the toughest management hitman I have ever encountered, told the unions point blank there was no way he would drop the vital clause on legally binding agreements. O'Neill, who gloried in the title of Vice-President, Personnel and Labor Relations, News America Publishing, was a poacher turned gamekeeper. Once a printer and union official on a Murdoch paper in Sydney, he was now hammering the British print unions. He had boasted at an earlier meeting with them, 'I've done it in Australia and America, and now I'm going to do it here.'

What provided the final clincher for Murdoch over the print unions was a letter from SOGAT national officer, Bill Miles, to Bruce Matthews on 23 December. It demanded guaranteed employment for print union members at News International's plants at Bouverie Street and Gray's Inn Road, plus index-linked pay rises. The fatal flaw was that the letter ended with a threat of industrial action unless these conditions were met.

That same day, the full weight – and that's pretty hefty – of TUC General Secretary Norman Willis was brought to bear. He wrote telling me his 'advice' was that no union should enter into an agreement or arrangement with News International covering any part of its Wapping operation without the agreement of the other unions. He also stressed it was 'imperative' and 'urgent' that the five unions should seek to agree a common approach. I regarded this as a massive extension of the TUC's and, indeed, Norman's authority. Who the hell was he to tell a union how and when to conduct local negotiations? I let the lot of them stew over Christmas and New Year.

Then, on 2 January, I wrote to Norman, asking for confirmation that his advice meant our hands were tied. We could not do deals of any sort without the consent of the other print unions; we had to agree with them all other matters, including the avoidance of disputes, flexible working practices and health and safety, and if we failed to comply we would be disciplined, starting with a report to the TUC's Finance and General Purposes Committee, its 'inner cabinet'.

My letter to Norman was blunt. It stated, 'I would be grateful for such confirmation of your "advice" in the interests of clarity, but cannot hide my concern as to where it may lead. You will know of the overwhelming decision of our members regarding public monies for ballots. That decision, taken under threat of suspension/expulsion from the TUC, was far more about our independence as a union than it was about acceptance of public funds. Our members cannot be made to conform to decisions of other unions even with the backing of your "advice". I fear that your letter is the beginning of an attempt to do so.' What I told Norman privately was that neither I nor my members would be bullied by the print unions, whatever the consequences.

The real intentions and underlying vindictiveness of the print union hard-liners was confirmed in Volume 1, Edition 1, of a rag called the *London SOGAT Post*. This anti-Murdoch, anti-EETPU publication carried an approving message from SOGAT General Secretary Brenda Dean on the front. The last page carried a 'Newsflash' of particular concern to me. This said that Norman Willis had told print union leaders that our union would be summoned before the TUC under Congress Rule 11, which could lead to disciplinary action, including suspension, if the TUC's advice or guidance was rejected by us. The piece added, 'This arises from complaints from the newspaper unions due to the refusal of the EETPU to join in a united front over Murdoch's proposals and conditions on his *London Post* where the EETPU has already manned the new factory in what is seen as a move towards a solo-union, no-strike deal.'

I told Norman that the SOGAT attacks on the union and myself would make it difficult for us to respond positively to his requests. It was clear to me now, more than ever before, that the print unions wanted us out of the TUC if they failed to beat us into submission. Norman started to get on his high horse. He invited us to a Printing Industries Committee meeting at TUC Congress House on 10 January. His letter confirmed the SOGAT story that failure to agree a common approach with the print unions would result in a report to the Finance and General Purposes Committee. The whole issue was becoming buried in TUC dogma, which could not save a single job.

At the Printing Committee meeting, Tom Rice restated our position, but agreed to put the TUC requests before our own Executive four days later. I was delighted that at that meeting my Executive, to a man, backed my actions. Further than that, they decided to continue negotiations with News International, but now at national level. We agreed not to conclude any agreement with Murdoch in the meantime. In a letter to Norman Willis later that day, I had to tell him that it was not possible for us to play a constructive part in joint negotiations because of the anti-EETPU abuse contained in SOGAT publications.

While all these TUC sideshows were taking place, Murdoch wasn't wasting time. The *Sunday Times* of 12 January proudly announced that part of the following week's edition would be produced at Wapping. A stunned Brenda Dean wrote to Norman Willis on the day of my Executive meeting asking for 'immediate intervention' to prevent a breach of the TUC constitution by the EETPU. She added, 'I am sorry to have to again trouble you with this problem, but unfortunately I rather suspect it is going to get more difficult before it becomes easier.' She was right.

Norman wrote to me the next day, 15 January, enclosing Brenda's letter. He said I should stop any EETPU members working at Wapping. I would not and could not accede to this TUC diktat. The *Sunday Times*, edited by Andrew Neil, brought out its 19 January edition. It was ninety-six pages, the biggest paper ever produced in the UK. In it, Murdoch allowed himself the luxury of boasting about his new 'baby' at Wapping, but he also had some telling words about us in one of his rare interviews. He made it clear that, as we had told the TUC, we had no agreement with him over Wapping.

Asked if we would become the key union there, Murdoch replied, 'We don't know that. We hope so. We have looked at other greenfield factories that have started in Britain in the last few years which have signed very interesting agreements with the EETPU and since enjoyed excellent industrial relations and operated at great benefit to both employees and employers. We would be happy to go down that path and only regret that our traditional unions were not prepared to do the same thing.'

Murdoch had just been on a skiing holiday with his wife, Anna, in Colorado. Although he had returned to the UK, he made it clear to me he was not planning to waste much more time on the print unions.

SOGAT and NGA members at News International, urged on by Dean and Dubbins, voted by large majorities (5–1 and 8–1 respectively) to strike even though Murdoch had told them it would put everyone in breach of their employment contracts. In other words, they would sack themselves. Coupled with this, the print unions demanded that we should be disciplined under TUC rules. A formal complaint was made. The picket lines were forming. The police horses were at the ready. The Wapping strike, which was to last a year until the print unions threw in the towel, was just two days away. And SOGAT and the NGA were baying for our blood.

On 22 January, Norman Willis wrote to me again. The General Council of the TUC was to hold a special meeting the following Tuesday, 28 January, on the Wapping crisis. Murdoch had sent a personal letter to the 5,500 destined to lose their jobs, expressing the hope of a last-minute deal, but also his determination to press ahead with Wapping. At the fifty-ninth minute of the eleventh hour, the print unions and Murdoch made their final attempt at peace at the Park Lane Hotel on 23 January. I didn't go. I am afraid to say that I didn't need to. Tom Rice went instead. The talks collapsed. The strike started the next day, 24 January.

After the meeting, the print union leaders claimed they had offered to give away chapel power, to offer Murdoch the best deal ever awarded to a Fleet Street proprietor, but careful reading of that final 'offer' shows that they wanted things they must have realized were anathema to a man like Rupert. After witnessing how he had outwitted them by setting up and operating Wapping, did they really consider it feasible he would agree to the TUC issuing binding awards on labour flexibility? Or were they living in a cloud-cuckoo land, trapped by their own dogma and crazy, outdated labour practices? My firm view is that they were living in the past and they could not win.

So assured were they of their God-given right to exist unchanged that the TUC Printing Industries Committee had not met at all in 1984 and hardly ever in 1985. Now, it was meeting every day as the crisis at Wapping deepened. Murdoch was to squeeze the print unions dry, and our union was to suffer the most vicious verbal and physical abuse ever endured by a union in more than a hundred years of TUC history.

The hearings which were called by our TUC brethren – spurred on by desperate print unions who saw their power being eroded by the minute – ignored the crucial facts. At least 400 former SOGAT and NGA members were already working at Wapping in addition to our 180 or so members. Just 32 of the 700 journalists working on *The Times, Sunday Times, Sun,* and *News of the World* quit rather than move to Wapping, despite the protestations of the National Union of

89

Journalists and its General Secretary, Harry Conroy. TNT, Murdoch's distribution arm, employed drivers belonging to the Transport and General Workers' Union, led by Ron Todd. They were driving past and, occasionally, through the massed ranks of men who were once Fleet Street's unconquered. The TGWU was clearly taking work away from SOGAT drivers and railwaymen belonging to ASLEF and the NUR. All this was forgotten by the selective memories of the men and women lined up against us at the TUC.

The picketing reached a crescendo when I turned up at Congress House to meet my accusers at the General Council meeting on 28 January. I was badly kicked and shoved and had a job staying on my feet as I made my way up the steps, only to be confronted by more pickets actually inside the reception area. This was democracy? I complained to Norman Willis inside the comparative safety of the meeting. It shook me up badly and I had residual pain in my leg for days afterwards because of the kicking I got. As I told Norman at the meeting (and there was not one word of regret from the print union officials) I knew that the picket and the intimidatory violence were obviously designed to sway the General Council against us. Not that they needed much of a push.

Afterwards, Brenda Dean staged a meeting within the TUC building with many of the pickets who had been baying for my blood earlier and who would have had their way but for the intervention of police officers. This unpleasant little gathering was transformed into a sort of victory celebration. I told Norman Willis I would not be attending a General Council meeting two days later, on 30 January, which would conduct an investigation into our conduct under TUC Rule 13. This can lead to suspension or expulsion from the TUC. Before attending another meeting, I had to be sure that EETPU representatives were secure from physical attack.

With Murdoch continuing his print run inside what became known as 'Fortress Wapping', the best the TUC fathers could come up with, apart from threatening our union, was to call on all trade-unionists and their families not to purchase News International titles. I demanded time to consider our response and asked Norman to provide us with specific charges.

What they did not know was that on the morning I was being kicked, Murdoch's lawyers, Farrer and Co, of Lincoln's Inn Fields, had delivered a letter by hand to my headquarters at Bromley. Cutting through the legalistic jargon, it basically said that there was no trade dispute between London Post (Printers) Ltd, the Wapping subsidiary company, and its workforce, and if the EETPU was daft enough to accept TUC instructions to tell our Wapping members to stop work, they would sue us. That would put our substantial funds at risk. This letter was, in fact, no great surprise to me because I had already obtained advice from our own solicitors. It turned out to be a trump card for us in the short term, in that it stopped the TUC from forcing through an instruction for our people to halt Wapping.

The General Council went ahead on 30 January in our absence. It decided we had a case to answer. We were accused of activities detrimental to the interests of the trade union movement and against the principles and policy of Congress. We were called upon to defend ourselves and stand in the dock before our accusers on 5 February.

Before this horrendous day, I wrote to every full-time official and branch of the union, so that no one could misunderstand our position within the EETPU. Despite the threats, I told my officials that we would fight to stay in the TUC; we believed the case against us was motivated by political prejudice and membership ambitions, and we believed our members had a right to develop their skills and opportunities as the impact of electronics advanced.

When we arrived at Congress House on the morning of 5 February, there were the usual hard-Left thugs outside, so we had to be smuggled in at the back. Before the General Council, I had with me Tom Rice, Tom Breakell, our President, whom Murdoch had described at one meeting as 'a gutsy little bugger', and Michael Short, a partner in Lawford's, our lawyers. That caused hiccups for a start, because it was unprecedented. They had never had legal people before when they were dealing with a union. They didn't like that, but they had to lump it.

The TUC staff said they wanted copies of the statement I was to make for all the General Council. They wanted to read our submission before we went before them. I said, 'Oh, no, we're not having that. I'm going to read it to you. I'm going to read every word, because I know people don't read documents properly. I will read my submission to you and make any other comments I feel necessary. Then, I will give you copies of it.' So we had this constitutional wrangle before we started.

The whole affair was to take fourteen hours. The worst thing from my point of view was that I had raging flu: I had a temperature, aches and pains, I was really ill. My voice had nearly gone, so I was stoking it

91

up with all sorts of tablets and throat sweets, and the document I read took me an hour and a half to get through. Then I had to do my own punching bit at the end.

Apart from the flu, I was at ease with myself intellectually. The only anxiety I had was a rather silly one: I am prone to bouts of hiccups and my fear was that I would start to hiccup in the middle of the presentation. Hiccups arouse no sympathy, only hilarity, so my concern throughout was not with what the TUC would do to me or my union, but 'Dear Lord – don't start the hiccups.' And so into battle with this simple unspoken prayer on my lips. I did not pull any punches.

I explained painstakingly that we had not colluded with Murdoch in the way suggested by our accusers. We could not be held responsible for the unemployment of so many Fleet Street workers. That blame lay with their weak leadership's inability to shape up to the future. Determined to get my message across, even in the face of expulsion from the TUC, I told the General Council, 'The immediate responsibility for that unemployment lies with the bad judgement – yes, I must say this, for the matters at stake demand plain speaking – with the incompetent leadership of SOGAT and the NGA.' Tony Dubbins and Brenda Dean flinched. It was no secret, I told them, that Murdoch sought to switch existing titles to Wapping.

But now, feeling sore about the 'Duke of York' marching over the ballot money issue, they had decided, regardless of our answer, to rid themselves of the EETPU. Some unions had calculated they could recruit EETPU members once we lacked the protection of the TUC's 'Bridlington' poaching rules. And some unions were under pressure from several factions of the Left who were making their cause the destruction of the EETPU.

I declared, 'You are probably outraged that I should doubt your integrity or political backbone, but is it a stranger construction on facts than that which you are asked to accept in the complaint?'

In conclusion, I asked the General Council to find in our favour, even though I realized this was hopeless with all the self-interest and political hostility lined up against us. 'We are supposedly practical people here,' I added, 'and we need a practical solution. That cannot be achieved by finding us guilty of charges which defy both commonsense and natural justice.'

It was lunchtime before I had finished. The Chairman said they would need to read the document themselves over lunch and then they would call us back in the afternoon. When we resumed, it was to face interrogation. I was more than prepared for it. I had spent the previous days and nights in the office and at my Kent home pouring over document after document to prove my case. I knew we were up against it. In charge of the meeting was TUC Chairman Ken Gill, General Secretary of the white-collar union TASS. Ken insisted at that time that he was a former member of the Communist Party, but, in fact, he had been expelled for being too hard-line.

Under a barrage of questioning, I nearly lost my voice as I insisted that our head office had no involvement in the recruitment being staged in Glasgow and Southampton. Once the TUC had intervened, we had ordered local branches to cease recruiting. Getting fed up with the barrack-room lawyers of the TUC, I told them at one stage, 'The print is a piddling industry as far as we are concerned, and the sooner we can get distanced from it the happier we will be.'

Ken Gill, whom I never could warm to, concluded by saying he wanted the record to show that our lawyer had been allowed to attend. I smiled and said, 'Well, we are used to making firsts. We hardly saw this as an inquiry, but a trial, and the fact that we attend it underlines the importance we attach to TUC membership.'

I left the room with my team. It was teatime, and I felt very rough indeed. They said I could stay because I was a member of the General Council, but I declined. I said I was there as the leader of our delegation. It did not seem fair or proper as an interested party – complained about – to take part in the consideration of the verdict, but the whole thing was daft, because SOGAT and the other print unions, who were our accusers, stayed. They took part in it all.

We went to a waiting room. It went on into the evening, so we started ringing our homes to say we weren't going to be back early and our wives and families told us, 'Oh, well, it's been on television that they've found you guilty.' We said, 'We don't know, and we're in the same bloody building.' So it went on past midnight and, apparently, the general councillors were falling away like flies. What started as a meeting of fifty people ended up with about thirty who actually made the decision.

They found us not guilty on two of seven charges, but it resulted in our being instructed to stop recruitment, not to sign any agreements with Murdoch and to try yet again to get recognition for the other print unions. Their real dilemma was whether to demand that we instruct our members to stop work at Wapping. That was the one I was counting on, because it was illegal. If only they had passed that, then I would have slapped a writ on them the next morning and we would have been free of all their directives, because they would have broken the law.

But the TUC had also had that advice from their lawyers. Even so, the Left-wingers, including Ken Gill, Ray Buckton of ASLEF and Jimmy Knapp of the NUR, were going for the order to stop work. The meeker and more moderate fellows were falling by the wayside and not coming up to the line to vote. When they finally voted on this issue there was only one vote in it. I had made the tactical mistake of not being in the meeting: if I had been in the meeting, I would have voted to put that directive on us. Red Ken would have used his casting vote and the next day I would have got an injunction against the TUC.

The hullabaloo which followed from that meeting in subsequent TUC Conference debates was not really directed against us. It was directed against the TUC General Council for not making a decision to direct us to order our members to stop work: that is what it was all about. It just shows a further degree of stupidity amongst them.

By this time, I was almost dead on my feet, so I had gone into Norman Willis's office to lie down on an armchair. I was covered up by some of the lads' coats, trying to get a wink of sleep. It was past midnight. They didn't call us back into the General Council. Ken Graham, the TUC's Deputy General Secretary, and Ken Gill came down the corridor to the room where we had set up camp to tell us the decision. They had come to tell us what we had known several hours before by ringing home, so, instead of meekly accepting this decision, I turned and attacked them. I said, 'How dare you keep us here when the whole world already knew hours ago through the television. You leaked it out like a sieve. The world knows our fate. This is no way to deal with people. The people to know first should be the people who have been subject to these charges.'

I heard the two Kens gasping. They were on the defensive and they didn't know how to handle the situation, because they were in the wrong. They had landed themselves in trouble by leaking the result to catch the television news. The place always did leak a lot. Since we left, there's been nothing worth leaking!

Then, much to my amazement, I discovered that the reason Norman Willis hadn't come down to see us was that at eight o'clock, because he had felt ill, he'd gone off in the middle of this. I couldn't believe it. I told the two Kens, who grimaced with embarrassment, 'Christ, I'm in a worse state of health than he is and he's disappeared.'

Norman had gone home. It was so bizarre, I could hardly believe it. But what it amounted to, in reality, is that Norman could not stay the course. He wimped out and left it to others. When it came to it, the rest of the TUC directives, without the biting one telling us to order our people to stop work, were easy for us to carry out, so I accepted immediately. But from then on, the razor wire was up between us and the print unions. Despite their obvious hatred for us, however, we ended up negotiating a better deal for their out-of-work members than they could obtain from Murdoch themselves.

With the strike on, and the print union militants fuming at their failure to stop our people working at Wapping, security became a problem for the EETPU, and myself and my family in particular. Ken Jackson, an intelligent and loyal Lancashire area official, now Executive Councillor and Political Chairman, was not himself a heavyweight, but he knew a few lads up there whose mere size was able to defuse many a potential punch-up with just a joke and friendly look. Chief among these was John Clarke, an ex-Wigan rugby union player, who spent many hours with me over the next two years ensuring my safety at meetings and public functions.

As the dispute grew wilder in the spring of 1986, a fellow appeared at our headquarters at Hayes Court, saying he had been sent by Murdoch to 'look after' Tom Rice and myself. We told him we could look after ourselves. He looked quite formidable – like a suit with muscles. We said we had our own resources to ensure that no damage came to our property or our persons, and we sent him packing. We didn't need a private security firm to do that job. By this stage, I know that Murdoch and his key men all had one of these fellas alongside them. Bruce Matthews was always accompanied by a large chap, just in case.

Shortly after that, there was an arson attack on a News International paper store in South East London, which was destroyed, burnt down. A couple of days later, I received a phone call. My secretary, Sylvia Hill, said, 'There's a chap on the phone, Eric. Says he's Bruce Matthews' secretary.'

I said, 'I didn't know he had a male secretary,' though I thought it might be a call to arrange another meeting with Murdoch. Anyway, I asked Sylvia to put the call through. A quite well-spoken voice said, 'You saw that we burned down the paper store in South East London and I just want to inform you that we're going to burn down your office, burn down your home. You and your family are going to burn, you bastard.' It was the voice that threw me. You expect threats more from uncouth types. I just said, 'You're potty, you silly sod,' and put down the phone.

The police had already told me that if I did receive any more threats, I should keep the person at the other end talking as long as possible and discover what I could. But I didn't, because I couldn't be bothered to listen to that garbage any longer than necessary. I rang the police at a number they had given me in Bromley and informed them of this call. Before I could get home – and I had never told my wife Brenda about this sort of thing so that she didn't worry – the police were round at my house. They wanted to fit an alarm and a panic button that alerts the police over the radio waves that something's up. The idea was that they would have a patrol car there within a minute or so. This was on a Friday evening. Brenda said, 'What's this all about?' I told her, 'It's just precautions, love. Nothing to worry about.' The police set up a panic button on the post at the bottom of the stairs and another one in the bedroom.

Early on the Sunday morning, Brenda, who is a light sleeper, unlike me – I go to bed to die – was disturbed by something. She went downstairs at about 3 am, and saw a parcel had been pushed through the door and was lying on the mat. It was bulky, addressed to me and marked 'Open with Care'. She came upstairs and woke me up. I said, 'I'll see to it in the morning. Don't worry about it,' but Brenda insisted, so I put on my dressing gown and went down to look at the parcel.

As I inspected it, I looked up at the bannister and saw the panic button. I thought, 'Well, I'm awake. Let's see if this lot are, too.' I pressed the panic button. Nothing happened. A whole hour went by, so I rang the local nick. I said, 'Is there anything keeping you lads awake there?' Within thirty seconds, there was a screeching of brakes and the police were outside. By this time, it was half past four and I had, I suppose rather foolishly, taken the package out to the garage and placed it on the freezer.

Two 'boys' from the police came along – well, they looked young enough to be boys to me – and these two fresh-faced lads and myself were looking at this parcel on the freezer in the early hours of the morning, with one saying to the other, 'Go on, it's your turn.' We were all leaning over this thing like idiots and opening the flap. If there had been anything in there, it would have taken our faces off. It was bloody foolish, really. Then one of the bobbies said, 'There's no foil there.' That's one of the signs that it's a parcel bomb. What it turned out to be was a whole bundle of papers from a member of mine who had got involved in a messy divorce action, and he wanted me to get his wife back for him. He hadn't slept and he had simply come along in the early hours and pushed this through my door.

The next morning, there was a big inquest within the police force about why the alarm hadn't worked. What had happened was that the battery had run down, so the technician they sent got real stick over it and had to fit a charger to make sure it would keep charged up. This wasn't the end of the farce. The technician then asked me, 'Have you got an extension lead I can borrow? Mine won't reach.' I had to give up my extension lead and stop mowing my lawn. It could only happen in England.

This was the funny side to the danger we might have been in, but there were more serious incidents, including a number of obscene and deeply unpleasant phone calls to Brenda, and an arson attack on our union's college at Cudham in Kent. That summer, I was alone one day shopping at Gravesend when a nondescript man of about forty came up to me in the street and said, 'Mr Hammond?' Suspicious and slightly on the defensive because I had no 'minder' with me, I said, 'Yes.' This charming fellow then started swearing at me. I rarely lose my temper, but I turned, as if to remove my glasses, and said, 'Get out of my way or I will drop you where you stand.' He let me pass. I think the aggression from a man almost twenty years his senior took him by surprise.

My most disturbing and frustrating experience came later during the 1987 TUC Conference at Blackpool. I was giving a television interview outside the conference hall and while it was going on, I was being jeered and barracked by a group of hooligans wearing SOGAT badges. One man was giving me some trouble from the heart of the crowd, and I felt a chill go down my spine as I thought, 'I recognize that voice. That's the bastard who threatened me.' He was the man who had phoned me at my office with the arson threat. For legal reasons, I cannot name this yobbo here, but he is well known in print union circles.

During that same TUC, this man threatened to 'do in' Tom Rice, and I wrote to Norman Willis about that. Norman came to me and said worriedly that if we reported it to the police, the man could go to prison. I wrote to Norman about it anyway, and those letters are still in my and Norman's files. Norman and Brenda Dean pressed me not to go to the police and I didn't, but, for peace of mind, Tom Rice did report it to them. No action was taken, but this loathsome creature did not threaten us again. Even so, he still has an honoured presence in SOGAT, despite the fact that he is a nasty thug.

After the TUC tap on our knuckles in February 1986, I saw no reason to shy away from Murdoch. In fact, I was being urged by Norman Willis to assist in reaching a settlement. In April, Murdoch came up with the highly original idea of offering the sacked printers the Gray's Inn Road site to print their own newspaper. I was to-ing and fro-ing like the Chairman of ACAS, the conciliation service – a union leader with a very strange portfolio. On 28 April, after Tom Rice and I had met Bruce Matthews in London with Murdoch, it was agreed that the offer of Gray's Inn Road, plus a £15-million re-dundancy payout offer would stay on the table until 30 May for the sacked men.

Despite last-minute talks between News International, the five print unions including us, and the TUC at Heathrow Airport on 25–6 May, the deal went to a ballot of print union members who threw it out.

On 18 June, Norman Willis, who by now was tearing his hair out with frustration, wrote to me confirming a formal request for us to use our 'best endeavours with our members at Wapping, and with the company' to get talks going again.

On 27 June, Tom and I were on our way to Los Angeles to see Rupert in yet another attempt to get the matter sorted out once and for all. I'm not sure who funded the five-day visit, probably Murdoch. But it certainly wasn't the TUC, even though we went on their behalf. We stayed at the Beverly Hills Hotel: it was beautiful, the service superb and the weather glorious. One irritant, however, was that we were followed there by Terry Pattinson, the diminutive Industrial Correspondent of the *Daily Mirror*. He had clearly been sent there by his proprietor Robert Maxwell, who was, to say the least, an arch rival of Murdoch's.

Pattinson got nothing from us and we tricked him by telling the bell-boy we were leaving on an earlier flight than the one we actually took. I felt quite sorry for him, really, because he had not come equipped for the weather. He spent most of the time in the air-conditioned lobby, wearing a thick wool suit. If he had gone outside, he would almost certainly have expired in the heat. It was an inglorious failure – he didn't get a word out of us. We were uncooperative because he had written a story for the *Mirror* which claimed we were staying at a luxury hotel under assumed names. Nonsense.

The day after our arrival and recovery from jet lag, we were picked up outside the hotel by luxury limousine and taken to a house Murdoch was renting in Los Angeles. On the way, we watched England playing in the World Cup on the in-car television. Murdoch greeted us with his wife, Anna, a charming and intelligent woman. Bruce Matthews and Bill O'Neill were also there as we enjoyed a splendid barbecue of spare ribs. One vegetable nearly threw us – artichokes – but Mrs Murdoch soon demonstrated the correct technique.

We talked on the patio. I had never seen Murdoch so relaxed. We pressed him to talk again with the unions and he agreed to consider our representations.

As Anna Murdoch brought us more ribs, Rupert asked her, 'What did you pay for these?' When she told him how much they had been per pound down at the local supermarket, Rupert, between mouthfuls, said, 'That was a good price.' Here was a multi-millionaire trying to shave the odd cent off the price of a few bits of meat. They struck me as a genuinely nice couple and much of their conversation was just as homely.

Having talked further business with Bruce Matthews, we rounded off the next day with Rupert and his family, plus Bruce and Bill O'Neill at a fine restaurant. The following day we relaxed, and Tom and Bruce both won around 500 dollars at the Hollywood Park horse races. We were not dressed smartly enough being without ties, so could only get into the general enclosure. Back in Wapping, the dispute dragged on – outside the fortified plant at least.

That summer had been busy on many fronts for Tom Rice and me. On at least two occasions, I have found in my diaries, we met the *Daily Telegraph*'s Chief Executive, Andrew Knight. The talks, at an office of what I remember as a trade newspaper in Farringdon Road, were at breakfast and lunchtime. The theme was that the *Telegraph* was considering 'doing a Wapping', but would look at other options first. In the end, the *Telegraph* titles did move to Docklands, but their transition was far smoother than Murdoch's – almost certainly because of his front-running. Later, of course, Knight was to become Murdoch's chief honcho at Wapping, so his interest in us was appropriate, shall we say.

We were not the only union Murdoch was involved with that year, for I clearly remember having lunch in London at Maxim's with Roy Lynk, General Secretary of the Union of Democratic Mineworkers, and

Joe Godson, now dead, who was a shadowy and influential figure between the British and American trade unions. I could never prove it, of course, but Joe always seemed to me to be some kind of spook. Joe wanted me to ask Murdoch for £250,000 for the UDM to bolster its recruitment campaign against Arthur Scargill's NUM. I passed on the request to Murdoch, but I do not believe the money was paid out.

There were no thanks from the print unions for our efforts to get them a better deal, even though in September 1986 Murdoch agreed to increase the payouts from £155 to £205 for each year of service. He also agreed to a national consultative committee, albeit with no rights at Wapping, and there was to be a request to print unions to provide the names of sacked printers. From these, management, at its own discretion, would provide some with jobs at Wapping.

The ballot to decide the deal, the last chance the print unions would get, rejected it. Even before that, there was an unseemly public squabble between SOGAT's Brenda Dean and Murdoch's personnel chief, Bill O'Neill. O'Neill wrote to Norman Willis, expressing concern that Brenda had mentioned the previous day in a statement that the union had 'a mechanism to monitor voting'. O'Neill said the company had no confidence in the voting system and was freezing the offer. He cheekily invited the TUC to conduct a newly run ballot. It mattered little. The game was over. And Tom and I had travelled half way around the world for nothing. After that, News International simply made settlements with its former employees on an individual basis.

At the September 1986 TUC Conference three weeks earlier, the print unions – still furious we had got off the hook the previous February – tried yet again to reopen the debate. They put down a motion expressing support for the Wapping dispute, calling upon other unions to give greater support and to intensify the boycott of News International publications. At the centre of their proposal was the rejection of the decision of the General Council made by fifteen votes to fourteen on 5 February not to issue a directive to the EETPU requiring them to inform their members to refrain from undertaking work normally done by members of other print unions at Gray's Inn Road and Bouverie Street. All the resolutions before Congress are considered by the General Council and an attitude taken to them.

At the General Council meeting preceding Congress, I got into an argument about another motion which was concerned with the equipment of the police. It came from the Inland Revenue Staff

Federation and argued against the provision of baton rounds, water cannon and disabling gas to the police force. Rather idly, and at first mischievously, I argued that we should not be seen in any way to be giving support to rioters, and that most of our members would not get involved in a riot, didn't want to be within a hundred miles of such goings on and expected the police to put violent assemblies down with all necessary force. I then said if police weren't properly equipped, instead of rubber bullets, we might end up by having to use real bullets. Someone said, I think it may have been John Daly of NALGO, that he hoped I wasn't going to use those arguments in Congress itself. The germ of an idea struck me. I looked up the order of debate and found that this motion 'Use of Anti-riot Weapons by the Police' was to be discussed immediately before the News International debate. I was prepared to find that my very presence would cause some uproar in the Congress, but I reasoned that if that hostility was directed at me in a debate in which I was defending the police, then the normal support I got outside of Congress would increase, and when it came to the next debate on News International, people would say, 'Ah, there's that reasonable Mr Hammond who defended the police – they are having another go at him.' That's exactly how it turned out.

I spoke immediately after the mover and seconder and said,

My union does not see policemen as enemies. Police do a hard but important, sometimes dangerous but very necessary job – a job we citizens have given them to maintain the peace. They deserve, they need our help and support in their task. Policemen are human beings too. Some react with more than minimum force necessary when confronted with violence. Some infringe laid-down codes, but the individuals concerned are properly accountable for such faults and correctly spotlighted by the media. What few mistakes they make are made in the course of duties we have put upon them. We have placed them in the front line of confronting violence and consequently we have the responsibility not only to deal with the erring policeman, but to back the 99.9 per cent who do a wonderful job in safeguarding our liberties and freedom.

This was too much for the hard Left and the barracking I had received from the beginning rose to a crescendo. I powered on. I said,

I am particularly grateful to the police. Without their help, I would not be able to speak to you today. There are some who will be ready to draw our attention to what they see as the causes for the increasing crime and violence. Yes, the conditions in our inner cities, the persistence of youth unemployment, miserable housing – a legacy of bad planning, are all powerful catalysts that create despair and provoke a breakdown in law and order. But these causes, these problems are dealt with elsewhere on our agenda. We do ourselves no credit in dragging the police into this debate. Those living in the inner cities, pensioners frightened to venture out after dusk, captives in their own homes, fearful of the would-be mugger, will look at us in astonishment. They recognize, and so should this movement, that the police are all too often the thin blue line between freedom and anarchy.

By this time the noise was like a wall, and even Red Ken, who was sitting in the President's chair, had to intervene, blaming it all on people in the galleries, saying it wasn't fair to Congress to have noise from them.

I took my second wind and repeated:

The police are all too often the thin blue line between freedom and anarchy. Dogmatic ideologues in single-issue pressure groups might not think so, but the great bulk of the British people look to the police for security and protection. Outside in the real world, our members are more eager to join Neighbourhood Watch schemes than they are to endorse the criticisms embodied in this motion. Only a very few have been part of a riot. The overwhelming majority who have ever got near one would want it put down with all necessary means. How many in this hall would be prepared to undertake the arduous duties, the tasks fraught with danger that are now imposed upon the police? How many of you would readily volunteer for a place seeking to restore order in the midst of a serious riot? How many in this hall would be eager recipients of petrol bombs, bricks, stones and debris? How many of you would have enjoyed receiving such comforts at Brixton, Toxteth and Moss Side, or, indeed, the riots of Tottenham, and then being told by the leader of the local council that you had got a bloody good hiding.

Let it not be forgotten that the policeman killed in those riots was PC Keith Blakelock, who had previously been an active member of APEX (Association of Professional, Executive and Clerical Staff), playing a leading role in seeking to save the Plessey plant at Sunderland from closure. PC Blakelock was hacked to death, defending the right of trade-unionists to go about their work, killed while protecting firemen going about their duties in an atmosphere of lawlessness and riot. It was the same PC Blakelock who contributed every week to the Miners' Defence Group in Harringay. When Bernie Grant speaks of a 'good hiding', he insults this movement as do other demagogues on police committees and so-called police-monitoring committees across London. Let them or any other loony understand that the British people invest more confidence in the British police than they do in those erratic revolutionaries. Place responsibility for the police in their hands, deny the police adequate equipment – you have a sure recipe for anarchy and lawlessness on our streets. I concede and advance all possible controls on the police and their equipment, but beware, deny the police plastic bullets and rioters may face real ones.

All this had had the desired effect and had got the hostile elements to a fever pitch – if not worn out. My youngest son, Shaun, was in the gallery together with our Education Officer, John Lloyd. John, perhaps wisely, advised Shaun not to applaud me so vigorously as they were seated in the middle of some SOGAT heavies. Shaun did not take his advice and I often tease John about his own discretion. Tony Dubbins moved the NGA resolution and expressed his chagrin with the General Council. He said:

They slapped the EETPU on the wrist with six directives and appeared to lock the door after the horse had bolted. They ducked out of directing the electricians to instruct their members in Wapping to stop doing printers' work. The General Council, by fifteen votes to fourteen, hid behind the skirts of the lawyers, the Tory legislation. They believed that to give the EETPU such a directive would be to risk an injunction being taken out against the TUC. What makes it even more incredible is that the threat of an injunction was not from Murdoch. It was from the EETPU. The General Council were too frightened of legal action even to try.

When I came to speak, I had a relatively easy run, having worn out the hostile claque on the previous motion. I ended by saying:

We have been advised that any such directive, if we operated it, would put our funds and TUC funds in jeopardy. We could, therefore, restrain the General Council not only from imposing that

103

threat, but also from imposing the rest of the package. With one bound, we would be free.

The General Secretary obviously had the same advice from different lawyers. We have made it clear that we will defend our union and maintain our membership of Congress with all legal means. We do not, however, want to react to our union's or other unions' problems with legal ploys. Rather we would look to the tools of realism that most of us use most of the time. We have in membership at Wapping only a minority of the production work-force. When it comes to a matter of stoppage of work we are, in any case, bound as the print unions did, to have a ballot. Does anyone doubt the result of that ballot? Whatever the result, our funds would be liable and, seemingly, having gone through such a charade, we would be shriven pure, like the T & G and the NUJ. They both had many more members than the EETPU involved in producing and distributing Murdoch's papers, as does SOGAT – 420 according to the *Wapping Post* – but with ineffectual instructions to their members and a ritual washing of their hands, they escaped condemnation. Why can't we be more like them? If we did that, then our influence with our members and with News International would be at an end. It is that influence that has secured the reopening of talks – negotiations on which the hopes of an honourable settlement must rest. We will continue to do all we can to secure just that.

All that Tony Dubbins secured in the debate was a reference back of the General Council report. Despite continued pressure, they failed to persuade the General Council to reopen the debate at that stage.

That same year, we had been invited to send a fraternal delegation to the Norwegian Electrical Workers' Union. The conference season was over and the trip to Norway was a welcome break from the battle. Moreover, we had been invited to the Conference, as is the Scandinavians' habit, with our wives. So Frank Chapman, Jimmy Egan and myself, together with our wives, looked forward to an enjoyable visit. It was not to be. On the evening we arrived, we were invited to dinner with the Treasurer of the union and had a pleasant meal, though he advised me that there was to be a demonstration against my visit by the NGA of Norway. I told him not to worry, we were used to such things and had handled them in the United Kingdom. He was obviously ill at ease and advised me further that there would be a demonstration inside the Conference when I got up to speak. I again assured him that I could handle this matter. He said that the Marxist/Leninist Group, as he deemed it, would walk out of the Conference. I told him that I would have a few parting words to send them on their way. He finally asked me to arrive at the Conference early. I said I understood – they wanted me to avoid the demonstration.

The Conference was due to open the next day after lunch, so we arrived at about half past eleven. There was a sprinkling of demonstrators outside the hall, but no real difficulty. We had lunch and the President of the union asked to speak to me. He said that he and the General Secretary of the TUC, whose building hosted the Conference, had decided that I should not speak. I was more than a little taken aback and asked him whether the proper authority within the Norwegian union had invited me. He said, 'Yes,' but they would prefer me to speak at the fraternal delegates' dinner that evening. I replied that I would be quite willing to do that as well as addressing the Conference.

He asked would I write an article for the Labour Party newspaper explaining our view. I said I would do that as well as, but not instead of speaking to the Conference. He said it was most difficult, there was to be a walk-out at the Conference by the Marxist/Leninist Group and this would give bad publicity because the television cameras were in attendance. He then had the grace to say that they were only there because I was there.

His final suggestion was that I speak at some other time in the Conference. I told him that I didn't want to be unhelpful and as long as all the other fraternal delegates from other countries were spread about the Conference, then yes, I would agree. He said, 'No' – the rest of the fraternal delegates were to be taken in the traditional way, at the opening of the Conference, and I was to be secreted somewhere else. I said I could not agree, and he then came back to his original point that he and the General Secretary of the TUC had decided I should not speak. I said if that was the case, then we would not attend the Conference. I had not come across the North Sea to give in to the very elements which I had refused to bow to in the United Kingdom and that if he thought that, by refusing me a platform, he was going to placate the Marxist/Leninist elements within his union, then he was mistaken. They had an insatiable appetite and they would demand that my voice be silenced today, but, in the end, they would not be satisified with that and the proper authorities within his union would be damaged. They would bite us today, but eat them tomorrow.

I consulted my colleagues and their wives, and they immediately supported the stand I had taken and we walked out of the hall accompanied by the interpreter, who said to me that he thought that I had made the proper decision and it was disgraceful the way the Norwegian union had treated us. We walked through the now formidable demonstration and the police group which was there to protect us without being recognized until we were half way down the street, when a journalist recognized me and then they gave chase. Our interpreter assisted us to our hotel and we immediately made arrangements to return home. We laughingly dubbed it afterwards 'the day trip to Norway', but, as we were to discover, the print union hardliners would continue the attack and use every trick in the book to nobble us.

The public threats and private entreaties from the print unions continued beyond the end of the official Wapping dispute on 5 February 1987, exactly twelve months after our marathon TUC appearance.

Wapping faced its most horrendous and ferocious demonstration on 24 January, the anniversary of the strike, in scenes which shocked the nation and left a bitter scar on the trade union movement. At the General Council meeting immediately after this riot, Norman Willis, in his usual way, sought to get a resolution on the one hand condemning the violence of the demonstration and on the other dealing with the violence of the police. Arthur Scargill said he couldn't go along with the condemnation of the demonstration because they were only defending themselves against the attacks of the police. I in turn said I couldn't go along with the resolution because it did condemn the police, and it was nonsense to equate the violence of the rioters with that of the necessary force the police had used to contain that riot. After all, that was a job that we as citizens had given the police. After some debate, Norman's motion was passed with only Arthur Scargill and myself voting against. I think, on this occasion, Arthur got the better of the exchange for I said to him after the vote, 'Arthur, you and I are the only two rational men on this General Council.' He responded, 'No. You're looking after your friends and I'm looking after mine.'

In the face of a threat in the courts to its assets, SOGAT threw in the towel on 5 February. The NGA and the other unions had no choice but to follow suit. The war of words went on. I had a union to run and, by then, we were under attack over no-strike deals, an issue dealt with elsewhere.

On 2 June 1987, at our Biennial Delegate Conference in Blackpool, I listened intently to some of our Left-wingers trying to justify the continued attacks on the EETPU. I had prepared plenty of background, as usual, but there was one particularly telling quote from the NGA's Tony Dubbins when he addressed his union's own Conference as Assistant General Secretary in 1978. Reminding my delegates of his words, I quoted him verbatim. Dubbins had said, 'I know that it is quite clear from the motions which are on the agenda that the general desire of our membership is to look back to the days when they had control over origination, and when entry to the union was solely through a craft apprenticeship. If we do not, it will not be a case like King Canute, of getting your feet wet, it will be a case of a massive tidal wave of changing techniques sweeping over this industry with the creation of an alternative non-union industry or an industry organized by alternative unions.'

I told my delegates, with some satisfaction, 'Brother Dubbins will never be more perceptive. It is a great pity for the NGA, it is a great pity for the whole movement, that he did not have the courage to act on his convictions.'

By the autumn of 1987, Wapping had begun to fade into the background somewhat. We thought that, at last, the print unions had run out of ammunition to fire at us. No such luck. On Friday, 4 September, an article appeared in the *Guardian* alleging that Tom Rice had breached the TUC directives by holding frequent meetings with management and staff representatives at Wapping. The article, by the paper's Left-wing Labour Correspondent, Patrick Wintour, also claimed we had started a check-off system for EETPU subscriptions with News International, prepared the production workers' pay claim, drawn up a draft recognition agreement and undertaken a survey of staff opinion, using names and addresses of employees supplied by the company.

The claims, which emanated from Stephen Seaman, who had resigned as Chairman of the Wapping Salaried Staff Council, were vehemently denied by the union and Tom Rice, who himself suggested to me that we set up an immediate internal inquiry. The print union vultures were swooping down on us again.

When our Executive arrived at the Norbreck Castle Hotel in Blackpool on Sunday, 6 September, we appointed Manchester-based President Paul Gallagher as Chairman of the inquiry, along with North

East Executive member, Barry Davis, and Jim Egan, the northern divisional Plumbing Executive member. Looking back, I suppose we should have shrugged it all off as nonsense, which the article was in large part. Unions have been written about in the newspapers for years and it is rare that the reports are that accurate. Our inquiry report, completed on 19 October 1987, showed clearly that Mr Seaman's claims were of little consequence, but my main concern was the physical condition of Tom Rice. Asthma, which had dogged him for years, had become much worse under the strain of Wapping. It was clear we would be unable to press him any further and I already felt at this stage that Tom would be forced to retire early through ill health.

When interviewed by our inquiry team, Mr Seaman was unable to substantiate his *Guardian* allegations. It emerged he had not even attended two meetings which Tom was supposed to have set up on a joint basis with the Staff Council and News International. There had been just half a dozen meetings in the early days of Wapping held by Tom with management, and these were designed to set up a decent redundancy scheme and eventual entry to Wapping by the print unions. This fell exactly in line with earlier instructions laid down by the TUC. Our inquiry proved it was totally untrue that we had tried to set up a check-off system. Tom did have occasional meetings with the Staff Council, which might have been misinterpreted, but there was no proof he had prepared a wage claim. The Staff Council had been specifically forbidden by Tom to use the EETPU's name in preparing a recognition agreement. To do otherwise would have been so obviously in breach of TUC directives.

The earnings survey which, by the way, covered members of other unions as well as ours, was innocent enough, but we did accept it could have been avoided because of the atmosphere of suspicion which reigned over any contacts with News International.

One thing that did emerge from our inquiry was that we had inadvertently admitted 20 further members at Wapping by accident, even though 330 other applications had been turned down. The twenty immediately had their membership terminated, even before I sent the inquiry report to Norman Willis on 6 November. The admission that we had taken in these members, albeit for a short time, led to a long series of meetings, hundreds of written questions and answers and interrogation sessions in which the KGB would have taken pride.

Before that began, however, and when I gave our report to the TUC, Norman Willis and I negotiated an agreement, which nobody knew about. Over Norman's favourite office tipple – a bottle of Mouton Cadet *blanc*, most of which he drank – I agreed to sign a covering letter which went further than the report, giving personal undertakings. Norman then produced a draft letter. He said to me, 'If you write this letter, I will see to it that the F and GP (Finance and General Purposes Committee) draw a line on this, and that's the end of it.' Rather strangely, he said I would not be able to prove his part in the letter as it had been typed outside the TUC. I have kept a copy of the changes Norman made, some on the back of an envelope. One extract, in Norman's own hand, says, 'It recognizes while there was a breach relating to some 20 applications, 330 had been properly stopped. Whilst this matter was not contained in the original allegations, as a result of the inquiry, this deviation was immediately corrected.' That was the deal. He said, 'Write this letter, and I'll see to the F and GP.'

I wrote the letter and kept my side of the bargain. Norman tried, it's true, at the Finance and General Purposes Committee on 14 December, but he didn't have the troops and they turned him down. I was fuming – I felt let down, but what it really amounted to was that Norman simply did not have the authority he should have to carry the day. I told that meeting:

At my Conference this year, I gave a pledge that I would do all I could to maintain our membership of the TUC. For that reason, I continue to speak as coolly and as measuredly as my temperament will allow. The further examination of my union which is now proposed is gratuitous. It is undignified for an organization like this – you are like a bunch of squaws hacking at a prisoner.

I don't know how my union will respond. From partial soundings taken yesterday I sense opposition to any further response from us. It is unnecessary. We have admitted a breach – a self-admitted breach of directives, one that was not even alleged. You can suspend or expel us, or accept my assurances on the basis of that breach. No other options are open to you after *any* examination or questioning. Indeed, there are really only two: expel or accept. For once you suspend, it is in the hands of Congress.

We then went through month after month of the TUC requiring written answers to hundreds of questions and I have volumes of them. It finally ended up at the General Council, and at their May meeting, there were moves to suspend us. We weren't having any of that.

I told the General Council this was completely unacceptable. What we were being asked to do was to answer charges in a newspaper. I told the assembled throng of TUC 'wise men': 'Far more serious charges have appeared in newspapers bringing discredit on the trade union movement, particularly about elections,' and I pointed my finger at Ron Todd, the General Secretary of the Transport and General Workers' Union, who had been forced to stage a rerun of his own election after widespread allegations of ballot-rigging. Ron winced, but said nothing. The TGWU had not been called to account at the TUC because something had appeared in a newspaper. There was no official charge against the union for us to answer.

'We can't be tried twice,' I told them angrily. 'We've admitted a mistake and we have put it right.'

Willis was trying to find a way out, because he thought if it got to the Congress itself then he was in trouble again. There was going to be another adverse debate: he wanted to avoid that. Even so, Norman was trying to impose some penalty on us and, to this end, he was using John Edmonds, General Secretary of the General, Municipal and Boilermakers' Union, the second largest in the TUC.

Edmonds was suggesting the idea of a three-month suspension for us, so I said when I came to deal with this at the General Council, 'You might find it strange that anyone would bother to argue against a three-month suspension from this body. The fact that you wouldn't have to come along here for three months would be seen as a benefit and not a penalty.' They had the grace to laugh at that one, but then I really went on the attack and accused them of abuse of their own rules in that they had us in the dock without charge. As soon as I had finished talking, Willis said, 'I've got to consult the lawyers.'

He backed off. When he came back, he told them, 'The lawyers say that what Eric says is right.'

But it wasn't over by a long chalk. At the next General Council meeting a month later, they said the penalty was to be a censure on us. It had reduced the TUC to a state of farce. At the base of it all was this inability of Norman Willis to keep his word. All this had happened because the letter he had cooked up with me the previous winter had been used against myself and my union. We were being sentenced for being open and above board. It would be putting the best possible gloss on the matter to say that Norman had let me down. However, one could interpret it differently – that he was being used by the Left there to encourage me to do this and then draw the rug from under me.

We were now in the run-up to the 1988 TUC Conference at Bournemouth where the issue of Wapping would be superseded by the no-strike deals affair which was to seal our final expulsion, but I was under no illusion then or now that it was Wapping which did for us. Clive Jenkins, the former General Secretary of the white-collar union ASTMS, admitted this to me while researching his own book two years later. We were sparring around, because he wanted something for his book and I wanted something for mine.

Clive was in the chair at the Bournemouth International Centre the day we were expelled. He told me quite clearly that we were not expelled because of the two infringements over no-strike deals. We were expelled because of Wapping. Clive, the man in the chair at Congress, pronouncing bell, book and candle on us in 1988, told me unequivocally in July 1990 that it was all down to Wapping.

Even as we faced expulsion for the no-strike deals, they were still demanding that the whole of our Executive went to the General Council to receive this censure. My Executive suggested a one-word reply, but I was more restrained. We told them, 'You haven't got the right to do that. We're not coming,' so they saved the censure up, because we refused to receive it. They decided it would have to be done at the actual Congress. It was ludicrous. They actually pronounced censure upon our union on the Tuesday, the day after the Monday they expelled us. We weren't even there. We watched it on television. First they expelled us, then they said, 'We don't like you, either.' It was a pantomime performance unrivalled in the history of the TUC.

With the union now free of its obligations to the TUC, I made it a priority to press Murdoch for a recognition deal for our Wapping membership. He had certainly shown more than a prick of conscience with regard to one of our members, namely Tom Rice. When it had become clear that Tom could take no more of the pressure being exerted upon him from both outside and inside the union, I picked up the phone to Bill O'Neill. I told him, 'You owe Tom a lot. Do something.' Tom, after taking early retirement from the EETPU, was made an offer he couldn't refuse. He was put in charge of Murdoch's Irish operations. His health is much improved and he raises horses in his spare time.

Despite all that I and the union had endured, and however much personal regard Murdoch might have for me, I knew that he was not a man to roll over and give us a deal unless he had to. This was made clear to us when we met Bill O'Neill early in 1989. By then, we had 330 members at Wapping, but no recognition rights. O'Neill was not a man to joke. Ill at ease and trying to smile, which emerged as a grimace, he suggested to myself and Roy Sanderson, who by then had taken over Tom Rice's job as National Secretary of our white-collar section, that we were only 'after the money'. In other words, we wanted Wapping workers in the EETPU for their subscription contribution only. He then hinted in a roundabout way, again with the peculiar half-smile on his face, that perhaps we might go away if they paid us the cash anyway as a regular lump sum. I never found out whether the offer was to Roy and me as individuals or to the union, for I responded with some heat that we hadn't endured what we had gone through simply for money. We had more long-term intentions, including the building of a proper partnership in industry and a model relationship, particularly in the newspaper industry. That was the challenge to them and to us. The smile, or what passed for a smile, went off O'Neill's face and he mentioned it no more. As Roy suggested to me after O'Neill and his assistants had left, it would have been as well to tease them out to see exactly what was behind this proposal.

In the meantime, our membership grew to more than 400: free of any TUC strictures, we set about recruiting as many as we could at Wapping to support our case for recognition. This was despite the fact that, years before other Fleet Street owners, Murdoch had introduced a system of personal employment contracts which, in his view, negated the need for collective bargaining.

On 4 April 1989, I wrote to Murdoch at his St James's Place flat, following talks I had had with him in London a few weeks earlier. I sought what I described as 'a proper relationship with News International, that is, recognition'. I pointed out that after our discussion, he had said he would consider what I had said and respond. There was no response.

On 5 June, I wrote again, this time in more detail. In my introduction, I used our mutual friend Woodrow Wyatt, a columnist on his biggest-selling paper, the *News of the World*, to break the ice which was rapidly forming around our relationship. I said that Woodrow had told me a week earlier that Murdoch was prepared to meet a delegation from Wapping, yet local management, in the form of Mr Reg Limb, had told employees this was not so. My letter added, 'You have not responded to my earlier representations. Second thoughts on meeting the delegation will only be seen as a move to diminish my veracity. I understand your concerns over recognition, but am convinced they are misplaced. Far more dangers lurk in a non-union future.'

I told Murdoch that while we had consistently opposed outdated trade union attitudes, we equally rejected their counterparts among employers. Pressing for a proper deal with the EETPU, I wrote, 'I know that you, like me, are not to be moved by threats and I am not arraying any. But you are also a careful calculator and I put these matters to you to be taken into your calculations. Your management/employee communication arrangement is not a satisfactory substitute for the independent representation based on the concept of partnership. Matters only reach you, diminished, through a series of filters and you are led to believe all is well. It is not and the truth of this will inevitably emerge if you continue unchanged.' I did not intend to let Murdoch off the hook.

My letter concluded, 'The world has seen a tacit alliance of our two organizations against all that was wrong in the industry. For us now to publicly divide would hardly be in the public interest and certainly not encouraging to others to be as bold. If we do so divide, it will be because you have abandoned boldness in favour of timidity. That the challenge of building a partnership, to fashion a new relationship in industry, is to be rejected in favour of old-fashioned management supremacy. That prospect makes me feel sad at such an opportunity lost.'

My letter hit its target. Murdoch's reply, marked 'Confidential', was sent by fax from Wapping at 5 pm the next day. He expressed his concern that EETPU representatives had allegedly been spreading the story around the plant that he planned to meet a shopfloor delegation on Friday of that week. He complained that the report had been relayed to the *Guardian*, who called to check its accuracy. Murdoch had told Woodrow Wyatt he was always happy to talk to those who worked for him. He confirmed that he did not react well to threats. However, he was prepared to meet me in the future provided the meeting was kept secret.

Murdoch was obviously displeased that his 'security' had been breached. He said this would make it 'dangerous' for us to have any communication, direct or indirect, despite his high personal regard for me which was reflected in his newspapers.

113

Never one to give up, whatever the odds, I pressed him further. On 8 June, I chided him for suggesting it would be dangerous for us to communicate. I said I had not perceived any danger. And I added, 'The communication has been rather one-sided.' I explained that I had sought Woodrow Wyatt's help as a mutual friend, and now he was qualifying what Woodrow had relayed to me – that he was prepared to meet an EETPU delegation from Wapping.

Even as I dictated the letter to my secretary, Sylvia, I knew the Fortress Wapping drawbridge was being raised before us. I still had shots to fire. Angrily I declared, 'I have mistakenly tried to find a way to recognition for my union at Wapping through personal discussions with you. It is obvious now that was never a possibility, given the power and influence of your local management and their misplaced fears of any union. In talking directly to you, I put myself on the line. If my position within the union was not so secure, this episode would be more than "dangerous" for me. As it is, I feel more than a little diminished. I have always put the issue of recognition to you as one of mutual advantage to our organizations, which would lead to a partnership that would be a model for industry generally. I have never argued the obligation News International has to the EETPU, but this I have to say, that I regard News International now as a bad debt. The world knows that you owe us and that debt can only be met by full recognition of the EETPU.'

Then, as my temper got the better of me, I added, 'Personally, I feel like advising our members to join SOGAT, for it is clear that your local management and SOGAT need, if not deserve, each other.' I ended by saying I would put aside my personal inclinations and urge my officials to pursue recognition in the proper manner with vigour. I added, 'I, too, regret all this because the personal regard is mutual. If, at any time, you want to talk, I would be glad to do so.'

It did no good. Murdoch sent me a six-sentence reply the next day which was bunkum. He suggested all would have been rosy had we signed a deal with him in 1987. Hindsight had enabled him to erase from his usually lucid memory that had we done that we would have been thrown out of the TUC even earlier and divided our union.

Murdoch said my letter saddened him. He could not agree with my version of events. He insisted that in late 1987 he was prepared to welcome a partnership with the EETPU. But our decision to abide by the TUC directive forced News International to create its own human

114

resources programme. Personal contracts were introduced and were working well.

Signing off with 'Best wishes', Murdoch claimed that had the EETPU formalized its position in 1987 events today might have been entirely different.

We took our case to the conciliation service, ACAS, but to no avail. Murdoch's mind was made up. He did not need a deal with us, or anybody else to operate at Wapping.

By 1991, the year of my writing this book, Murdoch's fortunes were less positive. Recession in his media empire's three main countries of operation – Australia, the United States and Britain – meant that years of borrowing had to end. As part of a deal with Murdoch's bankers, his massive News Corporation was restructured and loans extended to enable the company to repay £1.5 billion in debts due for repayment by June 1991. Other debts bring the total owed by News Corporation to £3.5 billion. In addition, five years after the Wapping conflict, workers at the plant are now threatening industrial trouble even without organized and recognized trade unions. One staff representative, Peter Goddard, was paid £20,000 to leave. Other similar cases are pending and may result in similar payments.

On 24 January 1991 – eighteen months after my last abortive effort – I wrote again to the now beleaguered Mr Murdoch. I could not leave our previous exchange as the last word between us. I told Murdoch it would be in both our interests if we talked about the future of industrial relations in News International. My letter homed in on the number of dismissals of union activists at Wapping. I added, 'When will they learn that above-average salaries and management diktat will not win the involvement . . . the hearts and minds . . . of modern man?'

I asked him for a confidential meeting, knowing of his previous concern, almost verging on the paranoiac, for secrecy. I also put him right on his assertion that we could have done a deal in 1987. I pointed out that we had accepted the TUC directives in 1986. 'We both knew,' I wrote, 'that if the print unions did not come to terms with new technology and the venue of Wapping, then the EETPU would be in difficulties with the TUC. Implicit, on the basis of trust, was the understanding that it would take time before we were free to make agreements. Recriminations I put behind me and I hope that you will see that the interests of both of our two organizations would be served with a fresh start.'

No joy again. No meeting. No deal. By now, I suspect Murdoch's mind is concentrated more on the bankers who are effectively running his business than a few loyal staff at Wapping without whom his British newspaper business would be in a sorrier state than it is.

His final reply from News Corporation's headquarters at 1211, Avenue of the Americas, New York, and signed 'Rupert', said that my letter was laden with false hopes! News International, in his view, had taken the right course which would remain unchanged. He said nothing could be achieved by a meeting. He then had the nerve to refer to my future correspondence with John Dux, the Managing Director of News International Newspapers Ltd, with responsibility for operations at Wapping.

Although Murdoch is rarely in Britain these days, he said he would be happy to meet me socially if I was ever on his side of the Atlantic.

John Bondfield, a former General Secretary of the NGA, said this of the Fleet Street jungle: 'They don't seem to think from one day to the next, let alone one month or one year ahead.' Events will press Rupert Murdoch to think carefully as more men are paid off for seeking union rights, and to think of the 'partnership of profit' he could have with the EETPU. Our door will always be open!

7

No-strike deals: a TUC farewell

Membership means business for trade unions. The subscriptions they receive maintain every activity, including the extravagant lifestyle of some union leaders. So when we began to increase our membership of the EETPU by recruiting new people through single-union, no-strike deals, those who were less successful and more fearful of the future set out to stop us. The fact that they were offering similar, though inferior, deals in a desperate scramble for membership money was irrelevant in their view. Through a series of threats and false dawns of an unrealized new relationship, we battled to stay in the TUC fold, but, eventually, dogma, stupidity and plain Left-wing spite combined to drive us out. Not, however, before we put up one hell of a fight. History will show we were wronged. The facts show we were right.

Today, everyone – from car workers to seamen – are signing no-strike deals as a matter of course, as if all the fuss when we started the trend was about nothing. We offered a glimpse of, and a hope for, the future. However, it came too soon for the TUC die-hards, who now send recruitment delegations to Japan, years after we welcomed the technology and expertise from the land of the Rising Sun. No-strike deals are nothing new. They are attractive to any industry which needs to maintain constant production. A strike means equipment and process breakdowns which can lead to lay-offs of workers for weeks or months after a dispute is over.

Our first single-plant, strike-free deal was with Anglesey Aluminium in the early 1960s. Aluminium smelting has an absolute need for continuous production. If work stops, it can take six months 'chipping out' before a restart. The deal we signed on behalf of 800 workers on this greenfield site was so successful that 20 years later, when the Finns were looking for an industrial partner at the Shotton paper mills in North Wales, we were approached again.

117

Bill Keys, General Secretary of the Society of Graphical and Allied Trades (SOGAT), was about to finalize the deal when there was a dispute at his Executive about whether the local Shotton branch or their 'brothers' in Liverpool should represent the workforce. They could not resolve the row at the Executive. Time wore on. The Finns became so impatient that they wondered whether it was worth taking on anyone from SOGAT, so they decided to comb the area to establish who else could supply a workforce and had experience of 'single-union' deals. By then, we were already under fire from the TUC for signing no-strike deals, but, unbeknown to us, the Finns went to Anglesey Aluminium, who told them, 'Look no further than our good friends in the EETPU.' The result was that we got the agreement by recommendation.

The funny thing was that I knew about the Shotton plan because I was a member of the Industrial Development Advisory Board, which helped the government decide how much aid should be given to inward investment projects. I knew SOGAT would be trying to get the agreement, so I said to Paul Bevis, our national officer for the paper industry, 'We probably won't get the paper mill, but get alongside your SOGAT counterparts and see if we can win a two-union deal with them doing production and our people the maintenance.' Paul did that to some effect and obtained an understanding with his SOGAT counterpart. In the meantime, cunning old Bill Keys had been up to his tricks and attempted to get a deal for the whole plant for SOGAT alone: yes, a single-union deal. Then, fortuitously, his Executive had their row and the Finns signed up with us instead. That was another one SOGAT owed us for later!

Our strike-free deals had their origins in our single-union national agreement in electrical contracting. It was the basic industry from which we sprung. In 1966, we reinforced the fact that we were the only union in membership by agreeing with the employers to settle disputes without recourse to industrial action. It worked well. There was some industrial action because, after all, a union cannot interfere with human nature. But it was nothing like before and any walkouts that did take place were not with our blessing. It became an oasis of order within the construction industry. Everything worked reasonably well until we ran into the incomes policy of 'Sunny Jim' Callaghan's Labour government.

In the autumn of 1977, we made an agreement with the electrical contracting employers. It was a cleverly designed deal to get around the incomes policy on behalf of 35,000 members: they would be paid a

'I didn't know they were this advanced!' (February 1986)

'Please, Brer Fox, don't throw me into de Brier-Patch,' said Brer Rabbit (June 1988)

'Free to choose': the EETPU delegation leaves the Trades Union Congress after its expulsion

Norman Willis, on the record, 1988

Norman Willis at the EETPU conference in 1987, and wishing he was somewhere else!

Norman Willis takes it to the vote, September 1988

With Norman in happier times

In joint harness with Frank Chapple

Frank Chapple, General Secretary (seated); Tom Beckett, President, and Eric, then General Secretary elect, saying goodbye to Frank Chapple at the EETPU conference

On to the twenty-first century (April 1983)

Buxted Park, the union's unique and historic country house hotel and management training and conference centre: Eric inspects the 312 acre estate for TUC infiltrators!

A meeting of minds, Eric with AEU President Bill Jordan as merger looms between EETPU and AEU

Eric and his successor, Paul Gallagher

At the EETPU conference, 1991, listening to a speech surely heard before!

Difficulties with the public address system

bonus for extra effort. The employers put their hand to it and signed. The Department of Employment gave the nod after it passed all their guidelines. It was to be paid on 1 January. Just as Christmas Eve dawned, however, the ministry reneged on the deal. They threatened the employers with disqualification from lucrative government contracts if they paid up. The poor old employers were squeezed from both sides: we wanted our money; the government feared it would lead to a pay explosion with similar claims from other groups of workers.

We told the employers our agreement excluded industrial action, except where it was in defence of our joint agreement. We dug our heels in. The result was extraordinary. The employers tried to take out a High Court writ against the union. They failed, then appealed. We ended up before Lord Justice Denning. By then the penny had dropped in Whitehall that we could not be stopped, for, unlike any other deal of its type, ours was legally binding. We had resisted TUC pressure not to sign agreements which were binding in law. They had wanted us to sign 'in honour' only, but that would have been foolish in electrical contracting. There were 3,000 employers, so we needed a deal that was watertight. Otherwise, every bucket shop would have got away with as low a wage as it wanted to pay.

I shall always remember the sight of the Attorney General, Sam Silkin, having to apologize to us in person before Lord Denning. That grand old gentleman of the English courts leaned over the bench and said, 'I should think so. Interfering with this fine body of men.' Since that winter's day in 1978, Lord Denning has always been a hero of mine. By using our heads and ignoring the TUC, we got our lads a ten per cent increase – twice the rise awarded under pay policy to anyone else.

It was two Anglo-Japanese electronics ventures in the early Eighties which began to seal our fate with the TUC. Neither Rank-Toshiba in Plymouth nor GEC-Hitachi at Hirwaun, South Wales, succeeded as joint projects. Both ended up with a British withdrawal. This failure was largely due to British management's inability to work to tougher Japanese standards; however, the fact that they happened at all was largely due to the efforts of the EETPU.

Some years earlier, Hitachi had indicated they wanted to set up a factory in Britain to make television sets. At that time, there was excess capacity, so any foreign newcomer was bound to kill off part of the native industry. For that reason, we were opposed to Hitachi's

119

entry. But areas of high unemployment like the North East, which was later to attract the giant Nissan Japanese car company, plus the South West, were lobbying like mad to secure the Hitachi investment. We found ourselves making common cause with directors of UK electronics companies, writing to ministers and every MP in an effort to stop the Japanese invasion. How things have changed since. Today, we welcome a new Japanese company to these shores almost every week, and the EETPU heads the list of preferred suitors.

Our protestations at that time had some effect, because the man leading Hitachi's bid asked to see me. We met in my office at Bromley. He looked me straight in the eye and said, 'Mr Hammond, why do you hate the Japanese?' I replied, 'I don't. We are hostile to this investment because it threatens the British television manufacturing industry.' I said I wanted the British industry to be even more productive than the Japanese, and then I put an idea to him. I said, 'If you change your proposal to one of a joint venture in which you prop up ailing British capacity and introduce your technology and know how, then we would support it.'

Our friend from Japan was taken aback by my suggestion, but not for the reasons I thought. He declared, 'British workers are some of the best in the world. In some ways, they are superior to Japanese workers.' I laughed. 'Come off it. Don't gild the lily,' I said. 'I know our limitations.'

But he went on, 'If we accepted your proposal of a joint venture, we would have to take on elements of British management – and that, Mr Hammond, we could not abide.'

Subsequently, I have told that story countless times to groups of British managers. I have used the 'lions led by donkeys' comparison to push the point home.

As we kept up the pressure over the Hitachi deal, we ended up at Number Ten. Jim Callaghan dismissed his officials from the room and had a good, old-fashioned hair-down session with Frank Chapple and me. Our reasonableness in suggesting a joint venture combined with the political necessity of saving UK capacity in the short term was too overpowering for the Hitachi project to be given the relevant grants and approvals. The issue went on the back burner, but within two years, there were two joint ventures – Rank-Toshiba and, shortly afterwards, GEC-Hitachi. But that little Japanese chap was right. They didn't work. It was like mixing oil and water.

Hitachi came into an existing factory with GEC, who carried on the same old inefficient practices. There was a multiplicity of unions and no real changes in the way management dealt with them. They just could not get a profitable business going. It was the same at Rank-Toshiba. Productivity levels were no better than before. Management would not change its style. Despite all our efforts, the British partners found the going too tough and pulled out of both factories. The Japanese were packing their bags to go home.

Toshiba was the first joint venture to collapse. They only stayed in Plymouth through the efforts of our national officer, Roy Sanderson, who had worked hard with far-sighted people in Plymouth, including the local MP, Dr David Owen, to work out a model agreement upon which the rest of our strike-free deals have been based. Later Roy and our South Wales Executive Councillor, Wyn Bevan, did a similar job with getting Hitachi to stay in South Wales.

In both cases, the EETPU signed a single-union, no-strike deal. It offered equality of treatment to manual and office staff, and involvement in an advisory board so that elected representatives were aware of the problems and prospects of the firm. It included training rights for all and, for the first time in this type of project, an agreement to solve any outstanding problems by pendulum arbitration, with both sides bound by the ruling of an independent arbitrator. Despite the jobs and the taxpayers' money saved, this caused great consternation with the unions who had represented a minority of workers at the two plants. They referred us to a TUC Disputes Committee over the Hitachi agreement, the first of a series of such events for us under the so-called Bridlington Agreement which, since 1966, had attempted to stop inter-union membership poaching – with limited success.

We agreed at the TUC not to take into membership anyone from other unions. If a rival union had a majority in a department at a firm where we had a single-union deal, we agreed to arrange for their members to be elected to the consultative board. In this way, we did not break the Bridlington rules.

The TUC kept us hanging on for a year, until its 1984 Conference, before they grudgingly accepted what we had done, but they decided that, in future, we had to consult all other unions involved before we made similar deals. Roy Grantham, the wily little fixer who was General Secretary of the Association of Professional, Executive and Clerical Staff (APEX) had pushed through at Congress a motion which closed our earlier Bridlington loophole. Now, everything had to be done with TUC permission. There were to be no independent single-union deals with companies looking for a new relationship. The TUC was intent on fencing us in.

As a white-collar union leader, Roy was not keen for the barriers between staff and manual workers to be broken down in case it reduced the status of his members. A second, more selfish reason, for his opposition to our pioneering deals was that our membership gains were his losses. Just six years later, those membership losses led to APEX being swallowed up by John Edmonds' General, Municipal and Boilermakers' Union.

At the time we clinched the Hitachi deal, there was opposition not only at national level in the TUC, but also amongst South Wales trade-unionists. Just before the TUC issued its verdict, I decided to go down there to stiffen up our people for a fight in case things went the wrong way. Apart from that, I planned to mix business with pleasure. England were playing Wales at Cardiff Arms Park that weekend, so the keen rugger fan could kill two birds with one stone.

To my surprise, when I arrived at the Hitachi plant, I was met with a deputation from the Shop Stewards' Committee, mostly men from other unions. They said, 'We want to join your union. We reckon you can get us the best deal.' I replied, 'But I've given my word to the TUC. I can't go against that. I tell you what. Speak to my local official after I've gone.' I know it was more than a little mischievous, but many of those lads then came over to us. These were men steeped in the old union ways who found change hard. But they had talked in the pubs and clubs to people like our South Wales Executive Councillor, Wyn Bevan, who did a tremendous selling job for the union to bring these old die-hards over to our side and into the future.

When I spoke to those stewards, their one niggling concern was that as members of the workers' board, it was all very well having details of balance sheets and production schedules, but half the time they did not understand them. They found themselves part of a radical departure from past practice, but they were impeded by managers incapable of putting over the information so it could be understood in a popular way.

This resulted in our starting courses at the union's Cudham Hall training school in Kent where we brought the two sides together in order to simplify the exchange of information. This involvement by us in one of the cornerstones of the new-style agreements has continued to grow. We have had a succession of Chinese, Japanese and large numbers of European and British managers down to Cudham to learn the language of partnership.

It is of great benefit to British industry in the long term. Those two factories in Plymouth and South Wales now have production levels on a par with their Japanese counterparts. They went on from threatened closure to produce two new factories on the same sites making microwave ovens and video recorders. The bottom line is that the agreements worked for the employers and the workers. They provided stable employment whereas before the workforce were in and out like yo-yos. They now compete in the highly competitive consumer electronics market on equal terms with the world leaders. But, most importantly, they have helped turn around the 'Made in Britain' label. It is no longer avoided, but sought after.

We didn't always persuade employers. Samsung, the giant Korean electronics company, approached the EETPU when they were planning a new plant at Billingham on Teesside in 1984. We were ready with our model no-strike agreement to step in and represent the workforce. But you can never take anything for granted in the industrial relations game, and, where the Far East is concerned, we were to learn that nothing is cut and dried.

At the presentation to their management, I gave the Eric Hammond Special on everything the EETPU could offer a high-tech plant – equality, involvement, training, partnership and efficiency. They listened very politely. Then the Korean boss said to me, 'Mr Hammond, we much appreciate what you have said. But we in the Orient have no hang-ups at all about treating manual workers equally with white-collar workers. We wouldn't dream of doing anything else. It seems to us to be against the interests of the firm to do otherwise. We certainly would not keep our workers ignorant of the company's problems and aspirations. We would involve them and gain something from their views. So, you do not need to press these things upon us. Again, in the interests of the firm, we have comprehensive programmes for training and retraining and we constantly update our techniques. Neither would we allow any disagreement to reach a state of conflict, and we would employ arbitration methods to settle any rows.'

My face fell as the little Korean added, 'If we do these things anyway, why would we need any union, including yours?' I felt a great hole developing underneath my feet and searched desperately for an answer to save the day.

My argument was, 'If you are absolutely certain that you'll never encounter problems which are not of your making, like the market going against you or cutting back the labour force, political matters outside, then I don't see why you need a relationship with any union, including mine.' But I added, 'If there's the slightest doubt in your mind that there might be some of these external factors which could affect your fortunes, organization might develop in the factory. That organization would be born out of confrontation, difference and division, and you might get a representative group spring up amongst some of your workforce. You would not then, once that immediate problem went away, get rid of that element from within your plant. It would be there to stay and would have been based on division and conflict. If you are not sure that situation can never arise, then you had better make a partnership with an organization now when you can choose who that partner will be.'

Even for an enlightened firm like Samsung, I thought it was an argument they could not reject, but I have still not persuaded them to do a deal with us.

I found out later that Samsung's fear of Western trade unions resulted from a long and unpleasant experience they had had in America where the company found itself at the centre of a ten-year inter-union row. I was a victim of his antipathy to American unions. However, I still hope Samsung will eventually accept that we are the future of trade-unionism in Europe and that their US experience will not be repeated here.

The self-serving Grantham initiative at the TUC was designed to stultify our efforts to modernize the rest of UK Limited. Inevitably, it began to point up our differences with other unions and ensure we would, from then on, be in constant conflict with the rest of the brethren. We had never been happy about the way we had been treated by the TUC over inter-union disputes. We never seemed to get the right end of the stick. Not once had any EETPU officer been invited on to a TUC Disputes Committee. They would say that we were directly involved in practically every dispute!

To our simple negotiating minds, it meant we didn't have anything to trade. Unless you were a member of those disputes committees and could fix it for your colleagues, you were not going to have anybody to fix it for you. Although unions never sat on the committees which handled their own cases, they did sit on those which handled those of their friends. So a vote the right way helped towards the next time they were in trouble. Deny it they might, but this was the way supposed fair play under Bridlington worked. We were excluded from the inner circle that made these decisions. We were without any cards in our hands.

Increasingly at that time, because we were becoming more and more unpopular for speaking our minds on a number of political issues, like the miners' strike and later Wapping, making stands on defence and the reform of the Labour Party, we were making a lot of enemies. So when we found our political rivals on TUC committees dealing with complaints against us we knew we stood no chance of success. The dice were loaded against us.

We were getting more than our proportionate share of the new agreements. The Wales TUC had looked at the problem of inward investment. Its General Secretary was George Wright, a leading Moderate in the Transport and General Workers' Union, who was later to twice lose ballots to lead his union against Ron Todd and Britain's first black union boss, Bill Morris. George had the sense to realize that once a foreign business had seen presentations from various unions and made a choice, the rest should fade out of the picture, otherwise there would be no members, no jobs, for anyone. George had in mind, no doubt, that the TGWU would get most of the jobs. But, having accepted the rules, people started to shout 'Foul' when we were more successful at winning these union beauty contests.

I was 'aggravating Eric'. It was bad enough that I had given the Left a bloody nose over government ballot money, the miners and Wapping, and forced the Labour Party to face the fact that unilateral nuclear disarmament was a dead duck and a vote-loser with the wider electorate. But with every union facing a declining membership, we were striking at their heart – the cash raised from membership subscriptions. Unions are not good at adjusting their spending to fall in line with dwindling funds. There are some whose principles do not allow them to sack staff they can no longer afford. Others have little managerial commonsense and only act too late for remedy. Recent years have seen staff go at the TUC, Labour Party and many Left-wing unions, including the transport workers and the miners, but never in time to reverse decline. Such economic pressure meant that by 1987, the scene was set for a fight to the death. No-strike deals were the excuse, if not the reason. As things started to get hot, I pointed out to our union's June 1987 Biennial Conference at Blackpool that the

125

TGWU had seventy-six single-union deals; the Amalgamated Engineering Union, sixty-five; the General and Municipal, twenty-five. All these excluded the EETPU.

Knowing that Norman Willis would address the Conference three days later, I went out of my way to say we were only 'beginners' in the business of signing single-union deals. We had dared, I told delegates, to make a few unconventional deals. And, with my sights firmly on Norman, I declared, 'There is overall an unwholesome hypocrisy about many of our opponents, particularly those in other unions who deliberately mislead and misinform.

'We face archaic industrial attitudes, and there is an element of envy, too, because we have a growing success in the quest for membership. Our efforts to substitute cooperation for conflict are no one-sided sell-outs of workers' rights; to suggest otherwise is an insult to our ordinary members who are willing participants in such agreements and, indeed, to this Conference which has over-whelmingly endorsed our viewpoint. We insist on a total deal in which employer and employee achieve a balanced trade-off of mutual benefit. We emphasize single-status conditions, parity of working hours, holidays, pensions and other benefits. We ensure that valuable training and retraining schemes are linked to job flexibility. And we gain from elected consultative bodies with access to the sort of company information which is still a closely guarded secret in much of British industry.

'Of course, our critics ignore all this; they concentrate on and vehemently attack the so-called no-strike element.'

As I set out my stall, I referred to two immediate points of conflict – deals we had signed with Yuasa Battery UK Ltd of Ebbw Vale, South Wales, and Thorn EMI Ferguson Specialist Com-ponents Division, High Wycombe, Bucks. Both had been referred to TUC Disputes Committees. In each case, I offered to try to renegotiate the deals, give three months' notice and seek to get an agreement to include the other unions. What we actually did was to wink to the employers, 'Don't you dare.' We got off the hook on that occasion.

But by 1988, the terms were more stringent and we were not allowed any negotiations or the chance of getting away with it. All the time, there was this narrowing, this squeezing of the options open to us until finally it became unbearable. I warned our Confer-ence that our continued membership of the TUC would not be at any price. Even then, I predicted the gathering storm which was to erupt. The deepening split in the movement could not have come at a worse time for Labour Leader, Neil Kinnock, who was to come second to Mrs Thatcher yet again in the general election one week later.

In introducing Norman Willis to our Conference, I said:

I do not have to ask this Conference to receive Norman with courtesy because that is your natural behaviour. We should also receive him with warmth. Whatever our differences have been, or will be, with the TUC, Norman has never been other than a candid friend, who has an almost impossible task of harnessing the energies and egos of a very diverse General Council. He does it very well. If he and I alone were given the responsibility of determining the future of the trade union movement, then I would rest content.

It is probably not generally known that he and I took up our appointments on the same day. We were wriggly greenhorns and we rubbed each other into some sort of shape. When you attain national prominence, you attract all sorts of attention and requests. Without knowing that the other had received it, we both received a request from a reverend gentleman who wanted to know what our favourite piece of poetry was. Norman is a poet, but I certainly would not claim that for myself. He was going to gather all these favourite quotations from people in prominence, publish them in a book and sell it for a worthy cause. He entitled the book, *Nuggets of Gold*. With the overwhelming work that we had coming upon us as new boys, we both threw the letter on the pile. Some months later, we both came across it, had a twinge of conscience and rapidly produced our favourite piece of poetry. We had the honour of ending up on the last page, under the heading 'Better late than never', one behind the other.

Norman's was that favourite piece from Robert Frost which Bobby Kennedy liked:

> For I have promises to keep
> And miles to go before I sleep
> And miles to go before I sleep.

Lovely and gentle – like Norman is.
  Mine was:

> Then out spake brave Horatius,
>   The Captain of the Gate;
> To every man upon this earth
>   Death cometh soon or late.
>
> And how can man die better
>   Than facing fearful odds,
> For the ashes of his fathers,
>   And the temples of his Gods?

Good friends though we are, we do not share the same temperament, but I ask you to warmly welcome Norman Willis.

It didn't throw Norman and he gave an optimistic speech despite our difficulties. Quoting from Isaiah 1, verse 18, he urged us to 'Come now, and let us reason together . . . '

Sadly, by then, reason had gone out of the window. An increasingly tight restriction was being placed on the freedom of action of the EETPU. Members who wanted to join us were prohibited from doing so, or we were prevented from taking them in on pain of exclusion from the TUC. We were unable to make deals with employers keen to take up the new type of agreements we were championing, and this all came to a head in 1988. The difficult day had been postponed at the 1987 TUC. Norman used the clever ploy of getting all the unions to withdraw their suggestions to reform the TUC structure by setting up a review body. They all wanted to tell us how to shape the future.

My union's motion sought to put aside past prejudices and conflicts and work together for a modern structure based on the interests and involvement of the members. I called on Congress to conduct a full examination and re-evaluation of trade union structure and to report back to the 1988 Conference. Little did I know that Conference would be voting for my union's execution.

In my 1987 Conference speech at Blackpool, I reminded the TUC of the large numbers of single-union deals signed by other leading unions. I questioned whether any of them could be against our style of agreement designed to end the industrial apartheid which blights so much of British industry. I suggested it was the no-strike element they so hated. I argued that our pendulum arbitration method of sharing power with employers was better than conflict. Most employers, I pointed out, would rather take their chance with a strike than share power. 'Think of the disputes of recent years,' I baited them. 'Think of the defeats.'

Much to the dismay of John Edmonds, I held aloft a model single-union agreement of his General, Municipal and Boilermakers' Union. I said, 'At the end of the procedure, it says that the difference may be referred by either side to arbitration and if arbitration is used, then both parties are considered bound by the findings of the arbitrator. Call it what you like, that is a commitment not to strike. You know that there are many others.'

I reminded them of the electrical contracting deal ten years earlier which had forced the employers to pay twice the going rate and led to a court apology from the Attorney General. With relish, I declared, 'Some sweetheart deal, that is.' I then pledged, 'During the period of the review, we will not conclude a single-union agreement without first informing Norman Willis and being exposed to his advice and guidance. We will not conclude such an agreement without putting it out to a ballot of the members concerned.'

That was the deal we gave. But it became quite embarrassing: I kept informing Norman about deals, and he would say, 'But what can I do about it?' I used to tell him, 'We're keeping to our pledge. We are taking these people in. What have you got to say about it?' Norman said all he could do was circulate any other union which might be affected. But I had to tell him, 'I didn't say I would agree with your guidance, just that I would take note of it, so I'm going to make these agreements.' And that's what we did: told Norman, then simply made the deals.

In my 1987 TUC speech, I was determined not to let our enemies of the hard Left, like Ken Gill of TASS, off the hook. I knew they were after my blood. The by-now-familiar barrage of hecklers and loonies was out in force with me as chief target. So I put it like this: 'All that we have done is to articulate the commonsense experience of ordinary people and we have been prepared in the process to take on the political theorists and the revolutionaries.' Then, in an iron-fisted swipe at miners' President, Arthur Scargill, and his ilk, I declared, 'There are plenty in our movement who hide behind the labels of "Left" and "Marxist" and who do nothing to gain wide support, who propose impossible claims and, when they lead, they lead to defeat. They pose no threat to the entrenched privilege of our class system. In fact they reinforce it. The establishment welcomes a choice between them, the status quo and the phoney revolutionaries.'

With my voice almost failing against the wall of shouting from those democrats of the Left, I added, 'Ours is a truly radical challenge to the established order. Our cause is reason; our weapon is democracy; our objective is freedom and dignity for our members and fellow citizens, in their homes and at work. We are the future, and we are not going to go away.' With speeches like that, you make few friends: even fewer if the truth hits home and hurts hard.

There followed a war of attrition to kick us out of the TUC. Inevitably, we soon ran into trouble with two more disputed agreements. These were Orion Electrical, a video-recorder manufacturing plant in South Wales and a Christian Salvesen depot at Warrington, Cheshire. The facts are bluntly that at Orion, a new company, the workers had a ballot and voted by a massive majority to stick with us. As was usual, all the unions had originally agreed to make presentations to the company, then withdraw once the company had made its choice. The TGWU was having none of that. Early in 1987, it claimed thirty-eight employees, even though not one had paid a penny to the TGWU in subscription money. The TGWU never had more than six people there. We recruited seventy-two members, all fully paid up, in just one week. A secret ballot on 23 April 1987 resulted in a 136–2 vote in support of joining the EETPU. The deal was backed by a vote of 129–10. Even though it must have realized the company would not agree, the TUC Disputes Committee ruled we should withdraw 'forthwith' and only approach Orion again in conjunction with the TGWU.

The TUC also went against us at Christian Salvesen, which had set up a subsidiary firm called Salstream at depots all over Britain to supply Marks and Spencer. The management agreed to recognize unions, but only one per depot from amongst the five involved: the TGWU, General and Municipal, Union of Shop, Distributive and Allied Workers (USDAW), Amalgamated Engineering Union (AEU) and ourselves. We won the 'beauty contests' at two sites – Warrington and Brentford in Middlesex.

The TGWU, GMWU and USDAW all complained to the TUC that we had breached the Bridlington Agreement. Our friends in the AEU, with whom we had started merger talks, let it be. We were told by the TUC to exclude from membership everyone we had taken on at Salstream. What infuriated myself and my colleagues was that it was the first time the Bridlington rules had been used to exclude people who had previously never been in a union. But, in the typical two-

130

faced way in which the TUC operates, the GMB, led by 'Honest' John Edmonds, that paragon of virtue, signed an identical single-union deal with binding arbitration at another Salstream depot at Neasden in London just two days after the TUC found against us. No complaint was laid against the GMB. Apparently, Edmonds and his crew were above the TUC laws.

I hate to claim we were the victims of a political witch-hunt, but that is exactly what it was. We were being pilloried for doing the same as everyone else, but our face, our politics, our desire to ballot members first and take decisions later, did not fit in with the cosy world of TUC ostriches who knew better than their members.

By the time we reached our industrial conferences at Scarborough in June 1988, our relationship with the TUC was in a state of crisis. I openly attacked the 'Alice in Wonderland' attitude of the TUC and took the rise out of John Edmonds and Ron Todd by comparing them to the Walrus and the Carpenter.

As we both prepare for retirement in 1991, I can hardly believe that the friendly, chummy voice on the end of the line I hear on an irregular basis these days is the same transport workers' Ron Todd who in April 1988 scuppered any possible chance of peace over no-strike deals. During a five-hour crisis meeting of the country's sixteen senior union leaders at Congress House, Ron twisted the knife in our back by insisting that no-strike deals should be banned completely if employers made them a condition for union recognition. Norman Willis was under intense pressure to chop off our heads and display them on the battlements. I asked the TUC to postpone the hearing of the case until after our industrial conferences and after we had staged a ballot of our members on the issue. Norman and TUC chairman Clive Jenkins of ASTMS said they would think about it, then refused to change the date.

Our trial was set for Wednesday, 22 June – mid-way through our conferences in Scarborough. Once it became clear to me that I could do nothing to prevent the TUC accelerating into the biggest crisis in its history, I won Executive support for a ballot. To ensure we could reclaim the majority of the costs from the government, we made it a rule-change issue. Members were asked to back our view that we could only remain in the TUC provided we were free to continue making no-strike deals. We won with a thumping 5–1 majority. The result was announced after the TUC suspended us from membership.

This decision was taken by what I can only describe as a kangaroo court conducted by dodos. Norman, with his usual clarity and accuracy, compared our ballot with the way the 'Albanian electorate are encouraged to reject the official party candidate'. The 'Albanians' in the labour movement supported him to a man! Besides no-strike deals, we were also under further investigation for our alleged wrongdoing over Wapping. We were getting choked by all this and seeing the inevitability of a parting of the ways with the TUC.

The night before we went to London for the sentence of suspension, I staged a council of war with my full-time officials. I knew things were going to get tougher than ever before, so I met them after Conference in the hall at Scarborough to steel them for the coming battle. I assured my people that there would be no break with the Labour Party, but I warned of the inevitability of a split with the TUC. Ken Gill of TASS and John Edmonds (GMB) had talked of 'bloody membership wars', I told them, but I added with some vehemence, 'We must be prepared for an effective counter punch – even if we get it in first.' I predicted an almost immediate 'exchange of prisoners', with hard-liners opposed to the EETPU leadership breaking away from us. That is exactly what happened – and with the connivance of Gill, Edmonds and others helping the Left-wingers set up 'accommodation' branches at their offices. I urged upon our officials to liven up their contacts to ensure that, after the initial break, we ended up with a new balance of membership in our favour.

Edmonds had spent a lot of money on his 'designer' union. He had succeeded in creating an image of a 'nice' union caring for women. 'Not unimportant,' I told our lads, 'but realistically hardly attractive to proud chauvinistic craftsmen.' I blunted the sword of Ron Todd's TGWU by passing on my belief that his hardline Executive gave the clear impression it was in charge not only of the TUC, but the Labour Party, too.

I added, 'Everyone is expected to kowtow. The General Council falls into line and the Labour leadership would be foolish to backpeddle to accommodate these outdated backwoodsmen. We won't do it,' I pledged. 'We won't fudge and compromise if it means jettisoning our principles. I suggest that if the Labour leadership took a leaf from our book and asserted its independence, it would gain enormously not only in public esteem, but also in support from within our movement from the very many people who are in despair at the current wobble and drift.'

Strong stuff, but necessary for the impending fight. Quoting from Shakespeare's *Henry V*, I gave this advice '" . . . That he which hath no stomach to this fight, let him depart; his passport shall be made, and crowns for convoy put into his purse . . . " That's the early retirement scheme,' I joked. But not one of my people took the money. They stayed on to do battle in the union's greatest war of all.

Paul Gallagher, the EETPU President, and I took the early morning train the next day to face our TUC accusers. The condemned men did it on a full stomach, thanks to a British Rail breakfast. The one light-hearted moment in an otherwise dreadful day came when we arrived in the late morning at Euston station. As we struggled to the taxi rank, a British Rail porter recognized me and shouted, 'Give 'em a hard time, Eric.' I replied, 'Don't worry, we will.' I didn't have time to tell the young chap that Jimmy Knapp, leader of his National Union of Railwaymen, took a very different view.

We appeared before the TUC General Council, knowing we were sunk, but determined to remain defiant to the end. Two days earlier, the TUC had completed a draft code to regulate single-union no-strike deals. Everything would have to be approved by a TUC Committee. In other words, they would reduce the odds against us winning deals in a fair and open contest by blocking our way with red tape. The TUC doesn't like pioneers: it prefers thick-headed dinosaurs.

I told my TUC inquisitors we would continue signing the deals even if it meant breaking every rule in the TUC rule book. It was they who should be in the dock, not the EETPU. I insisted on reading a prepared statement, which put on record the real reasons for their hostility towards us. I peered over my glasses in disgust as Gill, Edmonds, Todd and Willis sat impassively while I cut into them. I openly accused Todd, Edmonds and Rodney Bickerstaffe, the General Secretary of the National Union of Public Employees, of a carefully conceived plot, formulated in 1987, against our union. They had wanted us out from that moment on, not least because of our involvement in the Wapping affair.

I said we had been unfairly treated by TUC Disputes Committees and suggested the TUC should listen to members, to people, not just unions. 'In disputed membership situations, the individuals concerned should have the right to choose their union and, together with their employer, the type of agreement covering their employment,' I said.

My onslaught on those who had baited us for too long continued, 'We understand that our views and actions over the years have caused irritation, engendered opposition and made some feel uncomfortable. We can always rely on the unremitting hostility of the hard Left. They can never forgive our union for exposing and ridding itself of the corruption of the Communist era. Those not of that ilk but in competition with us for members do not scruple to make common cause with our enemies, hoping thus to damage us and gain business advantage. Others will go along with these two elements because it's the easier thing to do.'

I reminded the assembled jurors how we were labelled 'quislings' for taking government ballot money; how GMB delegates to their conference three years earlier had said, 'If you lie down with dogs, you only get fleas'; how another had said, 'This cancer must be cut out before it spreads.' All these remarks were displayed prominently in the GMB's official journal.

I then dug the knife in: 'Yet we read that now even the G & M is to ask for the tainted public monies – to risk the fleas – to succumb to the cancer and join the treachery. Seriously, I am sure they made that decision in the best interests of the movement. Let them and you reflect that, without our stand in 1985, they would not have had the gumption to do so.'

Time after time, I reminded them, the TUC had followed our lead after initially berating us for our forward-looking stance. After all the criticism we had endured over secret postal ballots, I reminded the TUC's finest how in 1984, soon after balloting procedures became law, we staged a vote of our members at Austin Rover. Other unions, including Ron Todd's TGWU, did not. When the company took the unions to court, they found they were mistaken in including the EETPU. We took action against Austin Rover to recover our costs. The result, as I took great pleasure in reminding the selective memories around that TUC table, was that we did a deal with the car company lawyers. The other unions, notably Ron's, had faced fines of £250,000, possibly more, but we fixed it for Ron so that Austin Rover dropped their action against every union in return for us withdrawing ours against them. I made Ron squirm as I read out the correspondence between us, confirming every detail, and I added: 'So this hard-headed, market-based, think-only-of-yourself union gave up the money it could have recovered from Austin Rover to protect brother organizations.'

My conclusion turned the shaft back on my tormentors. I refuted their assertion that we had acted in a manner detrimental to the interests of the trade union movement. I declared, 'It is the actions and decisions or, more accurately, the failures and indecisions of the majority here that have brought the trade union movement into disrepute.'

It was they who had adopted an ostrich-like attitude towards the employment laws; had given the impression that unions were prepared to go outside the law; refused to condemn picket-line violence in the miners' strike; foisted the election-losing policy of unilateral nuclear disarmament on the Labour Party; failed to silence the thugs who denied a hearing to myself and others at Congress; tolerated the shame of Dundee when Ford pulled out of a £40-million factory plan because the TGWU opposed a single-union deal for the AEU; allowed a minority of unions to sabotage the retraining of the jobless to prepare them for work.

'It is you who should be in the dock – not the EETPU,' I stormed, 'for our union has acted in the best interests of the trade union members. Where the members' interests and convictions conflict with what you regard as that of the "movement's", its ideology and its unrepresentative decisions, then, yes, we have supported the members and given voice to their opinions. We will continue to do so, even if that means breaking every rule in the book.' My words had no effect on the TUC dunderheads, but I enjoyed every minute of them.

After we left Congress House for a nearby hotel, Norman Willis told the Press we had two weeks to comply with the TUC directives on no-strike deals. The media circus scurried between the two camps in Great Russell Street. The most sensible comment Norman could come up with was that I had to start obeying the rules and stop being the John McEnroe of the trade union movement. My immediate response was that we were not involved in a game of tennis. But when I reported back to our Engineering National Conference at Scarborough the following morning, I had had time to reflect. I said that in ancient times, issues were settled between champions instead of committing armies. Bearing in mind the TUC General Secretary's rotund shape, I said, 'If Norman Willis declines tennis, then he can choose any form of combat – other than sumo wrestling!'

But what was happening to our union was no laughing matter. We had, initially, invited Norman to address us at Scarborough. We withdrew that offer after he brushed aside our plea to adjust the hearing date. Despite this, Norman released the speech he would have made. It said, 'Your union has still a few weeks before you pull out the pin on the hand grenade – while you are still holding it . . . ' That speech was written before the TUC General Council made its suspension decision. How could it contain such a statement unless the matter had been predetermined?

The TUC had argued that if it became common practice to seek workers' views as we did, it would be difficult to resist the claim of such opinions to be paramount. Their fear was that their own power, the power of decision without consultation, would be eroded. That was really at the heart of the rift. If Gorbachev was responding in Russia to the people's voice, how could the TUC ignore it?

On 8 July 1988, the very day our TUC suspension came into force, the hard Left in our midst came out of their ratholes with a threat to form a breakaway union called the Electrical and Plumbing Industries Union. This they finally did when we walked out of Congress in September. It was led by John Aitken, a *Daily Mail* newspaper electrician. The minority who joined were kept in holding branches by the TGWU, GMB and the Manufacturing, Science and Finance Union, which resulted from a merger of Clive Jenkins' ASTMS and Ken Gill's TASS.

Aitken, whom I had trounced in my election for General Secretary, said he hoped the new union would attract the 36,000 electricians who had voted for him. He was to be sorely disappointed. His target was said to be 20,000 in the first year. The result was just 3,000. Three years on, the EPIU claimed 4,200, but even that is looked upon with suspicion by my friends and theirs in the TUC.

The final conflict was to take place at the TUC's Conference at Bournemouth in September. My first thought was that it was not worth going as we would be expelled anyway. Other Executive colleagues felt our members would not think we were making a proper defence, so we paid in £75,000 in TUC fees for the honour of letting them kick us out. After our expulsion, however, we got £30,000 back. We reclaimed the money for the period we had received no services from the TUC, not that their services ever did us much good.

We were so sure of the TUC verdict that we booked our delegation in for two nights only at the Winterbourne Hotel, just up the hill from the Bournemouth conference centre. As soon as I arrived on Saturday, 3 September, there was a message that a number of colleagues on the General Council wanted to see us on the Sunday morning. The eleventh-hour bargaining had begun.

I met eleven of them the next day in a private room at the Palace Court Hotel. They included Bill McCall of the Institution of Professional Civil Servants, who initiated the meeting, and friends like John Lyons, of the Engineers and Managers' Association. Also on board were Tony Christopher, the leader of the Inland Revenue Staff Federation and John 'Jelly Roll' Morton of the Musicians' Union. They pressed me to find anything we might do to avoid expulsion. I explained that we were prisoners of our members' ballot decision and it was now a rule of the union that TUC membership and strike-free deals had to go side by side or not at all. But I knew that these union leaders at least meant well, and I promised to give their points careful thought.

When I met our Executive on the Sunday afternoon, I suggested we should make some attempt to bridge the gap. I put forward the idea that we would accept the Disputes Committees' decisions if they were accepted by the members concerned at Orion and Christian Salveson. The TUC could organize the ballot, and if our members wanted to abandon those agreements and join another union, we would accept their verdict. That was my final word in my speech to Congress the next day. The Executive were difficult to persuade, but after a long meeting, they accepted my lead. It was Norman Willis's failure to grab that last-ditch offer which guaranteed our walk-out.

After a full English breakfast, washed down with cups of strong tea, I led the EETPU delegation down the hill from our hotel to the Bournemouth conference centre. We arrived early to avoid a kicking from the cranks who would line the route later and bay for our blood. These were desperate times for the trade union movement, but not for us. My view then and now is that we set ourselves free from the shackles of a tired, outdated movement that day.

For the first time in years, I was able to make a speech without constant interruption. Norman had issued orders the previous evening that there was to be no heckling; no one but he and I would speak in that section. I tried desperately to bait them, but much to my chagrin it didn't work.

The execution began on a sour note when Clive Jenkins, who was in the chair, stopped my good friend Bill Jordan speaking by switching off the microphone. Bill, the boyish-looking President of the Amalgamated Engineering Union, tried to press for a vote to allow our continued suspension rather than expulsion to stop what he called 'the most vicious membership war' in TUC history. He warned that the members would lose and the employers would gain, and that his union would not vote to inflict 'grievous bodily harm' on the movement while the enemies of the working people went unscathed.

Clive accused Bill of behaving 'intemperately' and asked him to leave the rostrum. When Bill continued speaking, Clive cut him off. But even at the rear right of the 'stalls' where we were sitting – nicely placed for a quick exclusion in unnumbered seats – we could still catch Bill making his point.

Norman then proceeded to pontificate and mumble and bumble his way through the TUC's jaundiced version of democracy. He said the EETPU had to come to the rostrum, accept the TUC decisions on no-strike deals or face the consequences. He had a fat chance. I went to the rostrum as a hush fell over the hall. But there was to be no apology, no bending of the knee to these paragons of democratic virtue. They all thought they knew the background, but, just in case there was a vague chance they might have been misled, I felt obliged to explain why our heads were on the chopping block.

I introduced myself as: 'Hammond, EETPU . . . or, as you are now thrusting upon us – The Independent Union.'

To an almost eerie silence, interrupted only by the occasional cough, I declared, 'I represent my union today not to appeal . . . not to say "Sorry, we'll abide by your instructions," but rather to tell you – and beyond you, the British people – why you are expelling my union.

'Some of you might regard what I say as a statement of mitigation – I doubt if there will be enough. All I hope to do is sow some seeds of doubt – seeds that will grow in time to question with growing force your denial of our members' freedom, our citizens' freedom – to join the union of their choice and to freely make agreements with their employers.'

I said that they had got themselves into a state of mind that regarded the EETPU as the hated enemies of wartime against whom any action was justified. And I did not let Norman off the hook: not so much Stormin' Norman, more like Borin' Norman. I half-turned towards the podium behind me where Norman sat like some Buddha statue as I reminded my accusers of how their TUC General Secretary had bluntly refused to wait for our suspension until after a member-ship ballot had expressed its view. Our plea for member democracy had been brushed aside. I told them, 'If there is any one-sidedness in the matter of our ballot, it rests in Goliath's camp – that of the TUC – not in ours.'

Even then, as the axe was about to fall upon us, I warned we would be more than a match for them in a membership war. Today, that prophecy has come all too true, with senior officials of the Union of Construction and Allied Workers (UCATT) fleeing the madhouse politics of their hard-Left executive and bringing thousands of disaffected Moderates into our ranks. I told the TUC we wanted to cooperate with other bona fide unions. 'We are not looking for conflict and resent incitement to attack us, from whatever quarter,' I said, but I warned them, 'I can only repeat that, if attacked, we will respond with vigour.'

The TUC had become irrelevant to the members' needs. We were victims of the 'albino syndrome' – harassed simply because we were different. I expressed confidence that more and more workers would choose us, using secret individual votes rather than the 'cornflake ballot-box' rattled under their nose. They would choose the future, not the past; reality not political humbug; partnership and cooperation, not hard-Left, class-war conflict.

As I neared the end of my allotted time, I referred to the advice of the friends who had counselled me the previous day. They had properly said, 'Why leave now when you're winning the argument?' I added, 'Further, they say, quite legitimately, with the new laws on union elections, the days of the ballot-riggers are numbered and the "notoriously dirty elections" will be cleaned up. All unions will then shortly be marching to the tune of their members and all union members want sensible, moderate trade-unionism.

'It is a powerful and attractive argument, but I have to say to those friends that we do not just have a responsibility for the policy of the movement as a whole, although I do not think it can be said that we have shirked in this respect. We have worked, organized and incurred unpopularity in our mission to change the overall situation. But we have a primary obligation and that is to our members and our own union. That obligation I have been trying to discharge this morning.'

I then offered what I described as an 'honourable alternative to expulsion'. We would accept the TUC Dispute Committee awards in respect of Orion and Christian Salvesen subject to our members' agreement in a ballot. 'Will you do the same?' I asked. 'Will you let the members decide?' Those were my last words to Congress. I will never address it again – at least, not from inside.

I know many of those union leaders who signed our death warrant that day now regret what they did. With us on the outside, it can never be the same again. Unity is everything to the trade union movement. Without unity, it falls, just like a government.

Introducing us as 'the appellant union' – a phrase typical of the TUC bureaucracy – Clive Jenkins then reintroduced Norman to finish us off. He began, 'I did not think much of that.' It was downhill from there.

Norman insisted my version of the trade union world was distorted by a misplaced sense of persecution. He should have been where I was standing during those difficult years to find out what persecution meant. They were right and we were wrong, said Norman. The TUC advice stood and we should accept it.

With that, we stood as one man and walked out before we were thrown out. There was no signal from me. No advance plan. There was no point in staying. The stupidity of the affair was heightened by the fact that the overwhelming vote against us was taken and sentence passed after we had gone. My blood was boiling.

The clever thing for Norman to have done was to have said that, although he did not like what I was saying, they would have a meeting over lunchtime to consider it. They could have found a compromise, allowed us a vote and buried it. But Norman Willis is not clever. He lost us that day, because of his stubbornness and his inability to free himself from years of dogma and red tape which encircle Congress House like a noose.

There was an army of scribes and photographers, but I wanted to get out of there as quickly as possible. I headed a phalanx of our people and said, 'Just walk over them. Walk over them. Just knock them down and walk over them.' We were ploughing through and my adrenalin was flowing, having not been able to provoke the TUC. I had done my best to get them baying, but they were well disciplined for once. The orders from the TUC commissars had been obeyed to the letter.

We got out of the hall surrounded by Press people, all asking questions at the same time, and climbed up the hill towards our hotel. One radio girl poked a microphone under my nose as I walked and asked, 'Well, what are you going to do now?' At that moment, I felt like a conjuror being asked to top his best trick. It was a warm day, and I was very irate. So I replied, 'Climb up this bloody hill. That's what I'm doing next.' It was broadcast over Radio 4 as my vision of the future.

Questions came thick and fast at a Press conference around the hotel pool. 'Who are you going to take in, Eric?' one reporter asked. 'Anybody,' I said, 'from janitors to journalists.' Later, we did take in the Institute of Journalists. We've always taken in janitors.

That evening, we had been invited to the AEU do. It was only they and our good friends in the Civil and Public Services Association, like their President Marion Chambers and General Secretary John Ellis, who had voted against the party line. We always went to the AEU on the Monday night of Congress. They would normally come to our party later. We had been banned by the TUC, but not by our friends in the engineers. There was a spontaneous cheer as we walked into the room at the plush Highcliffe Hotel. I was taken aback. People were coming up, patting me on the back and shaking hands – not just our AEU colleagues, but employers who were there as well.

We decided to leave Bournemouth on the Wednesday. That left Tuesday free. After all, we had no conference to attend. Having done my national service in the 19th Armoured Workshop attached to the Fourth Royal Tank Regiment, I had always wanted to visit the Bovington tank museum. We enjoyed viewing this fine collection of fighting vehicles. We took our time, spent half the day there and had a drink on the way back. We were winding down after Monday's experiences. This did not please a BBC camera crew, who had been looking for me since breakfast-time. They had been assigned to follow my every move – something normally reserved for pop stars and Prime Ministers. The cameraman said, 'You've really made it now. But where have you been all day?'

I said, 'Sorry, but you missed out. I was looking at some hardware we're going to need. You missed some great pictures of the Bovington tank museum.'

The dismayed cameraman said, 'Why didn't you let us know? We could have done a good piece on that.'

It provided lighthearted relief after being wound up for days. Overall, I reckon we won on points, though. We left Norman Willis blathering away at nobody. I had dozens of letters afterwards from members congratulating me on making him look a fool by walking out before sentence was passed. We had deprived them of the pleasure of excommunicating us in public. It was a censure in thin air.

During our first twelve months outside the TUC, we made our first membership gain for a decade. It was only 1,200, but it was more than most unions whose membership slide continued apace. My only real fear was that employers might succumb to pressure from TUC unions like the TGWU and the GMB to stop them negotiating with us. Our members are no great warriors. They want an easy life. They would have been worried if we had been removed from negotiating committees, and that would have had a detrimental effect upon us. So I took advantage of being the man of the moment after our expulsion by accepting every speaking engagement. I must have spoken almost every night for six months to put our message over. I wanted to make sure we stiffened businesses up. I usually ended, if I was with a doubtful group of employers, by saying, 'You might feel that you have to give way to some pressure.' But, alluding to an influence I didn't have, I added, 'Understand this. There are no knighthoods in betraying the EETPU.' They all suspected I had the ear of somebody.

In fact, business and industry stood firm. Where there was an attempt to push them about, they said, 'No'. Though the other unions wanted an army to cut us to pieces, ordinary Joes out there were happy to get on with their work and to work with each other. The result was business as usual. Apart from a little local difficulty in the more bizarre local authorities like Manchester and on one occasion in the oil industry, we have continued to represent our members on negotiating committees alongside TUC unions.

A year after our expulsion, I had the chance of recruiting 7,500 disaffected cabin crew belonging to the TGWU. When their leaders came to me in my office, I was sorely tempted to invite them into the fold, but then I thought, 'What could be better than persuading them to merge with an existing TUC union, which itself could then face the same fate as the EETPU?'

My ingenious plot failed. I put them in touch with the British Airline Pilots' Association, led by my former EETPU colleague Mark Young. I reckoned that I would either win first prize, with BALPA outside the TUC before joining us later, or second prize, if BALPA rejected the cabin crew, by taking them direct into our union. But it didn't work out that way. I hadn't taken into account the fact that the Bridlington rules would fall apart.

Mark took in the TGWU dissidents, even though he formed a phoney organization called Cabin Crew '89. In fact, one of our officials, Graham Fowler, who had worked at Heathrow, left us to help out. The TGWU challenged Mark and took him to the TUC. At the General Council, Mark's final defence was, 'If you don't let us have them, the EETPU will.' Consequently the TGWU had to take it on the chin, so hard that they swallowed the camel of the cabin crew, having gagged at the gnat of Orion. This was despite the fact that their claim to half-a-dozen members led to a major organization like the EETPU being pushed out.

At the same time, a similar U-turn on a previous precedent took place. The AEU had, in competition with us, won negotiating rights for the Coca-Cola factory and an integrated canning plant, Nocanco, at Wakefield, West Yorkshire. Once again, the TGWU stepped in. They claimed canning was one of their traditional areas. They used the same arguments against the AEU as they had against us over Orion and Christian Salvesen, but the AEU stood firm and said, if ordered to scrap the Coca-Cola agreement, they would tell the TUC to get lost and quit in protest. Result: the TGWU was forced to swallow again. They accepted what they would not accept over our deals.

The TUC has had to change. They are subjecting the Bridlington rules to a major review. In other words, as I warned them, they're as dead as the dodo. So what did they put us out for? It was for being right too often. For spite. For Wapping. But it goes beyond that. It goes right back to the Communist ballot-rigging in our union in 1961. Even after they had been exposed and found guilty, the likes of Frank Haxell and Frank Foulkes, the ringleaders, were never subjected to the venom directed at Les Cannon, Frank Chapple and myself.

There was no twenty-minute silent and shameful goodbye for these ballot-fixers. It was full speeches, a major debate and reserved seats in the gallery for them. It was a different story when we were expelled.

We have never looked back, just forward to a future where the TUC will become an increasingly spent force. Many have speculated about whether we will rejoin the TUC club. I doubt this will happen even after I have retired, unless we merge with the AEU. Our members are an awkward bunch and they have long memories. It is not our way to forgive and forget. We do not need the TUC in order to conduct our business. They need us far more. So, it's not just *au revoir*; it is a final farewell.

The contradictions in TUC unions' attitudes to strike-free deals continue to emerge. Recently, NEK Cables, who have such an agreement with John Edmond's GMB, decided to end it. The local representative threatened a strike to maintain the union's no-strike deal!

Even outside the TUC, we were concerned in 1990 with the ambulancemen's dispute as I reported to our Conference that year:

All of us were concerned at the long drawn-out struggle of the ambulancemen and concerned as to how we might effectively assist.

You will remember that at the centre of their case was a desire to secure a mechanism that would determine salary levels without industrial action – as the headlines would put it, a 'No-Strike Deal'. It was no surprise that GMB's John Edmonds, Rodney Bickerstaffe and the top brass of NUPE kept away from the dispute – were unusually silent – and left it all to the acceptable Roger Poole.

In 1987, John Edmonds said, 'There are some things in life which are right and others which are wrong. No-strike deals are wrong.' Rodney Bickerstaffe in the same year said at the TUC, 'If any of the papers want to say, "This is a good union, it's promised never to strike any more," do not come to my union because we will never agree to that.'

Notwithstanding the muted general secretaries concerned, the Executive considered how we could assist the ambulancemen in their objective. They agreed that I should write to the Prime Minister. This I did on 9 January as follows:

Like every other caring person in our country, you must be concerned about the continuing dispute in the ambulance service. Advice you have had in plenty, but I think my union has shown by its deeds that we go beyond words when the public interest is at stake.

Last June, your government announced that it was considering prohibiting strikes in essential services. Our attitude has always been that we would resist to the utmost any attempt to impose a no-strike restriction on our members, but we would be prepared to talk to any employer about arrangements to end industrial disputes.

We see the present dispute not just as a growing threat to the well being of those needing the ambulance service, but as an opportunity.

The government and the public are concerned to maintain essential services. That objective can only be achieved if the employees involved willingly accept alternative mechanisms to that of withdrawal of labour. Could we not make a start and possibly find a way out of the present impasse if a conference was convened of those involved in emergency/essential services – government, management and unions?

The purpose of the conference would be to examine and recommend mechanism, formulae and procedures that would end industrial action in the services concerned. Not by one single option, but by a variety based on different experiences that employees in an industry/service could choose by ballot.

I understand (from Ivor Manley, the civil servant with the responsibility) that it was difficult to frame a reply to my letter. Eventually, I received it, dated 13 February:

Thank you for your letter of 9 January suggesting that a conference of government, management and trade unions might find a way out of the ambulance dispute in the context of a wider understanding on pay and industrial action in the essential services.

So far as the ambulance dispute is concerned, as you will know, ambulance pay and conditions are negotiated in the Ambulance Whitley Council. The management offer includes a fair settlement on pay with increases ranging between nine and 16.3 per cent over eighteen months. It also paves the way for a better service to be provided and for local management to have more flexibility to negotiate local pay increases for staff based on improved productivity.

I have carefully considered the procedure you propose, but I believe that it would be wrong for any government to step in in this way. The appropriate machinery for pay negotiations is in place; the right approach is for this machinery to be used effectively.

I persevered and wrote on 1 March:

Thank you for your letter of 13 February. I do understand the argument you array, but I think the prize of dispute-free essential services is one worth trying to achieve. In any case, some of your considerations no longer apply in the light of the settlement presently under ballot.

I am sure that an initiative as outlined in my letter of 9 January would be in the long-term interests of our country.

Only a note this time, from the Private Secretary, on 14 March:

I am writing on behalf of the Prime Minister to thank you for your further letter of 1 March concerning the essential services. She has noted your further comments.

145

I do believe that this was an opportunity missed: an opportunity to begin to build a constructive relationship between government representing the political citizen and trade unions representing the same person as economic man and woman.

This experience with government and the more recent NEK/GMB farce emphasizes the correctness of my arguments to the TUC's review body in 1988, before they expelled us.

I opined that we did not have all the answers within our own national experience and that we should ask the Russian and the American trade union movements for their experience of no-strike agreements. I am always at least half-serious. For I remembered that at the 1987 TUC, Lane Kirkland, leader of the AFL-CIO, had said to me rather enigmatically, 'Look at the experience of the American steelworkers . . .'

I did and found that some years ago, the pattern of negotiation and dispute had given birth to a remarkable change. As negotiations moved towards the due date, the steelmasters and their customers stockpiled steel in anticipation of a possible dispute. If the negotiations failed to produce a settlement, then there was a strike and all were out of work. If the negotiations succeeded, then with their huge stocks, the steelmasters laid off a considerable part of their workforce.

Reasonable men eventually concluded there must be a better way! They reached a binding arbitration strike-free deal. For the several years it operated, the steelworkers made better than average advances. Who ended it? Yes, the employers.

Early this year, I had a visit from the leader of the Swedish white-collar workers. He wanted to speak to me about our agreements. He told me his members had been on strike for three weeks to secure a binding arbitration – no-strike deal!

It is clear that many in other countries recognize the binding pendulum-arbitration mechanism for what it is: a means to extend rather than limit employees' influence. Most British employers are not prepared thus to share their power: they would sooner take their chance with a strike . . .

To my trade union colleagues, I say, think of the disputes of recent years; think of the trade union defeats – the miners, the teachers, the P & O seamen. Would not all concerned – the industries, the employees – have been advantaged if they had had access to binding arbitration?

8

Labour's odd man out

I have never been an easy conformer – and my relationship with the Labour Party, its policies and its leaders has been no exception. It is a body which has disliked change, and looked backwards instead of forwards. Its committees and caucuses usually close ranks when an odd man out like me questions the validity of a policy. They don't like a rebel, and I am certainly that. I am glad to say, though, that in recent years, change has been forced upon Labour's body politic if only because of the growing realization that without it the Party will never hold power again. It has taken years for them to realize that the electorate is suspicious of the degree to which Labour is beholden to the trade unions. Most of its cash comes from us. For decades, all but a minority of Conference votes have been bought and owned by the unions. At last, all that is changing, and the sooner the better. For without that crucial change in the public's perception of who controls Labour's directions, I believe there is little chance of a Labour general election victory despite what the opinion polls may say.

My links with Labour go back to my teens, but not to my upbringing in Canada during the war. Up to the age of sixteen my politics were fairly Right-wing. I had been living with a middle-class conservative family over there, but when I returned to my home in Kent, I came increasingly under the influence of my father, who was a strong middle-of-the-road Labour Party supporter.

I started as an apprentice electrical fitter at Bowater's, joined the union, and was exposed to industrial life and the new ideas which were discussed in the union branch, canteens and work shops. The war was over and the '45 Labour victory brought with it an expectation, an excitement, a hope of a better country than we had known in the Thirties.

My apprenticeship at Bowater's began with a shop steward, Albert Knight, a friendly and kindly man who became Assistant Branch Secretary of the Gravesend branch of the Electrical Trades Union. I must have been seventeen when he came back from one branch meeting and told me he had been elected Branch Secretary, but the election had been disallowed because the Chairman had ruled that he could not hold two posts at the same time. I told him the rule had never been intended to disallow somebody elected to a higher post. It merely meant that he would have to relinquish the Assistant Branch Secretary's job on becoming Branch Secretary. Albert asked me if I was sure and I assured him I was. So here was this new member of the union, seventeen years old, advising a veteran shop steward on the meaning of the rule. He asked me if I would go to the next branch meeting with him and say the same thing. I did. When the minutes were read, I challenged the decision of the Chairman recorded in those minutes to invalidate Albert's election. He was a wily old fellow traveller and knew that he was wrong and soon gave way. Albert became Branch Secretary, the position of Assistant Branch Secretary was vacant, and guess who was elected?

By the time I was seventeen, in 1947, it had all begun to make some sort of sense. The Hammond family had moved in 1938 from the two-up, two-down in York Road with its outside loo and no bathroom to what for us was relative luxury – the council house in The Crescent.

At the time when I was becoming politically aware, a unique situation developed in my local Gravesend constituency. It had been a Conservative seat apart from a brief period in the 1920s when George Isaacs held it for Labour for a couple of years, but the Tories had an unbroken run until 1945 when in the post-war election landslide, Garry Alligan, a journalist, gained the seat for Labour. Alligan, who originated from South Africa, did not last long, however. He wrote an article attacking the allegedly drunken behaviour of his fellow MPs in the House of Commons. This broke all previous conventions. Even though those of us who have made regular visits to the Palace of Westminster know its bars are the most popular meeting place for many MPs, it is not talked about outside – and certainly not written about. In 1947, Alligan breached this age-old convention and paid the price: he was expelled from the House of Commons.

It was a critical time for the Labour Party and they could have done without this extra irritant. There was a fuel shortage, there was even potato rationing, which had never occurred through the war years, so the Labour government's popularity was not exactly at its peak. The by-election was called. Labour, alarmed at the prospect of losing this seat, had to have a charismatic, larger-than-life figure to fight, and they brought in Sir Richard Acland, who came from an old Liberal family in the West Country. He had been a Liberal MP and turned to Labour.

Acland had formed the Commonwealth Party in the war years which had such notables as Tom Driberg in its ranks. Its purpose was to outflank and disrupt the pact agreed between the Tories and Labour during the period of wartime coalition that they would not fight against a sitting party in a by-election. Acland was a man of influence. He had become a champion of the Left after writing a number of books, including a reply to Hitler's *Mein Kampf* called *Unser Kampf* (*Our Struggle*).

It was on the eve of the election poll, after canvassing for this deeply committed Christian Socialist, that I decided to join the Labour Party. I have been a member ever since.

Acland was an exciting man to follow. The last election meeting could not have been more dramatic and, I believe, decisive. In the large market hall, filled to overflowing, the meeting began with darkened lights. Suddenly, down through the hall marched singing Kent miners with their helmet lights ablaze. Acland's passion moved us all to work till we dropped the next day. He became a role model, yet he was an awkward fellow, too. Against all the odds, Acland won, albeit with a slightly reduced majority.

Herbert Morrison, who was in charge of Labour's campaigning, took time off from Cabinet duties to send the constituency a telegram. *Oklahoma* was a hit show at the time, and the message simply read, 'Oh, what a beautiful morning.' It was indeed to all who had such great hopes of that post-war Labour government.

Acland increased his majority against the trend as the elections went by in the Fifties, but in 1955, he resigned to stand as an Independent in a by-election over the building of a British H-bomb. It was well before the Campaign for Nuclear Disarmament was formed.

I was, by this time, an active member of the constituency's General Management Committee. We had a particularly acrimonious debate in my local party at Northfleet about whether we supported nuclear weapons. I took a leading part in backing Acland's vehement opposition to them. After his resignation, we pleaded with Labour's National Executive not to put up a candidate against him in the by-election, but the Labour Party was a much more formidable machine than it is even now. The National Agent, Len Williams, who later became Governor-General of Mauritius, would not give way.

He refused our hero a hearing before the Gravesend General Management Committee. This was too much for their sense of fair play and they voted to hear Acland before proceeding further. Dick was accompanied by his wife, Anne, who had been suffering from TB and could only walk with crutches. She was universally liked throughout Gravesend. Frank Shepherd, the Labour Party's Regional Organizer, sneered that Acland was bringing his sick wife along for sympathy votes – he soon felt the displeasure of the decent people who attended that meeting. By the time Dick Acland had finished speaking, many on the Left, including myself, were in tears. I was part of a group which was not prepared to oppose our local champion – indeed, we supported him.

The situation became even more complicated for us when, in the midst of this dilemma, the Tories called a general election. I was of the view that what was now at stake was whether we were for a Labour government or not. The National Executive imposed a candidate upon us, one Victor Mischon, a solicitor who had been Chairman of London County Council and was later to become Lord Mischon and head one of Britain's richest legal practices. I found myself in the early stages of the election in a most unusual position, attending Campaign Committee meetings for both Acland and Mischon. Knowing that a split Labour vote would lose us the seat, I wanted to ensure that we could mend bridges in the months and years afterwards. It was a damage-limitation exercise, but it came too late to save the seat. The Tories won. Their new MP Peter Kirk was a decent, honest man, and I got to like him. He was later to switch to Rab Butler's old seat at Saffron Walden and become the Tories' leader in Europe.

On the night of the election at the Gravesend Town Hall Court, we were in desperate mood in the Labour camp when we knew we had lost. Others did not appear to be as sorry. I will never forget seeing Victor Mischon walk over to Kirk and overhearing him say, 'We'll have to have lunch next week, Peter.' Our team of election workers were distraught, yet our champion was booking lunch with his opponent as if he had been playing a game of cricket. I did not take to Victor Mischon.

He was our candidate again in 1959. By that time, I was Chairman of the constituency party, and it was my duty to move his adoption. Mischon said to me afterwards, 'That's the first adoption speech I have ever heard which did not mention the name of the candidate.' We weren't buddies.

Around that period, newspaper claims were made about alleged shady property deals centred around a man called Josephs. Mischon's name was being connected with all this. He firmly denied any link, but late in the election campaign, the *Daily Express* carried a front-page story doing just that. Mischon firmly denied any wrongdoing and nothing was proved against him. I lost touch with him after he dropped out of the Gravesend scene until the Electrical Trades Union, as it then was, amalgamated with the plumbers.

Mischon's firm had been handling the plumbers' industrial injury cases. Frank Chapple decided we could not retain two sets of solicitors; we already had Lawford's, so we could save money by keeping to one. I bumped into Mischon in the corridor at our union head office after he had been to the termination meeting with Frank. Beforehand, I said to Frank, 'I know I have nothing to do with this, but for old times' sake, could you hint that I influenced this decision?' By the frosty reception I got from Victor Mischon, who grunted at me in the hallway, Frank did just that.

Dick Acland and I retained respect for each other right up to his death in 1990. When I became General Secretary, BBC-2's *Newsnight* programme went to ask him about me for a profile they were doing. The *Newsnight* people rang me back to say that when they asked Dick about me, he more or less said, 'Eric who?' I was suitably humbled by this, but things were not what they seemed. Ted Rouse, who had been Gravesend constituency Chairman, went to see Dick, who told him, 'Of course I remember Eric, but they wanted me to give them some knocking copy about him when he was a lad. I wouldn't do it.' But they had come back with the story that Dick didn't remember me. Such experiences have convinced me seldom to trust a journalist, but, even more important, never trust the BBC.

The Co-operative Youth Movement was very important to lads like me in those post-war years. It helped give working youngsters a sense of community and brought girls and boys together, like myself and Brenda, who became my wife. We had several clubs in our area. I was a member and later Committee Chairman of my local one. We had numerous social events and summer schools at Bexhill – learning and enjoying. From this we were attracted to the Labour League of Youth and at nineteen I became Chairman of the Gravesend branch.

Ted Rouse, who became a life-long friend, was involved in this and virtually every other Labour Party activity in our area. A modest man, but very able, Ted was best man at my wedding in 1953 and godfather to my eldest son, Ivan. He was the best MP Gravesend never had. We pressed him to stand for parliament in 1959, but he declined because of the effect it would have had on his family. It's a pity, because Ted would have held the seat for years, whatever the national trend, and been a valuable addition to the Commons.

It was Ted who loaned me books and encouraged me to seek election to the local authority, first Gravesend council in 1957, then the authority he led in the neighbouring district of Northfleet. He's the sort of chap who made the Labour Party great. He has served it all his life. A measure of the widespread respect he has in North Kent was expressed when he was given the Freedom of Gravesend when the Tories were in control there. It was a great pleasure for me to be asked to propose the toast at the golden-wedding celebrations of Ted and his wife, Peggy.

I was still living with Brenda and her parents when I won a seat from the Tories in Gravesend. Labour had ten against twenty-two Conservatives. Gravesend council dates back to the thirteenth century, and in its early days had legal powers. It addressed itself as the Court and in the early times was led by a sheriff, not a mayor. Being an ancient borough, it had numerous traditions, including the wearing of rather splendid robes with fur trim. The aldermen had even thicker fur around the collars.

Immediately I was elected, the Town Clerk wrote to me saying they would be grateful if I could come in and be measured for my robe. There was no way I was going to prance around like a peacock: I was a young Leftie in those days and the idea of dressing up in all that regalia made me feel ill. Having consulted my good friend and local Labour agent, John Beadle, about my legal position, I wrote back and refused to take part in their fancy-dress parade. I told the Town Clerk I did not intend to wear the robes, there was no legal requirement and I would not be coming in for a fitting.

I arrived early for the first meeting of the new council to be met by a flunkie dressed in stockings and breeches ready to assist council members into their robes. Wearing an ordinary lounge suit, I walked right through the robing room. The attendant's eyes opened about three inches wide. He shouted, 'Sir, you can't go in there.' I said, 'I think you'll find I can. I'm a duly elected councillor.' I brushed past him and sat down in the council chamber.

Minutes later, the Mayor's secretary poked his nose around a door and whispered, 'Excuse me, sir, you haven't got your robe on.'

I replied 'No, and I don't intend to wear one.'

Back he scuttled into the parlour of the Mayor, Harold Goodwin. Panic had set in: more than 600 years of tradition was about to be thrown overboard. The meeting began, with E. Hammond, Esquire, the only council member not looking like something out of the Middle Ages.

The main item on the agenda was a Tory proposal to put up council-house rents. When I rose to speak against, several Conservatives jumped up and shouted, 'Point of Order. Point of Order. The councillor is improperly dressed. Will you rule he cannot address this meeting?'

I ostentatiously looked down at my flies and said, 'I think I am perfectly in order, Mr Mayor.' With true, impartial chairmanship, the Mayor said, 'I can't stop him speaking, but you don't have to listen to him.' The result was that they chatted with each other while I spoke and didn't listen very much.

I was working for Aberdare Cables at that time, fitting a new boilerhouse at Bowater's paper mills, Northfleet. On site the next morning, the foreman, Tom Hall, who was a firm Communist, ticked me off. He was the last person I expected to back the regalia-wearing, but Tom said, 'Don't you realize? You've not just upset the Tories. You've upset your colleagues on the Labour group, who have been wearing these robes ever since they were councillors. So anything sensible you have to say will be ignored and you will diminish your influence with them in the years to come.'

It turned out to be accurate advice, because a couple of days afterwards when we had a meeting of the Labour group they said they were going to pass a resolution stating that I must wear the robes. I told them they could be that daft if they wished. I believed it was a matter of individual choice and freedom. If they persisted, I warned them I would take the matter to the local constituency party. I knew who would win there – I would, I was the Chairman. So they withdrew the resolution, but it was quite clear they were sore. I never did wear the robes.

Another part of this uniform for councillors was a top hat, which had to be worn at church and on other civic occasions. To me this was a symbol of all that I was against, a class society full of Tories and capitalists wearing top hats. The whole thing was anathema to me.

Within three years, after I had left the authority, Labour had taken control. The first decision of the new majority was to scrap the wearing of robes: a minority of one came good in the end.

It was no thanks to the local paper, the *Gravesend Reporter*, whose hostility towards me became greater than any animosity I encountered with the Tories. The paper had the contract to print the minutes for the council; it also printed the confidential minutes of the key Finance and Law Committee, so the paper knew the decisions of those private meetings before the open council meeting. While the council was still under Tory control, it was suggested that officials should find out how much it would cost to buy their own printing press in order to print the minutes in-house. They discussed this at the Finance and Law Committee in private to make a recommendation to the full council.

The meeting was due on the Tuesday. On the Friday beforehand, a critical editorial appeared in the local paper attacking this decision. It was before the public knew anything about it. The paper had used its business relationship with the council to mount a campaign against the idea. I was furious about this. I told the Tory majority, 'I know what you are going to do. Many of you who owe your seats to the support of the local paper are going to change your mind. You're not going to pursue the idea.' It was about this time that somebody had taken a tape recorder into the House of Commons and there was a terrible kerfuffle because it was illegal. I told the wimps of Gravesend, 'The *Reporter* doesn't need tape recorders, because it prints the minutes.' It was a clear abuse of the business relationship the newspaper had with the authority.

The majority of the council backed off, as I had predicted. Thereafter, that paper would not print anything I said. I could have dropped my trousers and they would not have printed it.

The vendetta continued when two years later I was elected to neighbouring Northfleet council. I was among a group of Left-wingers who disagreed with the ruling Labour group over the Macmillan government's call for every council to have a civil defence force. We said it was a nonsense trying to kid the public that this kind of ill-equipped 'Dad's Army' could do anything against a nuclear

154

attack. Not a word of my argument appeared in the *Gravesend Reporter*, which also covered Northfleet. Instead, the paper ran a bitter editorial entitled 'Odd man out', which said I must be as big an embarrassment to my Labour colleagues as I was to the whole community.

I wrote to the paper complaining it must be the first time a local politician had been editorially criticized for saying something that had not been reported! I never received a reply and they would not print the letter. Now, of course, I am the darling of nearly all the newspapers and I have trouble stopping them quoting me – even when I've said nothing!

By 1963, I had become the union's Gravesend Branch Secretary and was on Labour's parliamentary panel of prospective candidates. My first selection conference was at St Albans where, even if I had been selected, I would never have won. I retained my position on the ETU panel even after the Right took over the union in the wake of the Communist ballot-rigging scandal.

In 1964, I had to decide whether to stay in union politics or try for the Commons. I was shortlisted for the Deptford seat in South London. The Left who controlled the constituency party backed me and I had a damn good chance of being selected. At the same time, the new anti-Communist Executive in the union was coming to the end of its first two-year period of office and I was being pressed to stand for the Executive as well. That was the choice I made, and I have never regretted it. There was a fork in the road and I decided to spurn the chance of a political career. The initial years on the back benches are pretty boring and dull for most new MPs, who are lobby fodder. I liked the real world of industry so I stuck to what I knew. As it turned out, given the many years Labour has spent in opposition, I took the right road, because I have been able to influence events far more from my union office than I would have in the Commons.

I began to make my mark in Labour affairs after the tragic early death from cancer of our General President, Les Cannon. Les led the unions in the vital electricity supply industry negotiations and his death in 1970 left a considerable vacuum. The gap left by Les was filled by Frank Chapple, aided by myself. I had worked closely with Frank in the electrical contracting industry and was already a member of the supply team. Frank used me to do the paperwork – to be his leg man.

We were plunged into an immediate crisis. The Seventies oil crisis was on and to make matters worse we had a bitter pay dispute which resulted in us imposing an overtime ban in the midst of Ted Heath's

Tory government pay policy. We had cooperated in productivity bargaining. The average working week in electricity supply had been fifty-two hours; some were working a hundred hours. We got it down to about forty-one hours on average. We arranged different patterns of working, so instead of people working from Monday to Friday, they worked any five days in seven. It was the first example of flexible rostering, with different hours worked in summer and winter by outside workers.

So successful were the incentive schemes that the workforce was reduced from 142,000 to 90,000 at a time when more power was being generated and more consumers being served, but with the incomes policy, Heath was putting a pay clamp on us. We had given all this and improved service to customers while other industries had not. Our work to rule included a ban on overtime and refusal to be upgraded if somebody was absent. Such was the effect of even this minimal action within the electricity industry that by the end of the week, the country was in chaos. The Energy Minister advised families to brush their teeth in the dark. The hostility our action engendered made a considerable mark on me. Press reports then of Frank Chapple made Arthur Scargill look like a Sunday-school teacher. Frank had loads of animal dung tipped in his front garden; he was threatened with a shotgun. It was a very difficult time. And it lasted less than a week.

We called off the action in return for the Wilberforce inquiry. That's when I first came to national prominence, because I wrote the trade union evidence to the inquiry. I had to work out all my calculations on an old slide rule. Calculators hadn't come in at that time and my eyes were swimming at the end of each day. I was helped by Fred Franks, a shop steward at Northfleet power station, who was later to become our national officer for electricity supply. We produced our evidence in record time and beat the Electricity Council with all their resources. *The Times* said how remarkable it was that our document had been produced in such a short time and compared it to writing a book in three weeks.

The TUC had formed a Fuel and Power Committee, which was initially chaired by Geoffrey Drain of NALGO and later by Frank Chapple. Its purpose was to secure more unity on energy matters between electricity and mining unions. However, the oil crisis, which was about price rather than adequacy of supply, gave it greater importance. The result was an integrated energy policy which was adopted by the Labour Party. It seems hard to believe now, but there was agreement all round.

The unity was such that Lawrence Daly, the General Secretary of the National Union of Mineworkers, moved a motion at the Labour Party Conference proposing that policy and I seconded it. There was room for all the trade union interests of coal, oil-fired and nuclear power. It was only when Arthur Scargill came on the scene that our unity was shattered. He was, of course, aided and abetted by Tony Benn who, when he was Energy Minister under Harold Wilson in 1975, was clearly against any form of nuclear power. At an energy conference at Church House, which Benn chaired, I accused him of prevaricating over which type of nuclear reactor to back. I wanted the SGHWR, the same technology as the Canadian CANDU reactor, which had proved its worth and would have the advantage of reducing American dominance of the market.

But power chiefs were at each others' throats, too. I likened Sir Derek Ezra, the Coal Board Chairman, and Central Electricity Generating Board Chairman, Sir Arthur Hawkins, to two jousting knights. I commented, 'Those two doughty knights can't be in the same room without throwing down the gauntlet. The trouble is they charge right past each other, miss and damage everybody else.' Derek Ezra never really forgave me for that. In Labour circles, the Left and Scargill from his Yorkshire base were destroying any hope of unity over energy policy. Doubt was cast about the safety of nuclear power. Unity collapsed and the splits widened, so that today Labour wants to dismantle those nuclear stations we have got.

Eric Varley was perhaps the Labour Minister I liked best. We had a good rapport, he talked sense and we got to know each other well over a period of years. I worked for him on the Industrial Development Advisory Board, which advised the Industry Minister on projects suitable for inward investment. The other union representative on the Board in the late Seventies was Harry Urwin, Jack Jones's Deputy General Secretary at the Transport and General Workers. He would have been top man at the TGWU instead of Moss Evans had his age not been against him. He could not stand because he was too old. Pity – he was running the TGWU while Jack Jones involved himself in the international scene, and he would have made a better job of it than Evans.

Before the disaster of the 1978–9 Winter of Discontent, government ministers were made 'minders' to major trade unions in order at least to keep open lines of communication despite the mounting difficulties over pay policy. Naturally, Eric Varley was given our union because he was Secretary of State for Energy before he was moved to Industry. Frank Chapple and I could see a nightmare unfolding before us, with the Tories gaining ground by the week in the opinion polls and amongst ordinary people, particularly skilled workers. We urged Varley to persuade Jim Callaghan to go to the country in June 1978. Had he done so, I am confident he would just have shaved in. June, July and August came and went and Jim stuck it out. By September at the TUC, Jim still hadn't made up his mind and made a fool of himself by singing his ridiculous 'Waiting at the church' song. It infuriated practically everybody at the TUC, because they felt he needed to announce the election and he didn't.

I asked Frank Chapple why Callaghan had not called the election when it was obvious to us things could only deteriorate if he hung on. Frank said, 'Don't you understand? He likes being Prime Minister. They all do. He'd sooner have the certainty of a few more months than the risk of never being Prime Minster again.' We sometimes forget that those in authority over us are human, too.

The Social Contract started to fall apart and attempts at wage restraint collapsed in front of our eyes. The TUC tried manfully to save the situation, but it could not deliver the goods to Callaghan. Just before the harsh rigour of the Winter of Discontent descended upon us, I told Varley, 'You are not going to get an agreement with the TUC and, if you did, it wouldn't be worth anything.' I suggested the government went over the heads of the TUC leaders. My idea was for the government to have not a Social Contract with union bosses, but a pact with the people. The nation would have been offered a referendum on what shape it wanted for incomes policy. It again went back to my basic philosophy of allowing a free democratic vote before deciding policy. I told Varley that, at the very worst, it would be a good platform upon which to go to the country. It would show Jim Callaghan was prepared to take on the union militants with the help of the wider electorate. Varley did not respond until early in 1979 when he asked me to join him on a trade mission to China with a group of senior industrialists. He told me, 'That was a good idea of yours, but it was too late.'

The Callaghan government fell in the May general election and we endured eleven years of Margaret Thatcher. Had Jim Callaghan held my suggested referendum, things might have been very different: an opportunity missed, I fear.

Despite the difficulties at home, Varley's China mission went ahead, even though he was checking back with Sunny Jim every evening as rubbish piled up in the streets and even cancer patients were turned away from hospitals. The China party included British Steel Chairman, Sir Charles Villiers, and Lord Nelson of GEC. At this time, China had invaded North Vietnam, and among the things Britain was trying to sell the Chinese were Harrier jets. Varley was in the midst of a furore over this, with people on the Left like Tony Benn saying we should not sell weapons of war to China, and the Russians issuing statements saying it would be a hostile act. Varley was treading on eggs the whole time he was there.

I indicated I wanted to meet the All-China Federation of Trade Unions during our visit. At that time, the unions in China were just emerging from the difficulties of the Cultural Revolution and every-thing in authority that moved had been beaten down by Mao's Red Guards. Because the Chinese say neither yes nor no to requests, I was surprised on the third day of our visit to be told by the hotel receptionist that a car was waiting to take me across Peking to the union federation.

I was driven to a great monolith of a building and found myself before the All-China Council. I was alone, without an interpreter, before a line of impassive faces. What could I say to these people? I started waffling about bringing greetings from my union in Great Britain, and then I remembered I had a cutting in my pocket from the *Daily Telegraph* in which Frank Chapple had berated Tony Benn and the International Committee of the Labour Party for their attack on the idea of selling Harrier jets to China. Frank asked how low could people get in cringing before the Russians. I pulled the cutting from my pocket and said, 'As you appreciate, not everybody wishes our mission well.'

I went on to explain Frank's remarks. As I looked up, I could identify those who understood English, because a big beam came on their faces. The ice was broken. They embraced me as a comrade in the cause against Russia. They gave me a long lecture on Soviet hegemony which they said was responsible for all the ills in Africa, the Middle East and Europe. It was a case of the enemy of my enemy is my friend. In other words, the Russians were enemies of the Chinese, and even though we had defeated Commies in the ETU, we at least had common cause against the Soviets.

Out of that almost bizarre meeting, our union developed a lasting relationship with China, which resulted in them sending students to be trained at our training college at Cudham. The students returned to

China as instructors in parallel schools there. These courses so pleased the leaders of the Chinese students that they personally reported back in glowing terms to their Prime Minister, who was on an official visit to Britain in 1985. I had been invited by Maggie Thatcher to dinner at Number Ten with the Chinese premier along with people like Norman Tebbit, the Trade and Industry Secretary, and industrialists.

On the way up to Downing Street in the car, I thought what a good idea it would be if British industry equipped these schools in China. This would mean that if they learned their skills on British gear, it could well lead to major orders for UK firms later. The first person I saw inside Number Ten at the pre-dinner drinks party was Norman Tebbit. He had been down to open an extension at Cudham only a few weeks before, so when I told him of my suggestion, he said it was a 'great idea'. But I warned Norman the problem was that British industry often does not know where its best interests lie.

I had divided the students into four groups and sent them for a fortnight's familiarization to four firms with business in China: Land Rover, the Central Electricity Generating Board, Racal and GEC. I told Norman I had asked the firms to pick up the hotel bills for the students while they were in their charge. After all, we would get nothing out of it, and each course was already costing us £50,000. Only one had given me a positive reply. Norman said, 'I can tell you which one – Racal.' 'Absolutely right,' I replied, 'and it breaks my heart that a non-union firm was the only one with the sense to see where their interests lie. The rest are so mean that I doubt if an idea to get equipment over there would take off.' As I spoke, GEC's Chief Executive Lord Weinstock came into the room. I said, 'He's the meanest of the lot.' 'Right,' said Norman and immediately walked over and wagged his finger at Weinstock.

Norman came back and said confidently, 'It's all right. Weinstock will do the right thing by you now.' I said, 'Norman, you've never understood us, have you? I've asked the man once and got no answer. I would rather complain about how mean he is for the next ten years and pay the bill ourselves.'

Then Weinstock, whom I didn't know very well at all, came over and said, 'I remember you.'

'That's flattering,' I replied.

Weinstock gritted his teeth and added, 'You're the b— who frustrated the nuclear programme in the Seventies. You denied British industry a great deal of business.'

I said, 'You're wrong.'

Weinstock: 'You were Chairman of the Trade Union Energy Committee.'

'No, you're wrong again,' I said. 'It was Frank Chapple.'

I was determined not to give in to his bluster, so I went on, 'It's true that I was standing very close to Frank Chapple's ear at the time.'

'That's right,' insisted the infuriated Weinstock. 'Thousands of jobs gone and billions lost to British business all because you opposed the programme.'

By this time, Weinstock was raising his voice and our confrontation was starting to attract attention in the Number Ten lounge. I thought, how can I stop this, get this bit of toffee off my finger? So I lowered my voice, looked him in the eye and said, 'Lord Weinstock, when things don't go your way, don't you ever ask yourself whether you might be wrong?'

Weinstock paused briefly and then said, with all the vehemence I have experienced from any of my enemies in the TUC, 'Yes, I was wrong. I didn't have you shot.' There was no smile. He meant it. It was too much for Tebbit. He took me by the arm and said, 'I have some other people I want you to meet.'

I rationalized Weinstock's outburst later when I recalled that he was quite close to Frank Chapple and they used to lunch together. I suspect that in order to get Weinstock off his back, Frank probably told him it was me rather than him who was opposed to GEC's favoured option of the Pressurized Water Reactor nuclear power stations.

Despite my life-long membership of the Labour Party, one of its biggest drawbacks has been its lack of genuine democracy when it comes to policy-making. The truth is that for decades, a small group of Cabinet Ministers and union barons have sewn together Labour government policy with the vote at Conference merely a rubber stamp. With just over six million votes going almost entirely to the unions, nobody else has had a look-in.

More than one sixth of the block votes are owned by the Transport and General Workers' Union. That's why successive Labour leaders have been forced to bow to the TGWU even if they knew the union was wrong-headed. What made it worse was not just that trade unions would use their votes in this way, but they were buying votes as well. The votes that unions wield at Labour Party Conference sometimes exceed the number who pay the political levy and, in the

161

past, exceeded the number of members they had in the union. There is no obstacle to this. You can have as many votes as you are willing to buy. All you have to do is make out the cheque.

It would become even more ridiculous if Labour took power and the Leader, who would then be Prime Minister, died as a result of accident or illness. It would be shameful to use a system under which the size of union funds would determine the next Prime Minister.

Our union continually objected to the block-vote system because it was not only unrepresentative, but capable of being corrupt, and probably was. This vote-buying was used, for example, by the National Union of Mineworkers, which paid for 'ghost' members at a time of falling membership in order to keep its voting power.

We used a different tactic. The EETPU allowed its payments to Labour Party headquarters to reduce as membership fell, but we used the rest of the money we would have paid to back Moderate candidates on an individual basis. We also used the rules the hard Left had forged to reselect, deselect Moderate members against Left candidates and MPs. Hardly a week goes by without someone whinging that John Spellar, the EETPU's hardworking National Political Secretary, has been packing a meeting – securing control of this local party or threatening the tenure of some hard Leftie. I only encourage him to do more – so long as we are denied a system based entirely on individual Labour Party member votes; so long as the Left organize and take advantage of every nuance of the Party rules, so will we with increased vigour. Dozens of Labour Moderates have reason to be grateful to John and our political machine. Messages come, via our AEU friends, will we lay off this particular Leftie – she's now behaving herself. Such messages get short shrift. We continue our fight to secure Labour representatives who truly reflect the aspirations and feelings of our people.

I was responsible for initiating the union's present political structure. So successful has it been that the AEU have paralleled it with one of their own and other unions are interested. When I first proposed it to the Executive, Les Cannon was hostile. He thought, with some justification, that it would be used in union elections. After Les's death, I persuaded the Executive and then our Conference to accept my idea of a political structure. Our representation to local Labour Parties was through branch delegates. My plan was intended to coordinate the activities of these then-isolated representatives. Now every branch delegate is invited annually to his Regional

Political Conference to discuss regional policy, and elect delegates to regional and national conferences of the Labour Party. The Conference would also elect a Regional Committee and send a member to the National Political Advisory Committee.

In 1977, that change was unique in that it provided a representative political structure not found elsewhere in the trade union movement. The proposals provided for the first time a means of liaison and unity to our political efforts and a permanent communication system. I said to our Conference, 'I am sure that those of our members who beaver away locally, sometimes feeling rather isolated, will wholeheartedly welcome this progressive change as a means to enhance our whole political activity.' They did welcome the change; we have enhanced our political activity and the Labour Party has benefited.

In 1982, a special conference at Wembley decided – against our union's advice – to elect the Leader and Deputy Leader of the Party through an electoral college. Forty per cent of the votes would go to the unions and thirty per cent each to the constituencies and the parliamentary party. It was a poor imitation of real democracy, and it ignored the people who really mattered – grassroots Labour voters. Could they not be trusted to help shape our future?

At the 1983 Labour Conference, I called for the electoral college to be scrapped and replaced by a one-member, one-vote system. They looked at me as if I was mad, for Labour had turned its back on the ordinary citizen. They believed they had all the answers in committees, Executives or local general management committees. They failed to understand why our own people had turned their backs on us.

I cannot write such words without feeling some responsibility for the rise of the idiotic Left in the Labour Party. They really blossomed when Ron Hayward became General Secretary of the Labour Party and proudly boasted that he had 'burnt all the files'. He obviously meant that the hard-Left nutters were free to do as they liked – and they did! Why did I feel responsible? Well, I knew and did not take to Hayward when he was Southern Regional Organizer. At Gravesend, we had the best agent in the business, John Beadle. Hayward did not take to him and, after John had a sabbatical break touring the world, Hayward effectively blocked him working in the region. I did not like, nor was I impressed with, the abilities of Hayward.

Some years later in 1969 when Frank Chapple was a member of Labour's NEC, the powerful Organization Sub-Committee had to consider a replacement for the formidable retiring National Agent,

Sarah Barker. The committee was deadlocked, evenly divided over Ron Hayward and Reg Underhill. Frank discussed the problem with me and I contemptuously responded that I wouldn't vote for Hayward to be my Ward Secretary! However, at that time, I was not seeing eye to eye with Frank. His unspoken reaction was, 'Well, if Hammond is against Hayward, he must be the right man.' He persuaded Andrew Cunningham of the GMB to join him in switching support to Hayward. Thus, Ron Hayward became National Agent and within two years, General Secretary, on the retirement of Harry Nicholas. You will, therefore, understand the responsibility I feel for the Labour Party's black years, albeit indirectly.

Soon after becoming General Secretary, I had a brush with the Labour Party that was to reinforce my view about legal challenges to those who libel and slander. The Labour Party's journal *Labour Weekly* produced a cartoon which had me kneeling down in front of Mrs Thatcher who was sprinkling coins over my head. From my hip pocket there protruded a document which had written on it: 'No-strike agreement.' The caption read, 'Thirty pieces of silver is the going rate, I understand, Mr Hammond.'

This was well before the Wapping bitterness and I was enraged. It was one thing to criticize our agreements – that I could accept. But to put forward the idea that I was in some way gaining personal financial advantage seemed to me to go beyond what was acceptable. I went to our lawyer, Ben Hooberman of Lawford's, a good friend and a wise counsellor, but this time I did not like his advice. He puffed on his pipe and quietly said to me, 'Look, son, you are now in the public eye and you must expect this sort of criticism.' I fumed for a while, then said, 'Well, if I'm going to have to accept this, then I can't think of any other matter upon which I would take legal action.' In fact, I instructed him to get rid of a number of cases which had been started in Frank Chapple's time.

Some little while afterwards, Roy Sanderson came to the Executive, again rather angrily, for he had read a piece in *Private Eye* which said he, National Secretary of the white-collar section of our union, had been around the country making speeches, trashing the TUC and making a great deal of money from it – so much money that he had formed a company to be tax effective. This piece ended by saying that Eric Hammond must be proud of him.

Roy wanted the Executive to support him in action against *Private Eye*. I retold the story about the *Labour Weekly* cartoon and then said that, in any case, truth was at least a partial defence in these matters and one needed to analyse point by point what *Private Eye* was saying: (1) that Roy Sanderson was going round the country trashing the TUC. I said I certainly hoped he was. (2) He was making money from it; so I said, 'If you are, good luck to you.' (3) He had formed a company. True or not, that was hardly libellous. (4) I must be proud of him. Well, I certainly was and would have to say so in court. Roy was hardly amused, certainly not as much as the rest of the Executive.

During my time as General Secretary, we have not taken a single action against anyone expressing an opinion about the union or any of its officers. But all credit to Neil Kinnock. He has done his damnedest to put us in tune with real people. When he became Leader, the loonies and the Militants could hold sway and come in and ride roughshod over everybody. Kinnock culled them. He kicked them out. He has done a tremendous job in a short time of putting the Labour Party into a position of possibly being elected, at least of looking electable. Though Kinnock didn't go fast enough for us, it takes no credit away from him.

At every Labour Party Conference, we worked hard to secure a Moderate majority for Neil Kinnock and the National Executive Committee. In 1985, despite the storm clouds of Wapping brewing, we were supporting Ted O'Brien of SOGAT and Gordon Colling of the NGA. Our own nominee, John Spellar, was working hard to secure the best possible result. He asked me to speak to Clive Jenkins of ASTMS to secure that union's support, not for himself, but for the two print union nominees. Clive, in turn, wanted our vote for his union's candidate, Doug Hoyle. We did our sums and found that, if we voted for Doug Hoyle, he would not have enough votes to get elected, but if ASTMS voted for the print union, then they would be on board. I went to Clive and said that I knew that it would be impossible for him to vote for our man John Spellar, but if he voted for the print men, then we would vote for Doug Hoyle.

Trust between us was not very apparent. Each wanted to witness the other's filling-in of the ballot paper in accordance with the deal we had done. 'After you, Clive.' 'No, you go first, Eric.' We finally ended up at the back of the hall, pens poised above ballot papers, saying, 'One, two, three – now' and filling in the ballot paper simultaneously. The result was that Ted O'Brien and Gordon Colling went on to the Executive for the first time and Doug Hoyle was not elected. We have continued to support them every year since despite our strained relationships with SOGAT and the NGA.

We have offered Neil our advice on a number of occasions and had fruitful meetings with him. One piece of advice was on defence. At the EETPU's 1985 Biennial Conference at Scarborough, I pointed out that TUC and Labour Party support for unilateral nuclear disarmament had proved to be electorally disastrous. I suggested Labour's next general election manifesto should include a commitment to hold a referendum on the issue. We tested opinion within our own union. Using our computerized records, we polled a weighted sample of the membership. We do this all the time to help us keep in tune with the ordinary member. We asked a number of questions about defence. Eighty-five per cent were in favour of a referendum on unilateral disarmament. It was overwhelming. Perhaps more significantly, seven per cent who were not planning to vote Labour said they would if a referendum were held.

Armed with this, I went along to see Kinnock in April 1987 – two months before the general election took place. I took Bill Jordan, President of the Amalgamated Engineering Union, with me. His is a much bigger union and carries more weight, if only because of the membership. Sitting with Kinnock in his private office at the Commons, I produced our computer printout, which I handed to him. I said, 'Look, don't believe us. You might think our members are giving me the answer I want to hear, so have a survey of your own, and if you do we'll pay for it.' I expected Bill Jordan to say that the AEU would pay half, but he didn't. He left me right out on a limb like a true brother.

Kinnock didn't make a decision on the spot, but within three days his office was on the line to say, 'We'd like to take you up on that offer.' They did a MORI poll of the general public. The first question they asked was, 'How would you vote if there was a general election today?' The answer was forty-three per cent Tory, thirty-one per cent Labour. It was within one per cent of the actual June election result when it took place. So all those expensive television advertisements by Hugh Hudson of *Chariots of Fire* fame, with Neil and the darling Glenys dancing around a cliff top, didn't matter a damn. However, in Labour's MORI poll, seventy-nine per cent said they backed the idea of a Labour referendum on defence. Then, they were asked how they would vote if Labour committed itself to a referendum. The Tory support dropped from forty-three to forty-one per cent, and Labour's percentage increased from thirty-one to thirty-eight. So, instead of a twelve-per-cent gap, it narrowed to three. With all the other policies we had which were attractive, we could have taken the Tories at the rush. Kinnock knew that. I knew that. I kept my counsel. I was pledged to confidentiality throughout that election, but I knew all the time what was beating Labour: its defence policy. That's why it was the first thing Kinnock dealt with after the election defeat.

Unilateralism is now a dead duck in the Labour Party. It came too late in 1987, because the likes of Ron Todd (TGWU) and John Edmonds (GMB) could not be swayed from their vote-losing stance. It's a different story today.

That wasn't the only advice I gave Neil. When the 1987 election was announced, the TUC was wrestling with a document telling trade-unionists how best to support Labour. In the middle of it was a pledge to reduce unemployment by one million. This made little sense. The people who were unemployed would probably vote Labour as would those around them. So this was being aimed at a relative minority. What were more relevant were the feelings of those with jobs about unemployment. If they feel anything about it at all, it is probably that they are fearful of being unemployed. Therefore, I suggested a revolution in the operation of industrial tribunals. Instead of workers going along claiming unfair dismissal and at best being given a bag of money in compensation, firms would have to prove that they had fairly dismissed people. The composition of the tribunals would be changed to be more friendly towards organized labour and the opinion of the trade unions in the plant concerned had to be taken into account. The effect would be an increase in union membership as more workers sought increased job protection. All this would have gone under the slogan, 'Your employment is safe with Labour.'

My idea had little chance of support at an open TUC meeting at that time, because I was still under attack over Wapping and the miners' strike, so I drafted a note to Norman Willis. He sent a note back during the General Council meeting saying, 'See me afterwards.' Norman thought it was a great idea. I said it was no good me putting it forward. 'You put it forward to the Party,' I added. Norman agreed, 'Yes, Yes, I'll do that.'

Nothing happened. I didn't see a mention of it anywhere. So I fed it into our candidates.

Nothing happened.

I wrote directly to Neil Kinnock: I told him he had taken no notice of my advice on defence, but here was an idea which might be too Left-wing even for him. There was still no response.

Then, at the end of August, Kinnock wrote apologizing for his failure to reply. Perhaps we could have a chat at the Party Conference in October. Of course, it got nowhere, but a year later, at the 1988 Labour Conference, we were describing ourselves as 'The Listening Party'. I couldn't resist leaning over to Kinnock at our reception and saying, 'I hope you're listening to me more than you were last year.'

We have been going through the same experience now over the National Minimum Wage. I have told Kinnock it simply will not work. So has Gavin Laird, the AEU General Secretary, among others Everyone in the world of work is paid and expects to be paid extra as they develop additional skills. They are not going to allow any government to diminish their earnings as part of a Utopian dream to guarantee a minimum to all. Employers will be dissuaded from taking people on. It will create more unemployment and chaos and conflict on the shopfloor. Already, the backtracking has started with news that Tony Blair says the scheme will exclude youngsters. It should include nobody. I have warned Neil Kinnock of the electoral consequences of pursuing a policy foisted upon them by unskilled unions not capable of doing their own job of representing lower-paid workers. They want it all to be settled by law.

At Labour's 1990 Blackpool Conference, they deliberately excluded me from speaking on the National Minimum Wage. I told the man in the Party chair that Monday afternoon, John Evans, of the Iron and Steel Trades Confederation, who is a friend, it was important I should speak in order to express a different point of view. I spoke to him during the break and he nodded as if he understood, but he obviously had been given his orders to see that I didn't get in – any more than they were going to let Tony Benn in. I felt like setting up a club of disappointed Labour Party speakers with myself and Benn as joint chairmen. But the party managers weren't going to have anything which was going to ripple the calm and peace of the Labour Party Conference.

However, I did rather redress the balance the next day. BBC television asked me to join a panel reviewing the day's conference with John Edmonds and Tony Blair. Instead of dealing with that day's events, I launched into an attack on the National Minimum Wage. It upset Mr Edmonds and caused Tony Blair to have a long discussion with me afterwards. I don't think he had fully understood our objections. As he stormed out of the studio, Edmonds said to me with all the pomposity he can muster, 'Thank you very much for that.' Blair obviously had not thought through the effects of the policy on skilled people like ours. That is now getting through to the Labour leadership and I think we shall see considerable attempts to soft-pedal the commitment to the National Minimum Wage. They would be wise to drop it, but this is unlikely with the general and public service workers so keen on it. Labour is between a rock and a hard place on this one. Government spokesmen will increasingly point out the contradictions.

At the 1990 Labour Party Conference, I came to the view that the leadership team would be strengthened with the inclusion of John Smith, the Shadow Chancellor. It was not politically feasible to do a Kinnock/Smith switch. It was just possible that we could persuade Hattersley to stand aside for Smith. Everyone approached felt the idea was sound, but how to bring it about? I understand that a private poll showed that Labour's position improved by four points if the public were asked how they would vote with a Kinnock/Smith leadership partnership. Nobody at Walworth Road would dare ask the other question – how would we fare with Smith as Leader?

I have done my best to secure harmony and peace within the Labour Party and not to disturb the unity within the ranks – from the period of the council robes to that of the National Minimum Wage! But from being the Odd Man Out all those years ago, I now feel like the Odd Man In. After all, they have followed my lead eventually.

There has been talk in senior Tory circles lately of the possibility of my joining the Conservatives. How little they understand what makes me tick. I could not see myself joining the Conservative Party. I admire some things which Mrs Thatcher did. I admire even more what Major is trying to do. But the Tory Party has round its neck a liability that I could never swallow and that is its failure to condemn outright and deal with the class system of Britain. For all its faults, the Labour Party doesn't have too many vestiges of that left. It's not a political or theological argument that I set against these class differences, because I believe there are differences between people and they ought to be recognized by society by reward according to ability. I'm all for a meritocracy. But I am not for people inheriting positions in society, which is what the Tories will not turn their back on. Continued support for the class system, or considerable parts of it, will be the insuperable barrier to my ever contemplating joining them.

9

Ambassador at large

It was Les Cannon, the EETPU General President for seven short but eventful years (1963–70), who brought home to me the importance of using my union position to influence others in a wider sphere. Union leaders are perhaps even more political than politicians themselves. We see problems at the grassroots as they happen, not months later in a vague written report. The seemingly never-ending list of government committees and quangos to which we have access enables us to express our view right at the heart of the Whitehall machine – even when Labour is in opposition. Our views have less influence in the Nineties than the Sixties, but we are still heard. We come face to face with ministers and opponents from our own side. We can act as sounding boards of popular opinion, a barometer of what's happening on the shopfloor. We are the voice of the members, their ambassadors at large, if you like.

Les died of cancer in 1970 at the tragically young age of 50. His death robbed our union and the entire movement of its best post-war brain. He was a member of the TUC General Council and of Harold Wilson's Industrial Re-organization Corporation, which monitored industrial performance and used government money to assist British companies in restructuring to face the growing internationalization of the world economy. Les used his membership of every committee to press home our union's view of life. What a blow it must have been to the Left when he quit the Communist Party after the Hungarian uprising and switched to the Moderate camp. Before he and Frank Chapple rid the EETPU of the Communist ballot-riggers, Leslie was once described by Harry Pollit, the hardheaded General Secretary of the Communist Party, as 'Britain's Lenin'.

Les advised all new Executive members to read Machiavelli's *The*

Prince – but it is some further advice which has stuck with me through more than twenty-seven years on the national union scene. He drummed into the EETPU Executive Edmund Burke's view of our function as union representatives. Addressing the electors of Bristol in 1774, Burke said, 'Your representative owes you not his industry only, but his judgement, and he betrays you if he sacrifices it to your opinion.' In other words, it was not enough simply to agree with those who elected us, to be compliant with the mob and whatever they believe, because that changes from day to day. We needed a vision of what went beyond that day, looking forward to the next week, next year, the next decade.

Years later, I came across a book entitled *British Historical and Political Orations from the Twelfth to the Twentieth Century*. In it was the full version of that Burke speech in which he elegantly chastised his opponent on the matter of mandating. To this day, Burke's words sum up more than any I have come across what leadership, certainly union leadership like ours, should be about.

The section of the speech before the sentence Les quoted hits the bull's-eye. Burke said,

> I am sorry I cannot conclude without saying a word on a topic touched upon by my worthy colleague. He tells you that the topic for instructions has occasioned much altercation and uneasiness in the city and he expresses himself, if I understand him rightly, in favour of the coercive authority of such instructions. Certainly, gentlemen, it ought to be the happiness and glory of a representative to live in the strictest union, the closest correspondence and the most unreserved communication with his constituents. Their wishes ought to have great weight with him, their opinion high respect, their business unremitted attention. It is his duty to sacrifice his repose, his pleasures, his satisfaction to theirs and, above all, ever and in all cases, to prefer their interests to his own. But his unbiased opinions, his mature judgement, his enlightened conscience, he ought not to sacrifice to you, to any man or to any set of men living. These he does not derive from your pleasure, no, nor from the law and the constitution. They are trusts from providence for the abuse of which he is deeply answerable.

I have used Burke's text many times when invited to speak to outside groups in order to explain our motivation and purpose: why we were different, what made us tick.

Soon after we were expelled from the TUC in 1988, I received an invitation from the Master of Eton to speak to his boys. I went along, had dinner with the Master and a couple of the pupils before speaking to their Keynes Society.

The speech and the evening went well. I got the questions from the boys out of the way with little difficulty, but then one of the teachers said, 'Mr Hammond, you've spoken a great deal about the need to support engineering and manufacturing, for men of ability to go into industry and take up the engineering profession. These are all boys of ability. They are all going to be leaders. How would you persuade them to go into the engineering profession?'

I thought 'You bastard. How do I get out of this one?'

I looked him in the eye and said, 'You do teach Mathematics here, I take it?'

He was taken aback with this. He said, 'Yes, yes. We do.'

I said, 'So these boys can count?'

He said, 'Yes.'

I replied, 'Well, I rest my case.'

While the City and other professions offered more, these young chaps were not going to be attracted into engineering. It is still a very underpaid profession.

After the evening had finished with a courteous vote of thanks to me, the Master said, 'I was very interested in what you had to say, Mr Hammond. You quoted Edmund Burke, so you might be interested in this.' He took me to the side of the splendid wood-panelled room and there was Burke's name carved with a knife in the woodwork. It gave me a great sense of history. My immediate thought was that Old Etonian Burke, the great politician and philosopher, had been a hooligan in his youth. It made me like him even more, to think he had been something of a rebel.

Shortly after my 'blooding' at the Brighton TUC Conference in 1984 over the miners' strike, I looked around the gallery and noticed there were as many employers in that section as union visitors and hangers-on. The attendance of the employers was handy for union leaders and delegates. They were taken to lunch and dinner by the bosses who, no doubt, used that as an excuse for having their meals on the firm. It's an incestuous business, the union/management game. I wasn't going to buy lunch for the CBI people, but why not take our message to them? So, for the first time ever for a trade union, we organized a fringe meeting at the CBI Conference at Eastbourne that autumn.

They gave me a visitors' ticket and I listened to their discussions. It was a very dry debate about industrial relations – about as exciting as cold custard. We had expected a dozen or so to turn up at our meeting, but the hall was packed. They were hanging from the rafters and queuing up the stairs. There were a couple of hundred of Britain's top bosses bending their ears in my direction. Some of them couldn't get in. It was standing room only. This was all very gratifying, if not exciting. I was feeling for a humorous remark to get into the serious side of my speech, so I said, 'After the passion of today's discussions, I feel emotionally exhausted. TUCs are one thing, but CBI conferences are something else. I listened with interest to most of the industrial relations debate. I would have liked to have made a contribution myself, so much so that I'm going back to my office to examine the CBI articles of membership to see whether the EETPU is eligible.'

None of the serious thoughts I had to expound about training and partnership and industrial involvement got quite so much attention as those opening, semi-humorous remarks. The assembled scribes had headlines the next day declaring 'Hammond to Join the CBI'.

It grew as the week went on from this Monday meeting. Each paper made more of it, so much so that I had letters from members and EETPU officials asking, 'Are we really going to join the CBI?' To keep it going, I said we were a medium-sized employer: we employed more than 300 people, and we had a right to go along and join in. By the end of the week, many of our branches were in uproar saying we should not link up with the bosses.

Thankfully, at the end of the Conference on the Saturday, an assistant director of the CBI got me off the hook. With great pomposity, he blew his chest out like a big venomous toad and said they had looked at the rules and the constitution and the EETPU was not eligible for membership. What a relief! It enabled me to issue a statement saying, 'If they won't let us into their club, I am certainly not going to apply.' It made me resolve never to indulge in light-hearted banter again, but I've never been able to resist a wind-up and the resolution was soon broken.

However, there was a serious point to my frivolous remark. We had gathered for the TUC Conference in Brighton to discuss many things besides the miners' strike – training, the state of the economy, the involvement of work people, education, health. The CBI gathered for their Conference to discuss the very same things. We might have benefited from discussing some of these subjects together. We were citizens of the same country. It was the same economy. It was the same lack of training we were talking about, and we just might come to more apposite answers if we did it together.

This wasn't pie-in-the-sky theorizing, because in the electrical contracting industry, the confidence we have built up with each other has, indeed, led to a Joint Industry Board Conference at which shop stewards, officials and Executive Councillors from our union come together with managers of all levels and discuss the problems of the industry. This has been of considerable benefit to everyone involved. We don't discuss problems separately and argue with the fellow in the other camp about who is responsible for all the ills, saying, 'It's that bloody management,' or 'that damn trade-unionist'.

The next great challenge of this system is to get that feeling of working together down to site and the workshop level. To get the ordinary Joe feeling that he is involved. Japanese firms have been far more successful at it, because they seem to be serious and do not use it as a way of being trendy. They actually believe that involving work people, training them and treating them as equals is good business. That's a lesson British industry has yet to learn. British managers actually believe it costs them to train and involve workers rather than realize it is an investment in the future.

I spent many years on industrial sector committees of the National Economic Development Office. It was only in early 1989 that I made it to the top table. Tradition was that the TUC had a 'Neddy Six' represented on the NEDO Council, opposite government ministers and employers. Our union had been kicked out of the TUC, and I could not join that select band, so the Tories came up with a unique ruse to enable me to express not only my members' views, but those of all independently minded trade-unionists.

Just before Christmas 1988, Nigel Lawson, who was Chancellor of the Exchequer, asked me to come and see him at the Treasury in Whitehall. I worked out in advance what it was about, because Clive Jenkins had left the TUC's Neddy Six. I thought Lawson was going to cock a snook at the TUC and replace Jenkins with me. Lawson was very affable as he offered me an early evening gin and tonic. He confirmed he was asking me to join the Neddy hierarchy. I said, 'I am more than pleased to accept, particularly as it means kicking off one of those TUC bastards.'

Lawson's response gave me the first indication that the government was remotely interested in the continuance of NEDO, or that it put any weight upon the involvement of the TUC. He said, 'No, no. this is an extra seat. You will be part of the independent group.'

I replied, 'Oh, well, that's second best. I don't mind.' But Lawson was at great pains to explain I wasn't kicking off one of the TUC members.

I had served my time at NEDO on its industry committees. They are made up of unions and employers from each major industrial sector plus representatives from the Department of Industry. My involvement came in the electronic components industry in the late Seventies. The microchip and the electronic revolution was going to be of great importance throughout industry. There's not an activity or service which has remained untouched.

I have done my best to promote the cause of the British electronics industry and ensure it stays healthy. Sometimes, I have experienced great difficulty in trying to convince government it was worth backing. I crossed swords with Jim Callaghan when he was Prime Minister in 1977. He had called a conference under the auspices of NEDO at Lancaster House about our competitiveness abroad. At that time, we were concerned about the effect too much inward investment would have on the British electronic industry. I had been asked to make a speech about some non-controversial aspect of the conference subject matter, but, seizing the opportunity to speak directly to the Prime Minister, I discarded the version NEDO had prepared for me and spoke instead about the threat of uncontrolled inward investment.

I said, 'If I used the prepared speech, my sector working group would think I had an obsession with an ingrown toenail while they are being throttled.' Jim was going several colours of purple on the platform and he savaged me in his speech afterwards, claiming his government had it all under control. However, many employers from the leading electronics firms said, 'You were right to speak up, Eric.' Like many people in all walks of life, they want someone else to declare the emperor is naked!

Equally important were my attempts to improve the performance of the British construction industry. For years, its efficiency was sadly lacking. Our NEDO committee produced a Large Sites report in the early Seventies which argued for change along the lines we had used in electrical contracting, with a proper grading system and simplified agreements. There followed a number of detailed studies which compared the British industry with its counterparts in North America and Europe. The results showed we were bottom of the league in performance terms.

My work to change this shocking state of affairs earned me the OBE in 1977. The same honour also went to three others on the same NEDO working party – Charlie Lovell, head of the EETPU plumbing section, Johnny Baldwin, of the AEU Construction Section, and Ron Burbridge, of the Central Electricity Generating Board. It was with some pride that I went to the Buckingham Palace investiture with Brenda and our two sons, Ivan and Shaun. Delighted to have a day off from school and university, they properly brought me back to earth by their enthusiasm at seeing David Wilkie, the swimmer, receive his honour, but I am sure they were as proud of their dad as I am of them.

The British construction industry was in a sorry state. It was not completing jobs on time. It was using more man hours than like projects in other countries we studied. It was costing more. Deadlines were being ignored. During one NEDO meeting, I said, 'Christ, can't we find somebody who's worse than Britain?'

At that time, Italy was full of turmoil, so we decided to look at a power station project over there. When we arrived in Milan, the omens could not have been better. The streets were full of demonstrators with red flags and slogans. I felt all my youthful nerve ends tingling. But after examining the figures at the power station, it turned out, to my disgust, to be more efficiently built than any we had made in Britain. The Italians had built their power station more quickly at less cost and with fewer man hours, but it was the twenty-third of its kind. All problems had been ironed out. They had built so many it almost put itself together. In the UK one power station was rarely like another and we kept moving on to new and larger generating sets.

Figures NEDO compiled at the strike-happy Isle of Grain site long before the infamous laggers' dispute showed that only eighteen per cent of the time workers had available for work was actually spent working. This excluded any tea or meal breaks or going to and from a job. In other words, eighty-two per cent of their available time was unproductive. This was a measure of the depths to which the British construction industry had plummeted.

We saw, right from the start, that the principle instrument of reform had to be a national agreement covering all trades. It took the bitter 1979 Isle of Grain dispute before it was signed, but since then there have been massive improvements in skill and productivity. The agreement has largely removed the strife that once bedevilled the industry, with groups of workers demanding leapfrogging pay deals in a chaotic bargaining scene at their sites and at others where they discovered men earned more. The result was that the cost of major projects would double. The national agreement has been a considerable influence in containing these costs, so I believe my work with NEDO has been of value. It has widened my experience and knowledge, but it has also given me a forum to influence matters, benefiting not only my members, but also the economy as a whole.

The discussions on the supreme NEDO body, the Council, have given me some surprising allies. On 10 January 1990, we were discussing a paper the TUC had produced on our poor performance in training. To underpin its argument, the TUC spotlighted the figures for craft and technician grade engineers. There were 30,000 in Britain compared with 100,000 in France and Germany's 130,000. I said it was alarming, because countless studies had shown the very direct relationship between performance, productivity and the levels of skill employed within an industry.

I had only been a member of the NEDO Council for a year, but one of the less attractive features of the forum was the tendency to define broad-brush shortcomings, though seldom accepting that any authority, other than government, had a responsibility to remedy those problems. I illustrated my point by quoting that comparatively miserable figure of 30,000. Some 4,000 of that, I said, came from a minor industry in terms of size – electrical contracting, which had a total of 40,000 employees. This was an industry in which sixty per cent of my members received their training. I told NEDO colleagues that if every other sector did as well as electrical contracting, we would be well ahead of the Germans, with all the beneficial effects that would have on our industrial performance.

I explained the reason for our industry's success was that everyone involved – unions, employers and government – had worked together in partnership to increase the number of apprentices. It wasn't enough for the TUC to come along and say how terribly we were doing on training and ask what the government would do about it. The unions themselves needed to help improve the training situation. This moved Ron Todd to say, 'If I wasn't going to be quoted outside this room, I would say how much I agree with Eric.' What he didn't know was that there was some wag who included that in the NEDO minutes.

A momentous meeting of minds between NUPE General Secretary Rodney Bickerstaffe and myself came on 3 July 1991. The fifteen chairmen of the NEDO industrial groups produced a paper for the full Council about the lessons Britain could learn from the success of Japan and Germany. The report brought together the expertise of all the NEDO activities. The chairmen included the heads of several major companies, the directors of the two leading schools of Economics and Business, together with the AEU's Bill Jordan, Sir Brian Wolfson, who runs Wembley Stadium and the National Training Task Force, and myself: a good cross-section of concerned industrial experience and know-how. Our findings showed Japanese production management could be successfully transferred into the UK environment. The Japanese, said the report, had succeeded in areas of the UK where British-owned firms had failed.

The Director General of NEDO, Walter Eltis, introduced the report on behalf of the Chairman. He posed three considerations for the council:

1 Those who run British business have had to spend far more time and energy than their German and Japanese counterparts on questions of financial management and they have therefore had less energy for their products and customers. Hence the priority the chairmen attach to the achievement of sustained low inflation together with exchange rate stability. Would the whole Council accept that getting inflation down is the only way of getting and keeping nominal interest rates down and that 'this deserves a public commitment by government, all political parties, industry, unions and other institutions', and 'the adoption of actions and policies by all concerned to turn that commitment into reality'?

2 The chairmen attach significance to the way in which the Japanese industrial model involves long-term partnership, (a) between workers and their companies so that poaching between companies for labour rarely occurs and there is far more incentive to train; (b) between companies and their suppliers, so that relations of trust concerning quality develop; and (c) between companies and their bankers. The Anglo/American model involves upwardly mobile workers and executives frequently changing companies as their careers advance, companies all the time seeking cheaper suppliers, and finance managers searching between the world's finance houses for the cheapest loans. Would the Council recom-

mend that there are potential advantages in the Japanese approach and would it wish the sector groups to report back on whether it is practical and desirable to move in this direction, and if so, how?

3 The chairmen were impressed by the way in which unions and managements work together constructively in Germany. Would all parties to the Council regard it as highly desirable that our unions should increasingly 'see themselves and allow others to see them as part of the team' so that energy is not wasted in conflict where there should be partnership, and the workforce is wholly committed to industrial success? The unions are extremely anxious to participate more fully in the decisions companies take and to become more involved in their successful implementation, but British employers are in general strongly opposed to a German degree of union participation. What changes would the CBI and the TUC expect to see before there was a realistic possibility of establishing the degree of partnership that German employers and unions apparently enjoy?

Vital issues for our country, but CBI's John Banham poured cold water on it – seemingly miffed that an earlier CBI paper had not been warmly greeted. Norman Willis for the TUC was tepid in his support.

I was more than irritated. Here were important proposals, vital questions supported by eminent men of all parties and they were being ignored. I said sarcastically, 'The chairmen must be feeling exhilarated by the response to their paper. The problems of individual industries which chairmen put to each Council meeting are fundamentally the same – investment, training, and training employee involvement and performance. They have not submitted their collective thoughts to be sniped at from the trenches. They have not blamed anyone, but have noted a shared responsibility. We all sail in the same ship. Response from the principal institutions (the TUC and CBI) has been disappointing. It is wrong to say we cannot learn from Germany and Japan.'

British workers in Japanese-owned factories had been treated like people by the Japanese, trained hard and, as a result, now had the same productivity as their Japanese counterparts. This proved British workers were not innately idle. It depended upon how they were trained and involved. I put the knife into the CBI by saying they were being unhelpful because their own document had not been treated seriously. The important thing was to get on with the real issues.

179

Rodney Bickerstaffe, Chairman of the TUC Economic Committee, to my amazement almost repeated Ron Todd's conciliatory words and said, 'If it's not going to be reported, I'd say how much I agree with what Eric has said.'

I had previously made common cause with the CBI – they asked me to join a task force on wider share ownership. Half way through our deliberations after a series of meetings at the CBI's Centrepoint headquarters, the task force gave an interim report to the NEDO Council on 4 July 1990.

I said I was handicapped in some ways in approaching the issue, because my union had a different view than most others. For most of their existence, unions had regarded share ownership as a manifestation of evil. Accordingly, union funds were invested avoiding equities and as a result failed to benefit from the growth in the value of shares. 'The present financial difficulties of some unions spring from this fundamental error,' I told them.

I could never understand this attitude. Employees, members of unions, contributed a great part, a decisive part, to the success of their enterprises. It was upon that that the appreciation of the share value of those companies was based. Why shouldn't trade unions and their individual members gain some of the fruit they themselves had grown? So I welcomed the TUC's tardy, but more realistic approach in its recent economic paper. Looking across at Norman Willis, I described how we had entertained at our Buxted estate in Sussex – paid for by market gains – a group of Russian miners, representing their newly formed independent union.

The discussion had centred on what they needed to assist their fledgeling organization. One of my colleagues, the union President Paul Gallagher, asked, 'What is it you most want in Russia?' He expected the answer would be a printing press or some such immediate need. The reply from the burly Russian leader was instantaneous. 'What we most want in Russia is capitalism,' he said.

I told the NEDO Council, 'There were no euphemisms about free or private enterprise. What he wanted was capitalism. Employee shareholding helps to bridge the gap between ownership and control, which is at the heart of many of our economic problems.'

The meeting was chaired by the then Chancellor, John Major. I took the opportunity to remind him that he and his colleagues in government had a great opportunity to give a boost to employee share ownership with the impending electricity industry privatization. I described how the record of cooperation and productivity in the electricity industry, particularly amongst manual workers, meant that the value of those shares had been greatly enhanced because of their work. They had earned a considerable stake in their industry.

I added cheekily, 'I urge you and your colleagues not to be conservative in this matter. You can, by maximizing the employees' shareholdings in the electricity companies, reward the unique enterprise and effort of employees and reinforce the stability of this vital industry.'

I had already arranged a meeting that afternoon with the Energy Secretary John Wakeham about increasing the shares available to power industry workers. As I walked into Wakeham's office, I joked, 'Don't worry, John, I've already sorted it out with the Chancellor of the Exchequer this morning.' Subsequently, I produced a document for Wakeham repeating my arguments at NEDO.

While I was on holiday, Wakeham rang my colleague Roy Sanderson to say that following my approach to him, he had persuaded the Treasury to increase the number of free shares for employees when the electricity supply industry was privatized. Wakeham flattered me and said he was able to use my name in pressuring the Treasury – I should have such influence! But our people got a better deal than workers in other industries which had been privatized.

When it came out later, my friend John Lyons claimed it was pressure from his Engineers and Managers' Association which had won the day, but, in fact, it was the solid arguments I had put forward which had tipped the balance.

When the Task Force report was completed, I was invited to the CBI Conference in Glasgow, held in November 1990. At last I was inside with a delegate's credential. The day before the debate of the report, I listened quietly to a debate on unit labour costs, inflation and the economy. Although it was the end of the afternoon, I was shocked to find only a quarter of the delegates in attendance. I tell employers since that I know they are not worried about wage costs, recalling that afternoon's experience. The only clear remedy that emerged to rising wage costs was that employers should stand firm!

The next day, I spoke about our report on wider share ownership. I said:

The hard Left throughout the world is in disarray. Their holy land of Russia hovers on the precipice of anarchy. Seventy years of control, regulation, backed by the fiercest of powers – control over a country as rich as any in raw materials with an innovative and brave people – all that has brought them to bread queues, grinding deprivation and the prospect of worse . . .

Understand this, that we in the West are their Mecca, their hope. There is no alternative economic ideology available and viable. When you get downhearted, disappointed, at our performance – I detected a little yesterday – just remember you, we, have much to be proud of; you have played a decisive part in holding together a political and economic system that has provided freedom and material advancement for all its citizens and now holds out a light for those emerging from Eastern darkness.

But I do not encourage smug satisfaction. This is not the best of all possible worlds. Our report *A Nation of Shareholders* is a step toward a better one. We all understand the development of our democracy: political power wrested from the king by barons and landowners, grudgingly shared with factory owners, and then won by the common man with a political vote. I see a parallel development of the economic citizen, with economic power passing from industry's owners to management, to the shareholder, particularly the employee shareholder, winning him at last an economic vote and influence.

Employee share ownership is a valuable way of helping to bridge the gap between ownership and control which is at the heart of many of our economic problems. I am attracted by the prospects of collectivizing those individual employee share stakes through an Employee Share Ownership Programme or other more appropriate vehicle. But employee share ownership, whether of an individual or collective nature, should not be seen as a substitute for good industrial relations procedures. Employee share participation is in addition to and not instead of their proper representation by responsible trade unions making use of agreed procedures.

Share ownership has to be buttressed with a total new deal for the citizen at work: equality – with the obscenity of industrial apartheid of blue and white collar workers swept aside; involvement – with the employee understanding the firm's problems and prospects and contributing to their solution; training – so that the individual's ability can develop to its maximum . . . and industrial peace – with outstanding problems settled by arbitration, not conflict. No, the answer to our problems like unit labour costs, lies not just, as we heard yesterday, with management standing firm – a rare enough event – but rather in building a genuine partnership to which I am sure our report will make a valuable contribution.

It was well received and I felt I had made another small contribution to diminish the barriers of them and us that so hinder our progress as a country and a people.

The events in Russia were very much to the fore, particularly for me as I had then just returned from my first visit. When I reported to our Conference, I led in by saying that we were a members' union through and through and I continued:

Many of you have given much to sustain and build such a union. Nothing gives me more pride than the part I have played. Not just pride in our union, but for what it has meant and the help it has given to others struggling for freedom and independence.

When we last met – celebrating our centenary – those struggles were growing in intensity. Now the Berlin Wall has been smashed. That monstrous scar dividing Europe, imprisoning its people, is no more. How does our union relate to that? For much of our existence, not at all! During the pre-Great War years, we were just trying to survive and that was in doubt at times. The between-war years had us nearly part of the AEU or the T & G and were characterized in the latter part of the period with growing internal political battles. The immediate post-war years saw both growth and the triumph of the Communist Left in the old ETU.

It cannot be claimed that anything we did in that period added to the sum of human freedom. To the contrary, it was precisely that rejection of individual freedom and rights and, above all, votes that led to the most shameful of trade union scandals – the ETU balloting fraud and conspiracy. That same rejection by other Communist comrades elsewhere led to the Berlin Wall and the enslavement of millions in Eastern Europe, Russia and China.

In the last quarter of our existence, we have placed our organization firmly in the hands, the votes, of all the members. In representing their views, in standing for their rights, for the individual, we have been fighting alongside those who have finally triumphed in Eastern Europe. Directly, we supported and campaigned for dissident voices raised for freedom. Almost alone, we championed and succoured Solidarity. When the TUC, the hard Left and Arthur Scargill were hesitant and hostile, *we* went to their aid. Throughout the dark years, we materially supported Solidarity and kept their voice alive.

One cannot look at the sequence of events in Eastern Europe and not recognize that the endurance of Solidarity, the success of our Polish colleagues, encouraged the human striving for freedom that at last has smashed that wall of tyranny. We can be rightly proud of the part we have played in this dramatic advance.

I believe that the progressive, people-based, directions we have taken, the battles we have fought – fought against those very forces within our own movement, forces that supported, or tolerated, the repressive Communist regimes; that these struggles are at one with those undertaken by progressives in Eastern Europe. Indeed, we have materially assisted the Independent Miners' Union of the Soviet Union. That union has been in the forefront of a courageous struggle for real trade-unionism.

Ken Jackson and I went to Donetsk last October to their founding congress – 2,000 strong – a delegate from each pit represented two million miners. We arrived after an 18-hour train journey and went directly to the conference.

Not unnaturally, seated in a comfortable chair, I started nodding, when I suddenly heard from the platform, amongst some Russian words I didn't quite understand, my name. Our interpreter assured me that there was no problem. They merely wanted me to address the conference. No problem! I told the interpreter – whatever nonsense comes out – make it sound good. As it was, I think it conveyed our experience and friendship concisely. I said:

> I bring warm fraternal greetings to you all from the Electrical, Electronic, Telecommunication and Plumbing Union of Great Britain: an organization, like you seek to build, both independent and democratic, accountable to its members – not to an élite of political bureaucracy. Indeed, I feel that I speak on behalf of not only the trade-unionists of Britain, but also the overwhelming majority of the British people, a people who both love and cherish freedom and the rights of the individual. From our little island, but from a great depth of tradition – democratic tradition – greetings to all who will speak and act for freedom.
>
> We, my Executive colleague Ken Jackson, Chairman of our Political Committee, and I have had some difficulty in coming to speak to you. It would seem that some in authority were very

reluctant to let us enter the Soviet Union! Why did they try to stop us? What possible words of mine could add to the troubles of your country?

I speak of liberty, the rights of the individual, of democracy. It is not these values that have brought your country to its present sad and dangerous condition. It is the persistent, continuous denial of freedom that does so! Without freedom, man cannot innovate, cannot develop, will not create the resources, the wealth to meet the growing expectations of modern society.

No, it is not free independent trade unions, not the democratic labour movement that threatens. To the contrary, they provide a genuine hope, a proper way forward to a better, more rewarding society, both materially and in the relations of man to man.

We are here to learn, so it would be discourteous to comment in depth on your problems and the historical background to them. But that historical background, the aberration of Communism, was not confined to the Soviet Union. Communist zealots, Communist crooks, have permeated the trade union movement throughout the world. In Britain, for many years, they determined the agenda not for debate but for division. In my union, Communists gained control by manipulation and maintained it through corruption, by stealing workers' votes.

Our members – people like you – stood up and fought them – beat them. I do believe that the intellectual and electoral victories we won helped, to some degree, your struggle here in the Soviet Union.

Friends, you have hard and exciting years ahead of you. Be assured not just of our good wishes, but of our experience and material help. We are independent and proud of it: independent of employers, independent of government – but not independent of workers in need.

Your cause is our cause. May it triumph throughout the world.

After seventy years of repression, the miners' representatives there were bubbling with enthusiasm for the freedoms they were now starting to enjoy. It reminded one of Wordsworth's words at the start of the French Revolution: 'Bliss it was in that dawn to be alive'.

Soon after we returned from Russia, a sorry pilgrimage took place from Britain to Moscow. Several of the old lags – the deadbeat Left of the TUC – trekked to the Congress of the World Federation of Trade Unions (WFTU). This has been dominated by the Communists and more particularly by the Soviet Union over the last forty years and used as an instrument of Soviet foreign policy. It is completely discredited, particularly in Eastern Europe, so much so that the Czechs ordered them out of their Prague offices. This total rejection from those who experienced appalling suffering and indignities over forty years did not affect our British fellow travellers. Predictably, firemen's representative, Ken Cameron, trotted along to the Czech Embassy in Moscow to plead with them not to make the WFTU homeless. But what would you expect from a friend of the PLO?

More unexpected, but even more amazing, was the appearance of John Edmonds at this wake. We expected Ken Gill, but John Edmonds? This representative of a once proud moderate union, the General and Municipal Workers, went not to bury the WFTU but to praise it. When the workers of the world were walking away from this dying ogre, he tried to breathe life into it. It is amazing the sacrifices he is prepared to make for international trade union unity. He rejects the advice of the international free trade union movement to stay away. He is quite happy to cuddle up to those who supported the invasion of Czechoslovakia, the building of the Berlin Wall, the outlawing of Solidarity and the vicious repression of freedom right the way across Eastern Europe. It is even more remarkable when you consider that he was prepared to divide the trade union movement in his own country over such an earth-shattering issue as whether workers should be free to join the union of their choice, the EETPU.

Maybe if I had been to Oxford, like Edmonds, I could understand such logic. As it is, I increasingly wonder whether our members would ever want to rejoin a TUC dominated by such people.

The development of free and independent unions in Russia and Eastern Europe, indeed throughout the world, is an exciting and heady development, but some might still say, trade-unionism in Russia or anywhere outside of Britain is not our business. I do not agree. They need our help and, in practice, it is also in the best interests of our people, our members – to give it as Herbert Spencer put it – 'No one can be perfectly free till all are free . . . No one can be perfectly happy till all are happy . . . ' We are presently working out, together with our Russian colleagues, a programme of training in

186

trade union and technical matters. Such training will be designed to produce trainers so that they in turn can train fellow workers in Russia.

Influence comes in various forms, and perhaps one of Britain's most influential institutions is the Monopolies and Mergers Commission, of which I was a member from 1978–83. It was a splendid education being exposed to the keenest minds in the industrial, financial and legal world. I was one of twenty-five part-timers on the Commission under full-time Chairman Sir Godfrey Lequesne, a real gentleman, who could be both kind and firm when dealing with the captains of British industry. Among the latter was Tiny Rowland of Lonrho, once described by Ted Heath as the 'unacceptable face of capitalism'.

I was with Sir Godfrey on the committee which refused Rowland permission to take over the House of Fraser and Harrods. It is the only decision that gives me any retrospective doubts. Although I did not vote in Lonrho's favour, I now believe that perhaps Rowland should have been allowed in to shake up the organization. Certainly, Harrods' new owners, the Al-Fayeds, have had anything but a smooth ride since they took over.

In 1981, soon after I had dealt with one Lonrho reference, Tiny Rowland featured in my diary once again. He was trying to take over the *Observer*. It was my first newspaper case, and it brought me into a quite different world, one I was to discover much more about when I became embroiled in the Wapping saga with Rupert Murdoch. Everyone we dealt with, from management people like David Astor and the Editor, Donald Trelford, to journalists like John Cole, later the BBC's political editor, came along to plead that a Lonrho takeover would be a disaster. One of their main arguments was that because of Lonrho's great interests in Africa, the *Observer* would no longer be able to pursue its missionary role over there. It's surprising how speedily they settled down to the Rowland yoke and wrote such flattering pieces about Lonrho's friends. They have continued to write in a way which clearly supports Lonrho's operations in Africa.

When the journalists came to state their case to the MMC, they were whinging about the prospect of working for Tiny Rowland. It was the only time during my years on the Commission that I experienced any interference from outside. We were appointed as commissioners to do our best according to our judgement after considering the submissions made to us. One day, I had a phone call from Len Murray, the TUC General Secretary. He asked me if I would meet privately with the journalists on the *Observer*. I really got on my high horse and said that anything which needed saying about their position, their jobs and their prospects should be said across the table at the Commission. I gave Len a very cold brush-off. It was the only time during my period with the MMC that I felt anybody was trying to interfere with my role. Len very quickly backed off. If I had agreed, I expect I might have been in a back-room meeting being nobbled.

During the *Observer* inquiry, the whole of our MMC team trooped along to the paper to see it being printed. I hadn't had much to do with newspapers before that, but one of the things that struck me was how many people there were in the despatch area. They seemed to be getting on in years. There were so many of them that even if they had been ill, they couldn't have fallen down, because the colleagues around them would have supported them, so tightly packed was the crush in that department. There were probably as many men there then as there had been in the days when they tied up the newspaper bundles with string. The advent of machinery had had no effect on manning levels.

We were invited up to the boardroom for drinks to send us on our way. The Editor, Trelford, came and said 'Hello' and assured me that he had good industrial relations. In particular, this was the case amongst the electricians. They had accepted new technology and their representative was foremost in seeing this was done. 'Oh,' I said, 'and who's that?' Trelford replied, 'Len Dawson.'

Now, Len Dawson was the Communist Party's man in the EETPU. If he *was* acting as a representative, he should never have done so, because the Communists were banned from holding office in our union. Dawson was committed to opposing everything that we were doing. Not only that, he was convener of the hard Left Shoe Lane Progressive Group in Fleet Street: a group that wielded tremendous influence. Other key members included George Jerrom of the NGA, and Bill Freeman of SOGAT. Even worse was the fact that Dawson was a recruiting officer for the Bulgarian Secret Service, who are noted killers. At one stage, Dawson was rejected by a journalist on the Communist *Morning Star* after approaching him to become a Bulgarian agent. Dawson, who died on holiday in Bulgaria in 1990, may as well have pulled the trigger himself on the Bulgarian hit men's victims.

The fact that he was embraced so warmly by this little Editor, Trelford, greatly affected my thinking about whether the hard-nosed capitalist Tiny Rowland should have the *Observer*. Rowland went up several marks in my estimation. I thought, 'This haven, this incestuous relationship they have built up at the *Observer* needs the hand of Rowland upon it. They deserve him and they're going to get him.' Having looked at all the facts and listened to all the submissions, that minor incident with Mr Trelford over drinks late on Saturday night did influence my decision.

The union ambassador had done his job using his judgement, but putting his members' interests before any other – just as Edmund Burke advised.

10

Freedom and the future

Unions are not that much concerned with the future. They are, in the main, day-by-day organizations, reacting to events as they happen, or the initiatives of employers and governments. This is where my union has been different from the pack. We have tried to recognize what was happening in society and to adjust the EETPU to any changes. In all our arguments with the TUC, there were a number of underlying trends which we recognized and others ignored. There was a crying need for greater recognition of individual rights. If unions were to survive, they needed to be not only attractive to potential members, but also to have a relevance to employers. Bosses can, in innumerable ways, frustrate union organization and prevent it existing within a plant or industry. At the very least, if they are hostile to the union involved, it can mean recurring confrontation and trouble.

The continuing batches of Tory industrial relations legislation are born of a concern that there is a need to put right a fault that has developed within the trade union movement – that it no longer represents the individual member's interests. Thus, the Conservatives have been able to proclaim that they are the defenders, the proponents of union members' rights. Their slogan is that they have given the unions back to the members. There is too much truth in that assertion for unions to be comfortable in their outright opposition to the legislation.

The most revolutionary components of the new laws were the provisions to give the individual member the right to elect his leadership and General Secretary periodically by a secret postal ballot counted independently of the union. That is a change we found easy to accept because we have been operating the system for more than a quarter of a century! We could hardly join with the others in their hostility to government legislation which made this an obligation upon all.

Our differences with the government in trying to change the industrial relations scene occurred when they went further than this major principle. Our view was that once unions were in the hands of their members, then all further benefits for the public interest would follow. Any objective observer of the activities of the EETPU over the past twenty-five years would say that that was a well-founded assertion. Instead, the government started from the sound base which Norman Tebbit laid, then proceeded with increasingly esoteric changes that they forced upon the unions, changes which had nothing to do with making them more responsive to the members.

I did not hide my support for that early legislation. In fact, I told the TUC General Council that, before the end of the century, we would be erecting statues to Norman Tebbit for making them listen to the members and consequently saving the unions! For whatever was in the minds of those who drafted the legislation, the fact of the matter was that by making unions more representative they would become stronger, more influential in society. That's why we owed Norman Tebbit a debt. If the movement had gone on as it had in the Seventies, the trade unions as presently known would have come to an end with mass desertion from their ranks by people no longer able to stand their extreme political excesses.

One union procedure which has remained untouched by the law is the nomination process. This is unsatisfactory, and I would welcome changes in existing law to provide greater access to nomination for all members. In most unions, you get on a ballot paper for election to high office by way of nomination by a certain number of branches. The same argument which says leaders should not be elected from those who attend branch meetings must surely apply to nominations as well. Less than one per cent of union members attend branch meetings so, effectively, if those appearing on a ballot can only get there with the approval of that minority, then there is a restriction on the choice of members.

I would prefer a system, backed by a polishing of the legislation, in which a minimum number of supporting members, say 200, would be needed before a name can appear on the ballot paper. This may not seem many, but to win a nomination for General Secretary in my union, you have to get the support of twelve branches. In many branches, there would normally not be more than five members in attendance: just three dozen people can give candidates a leg up to the top union jobs. So, 200 is a pretty reasonable minimum requirement if we are to bring democracy to yet another inadequacy bordering on malpractice.

It is chiefly the Left-wing activists who attend branches, and the more Left you go, the more assiduous they are in their attendance. That has kept Moderate, more acceptable candidates off the ballot forms for years. But I am equally opposed to the use of the 'nomination squeeze' by Moderate activists, including those of my own union. Legislation needs to deal with this undemocratic restriction – the unions will not do it themselves.

However, I am at odds with other parts of the legislation, because it shows all too clearly that there are parts of the Conservative Party which are essentially anti-union. It's not simply that they want us to operate properly and within the law. They are anti-union even when we have shaped up and accepted all the democratic amendments that the legislation has put upon us. Even then, some Right-wing Tories are still hostile. They keep digging up the plant to see if the roots have taken, or whether it needs another law grafting on. With that attitude, the plant will not survive. Governments really have to accept that trade unions are here to stay. It may not be in the form we now see them, but there will always be representative organizations of people at work – not fighting employers, but providing a proper means of making agreements and doing deals in a collective way.

There's no way that the individual can match the power of modern corporations. It's only in an organized, not combative way, but in proper partnership that industry can be effective. So, whither the trade unions? Most would recognize that trade unions have a bad press. This is partly because of the prejudices of newspaper owners. It is partly because government is tempted to make trade unions the scapegoats for social unrest. This often has a great deal more to do with hiding from public resentment at their own economic policy failings. It is, however, often due to our own failings. Some trade-unionists blame it all on poor presentation of our affairs; if only we had better publications, zippier pamphlets, access to television advertising, everyone would suddenly value the trade union contribution to our national life. There might be something in that; however, we shoot ourselves in the foot too often.

First, our icons and language are firmly fixed in the 1920s. There are far too many televised trade union leaders who ask us all to 'take cognizance' of the following statements rather than 'pay attention' to them. All of our 'brother' this, 'comrade' that, means little to the new generation of well-paid, highly educated 'knowledge' workers in modern industry. It may help us to warm our hands at the after-glow of the fires of the last fifty years' struggle, but it alienates the modern member. More important, it alienates the potential modern member even more.

Equally, there are still too many trade union leaders who believe that trade union action and trade union campaigning on economic issues is a clever way to attack governments they do not like. To use trade union power in contradiction of the parliamentary system is rejected time and again by the British public. Revolutionary action against the law – however foolish in conception and partial in operation that law may be – is not the chosen path in Britain, and it brings discredit on those who seek to use industrial power for political ends.

Just because trade unions ought not to be a government-in-waiting or the political opposition to the current government is not to deny them a crucial role in the development of our modern economy.

The most obvious feature of our economic system is its complex of interdependent relationships. The British economy is increasingly just one base of the world economy; the growth of trans-national corporations from America and the Far East has wholly changed our capacity in Britain to be complete masters in our economic house. As we develop yet more international connections through the growing interdependence of the Western European economies and con-template the arrival of the East European economies in our system, this sense of being an important part of very large teams will become yet more dominant in our economic life.

Modern companies will then need to develop their internal democracy in order to achieve the motivated performance that alone will produce a response equal to the challenge of international change. Totalitarianism in the politics of Eastern Europe has pro-duced the social tensions that are expressed today in the demands for democratic freedom. The only way they can free their economies from the dead hand of bureaucracy is to free the people. The same general point applies at work in the West. Decision-making that ignores the feelings and the sheer knowledge of working people is doomed to eventual failure. This is where trade unions have an overriding role. They must be independent of the single company or single workplace if their organizing of opinion is to count for anything. Their structures can encourage democratic participation in a company's affairs. They have expertise in similar companies and totally different companies alike. This produces a consultant capacity that private industry would pay vast sums for from so-called 'consultants' whose direct experience of industry is minimal compared to modern trade unions.

Trade unions, then, ought to be welcomed by wise managements who know that simply being called 'manager' does not guarantee their understanding of economic forces, or entitle the job-holder to deference or obedience. In the democratic workplace, the manager welcomes advice, not ignores it; he will act on the advice, not sneer at the pretentiousness of the lower orders who offer it. Much of British industry – indeed many of Britain's institutions – pay too much attention to status and hierarchy and too little to skill and competence. Trade unions have a modern role on the side of the angels on behalf of us all.

This pace of change, exemplified by the growing interdependence of the world economy, does produce enormous insecurity. Cheerful commitment to change is impossible to achieve if men and women think that the reward for helping companies to modernize is a one-way ticket to the dole queue. Here again, trade unions have a distinct, independent role to play. My union has been struggling to make sense of insecurity at work in a world of change. We now provide part of the answer as a service to our members and as a service to the nation. Whether we have an apprenticeship or a university degree as our first qualification, it is intellectually foolish to expect it to last all our working lives in the modern era. New industry requires us to retrain in mid-career to accommodate the new demands of the modernization process. Training is perpetual and never-ending, and our union has spent several million pounds on our training facilities to help keep our members up to date with their vocational skills. The great trick with training is to convince everyone that even if their particular job function is no longer required they, as personalities, most certainly still are. In that way, retraining reassures every individual that change may be irritating without being catastrophic.

Perhaps this is the way forward for modern unions following the first faltering pioneering steps of the EETPU – perhaps it is not. Perhaps the class war is merely dormant and the traditionalists will have another day – I think not. What I am sure of is that the educated workforce of today will only add their talents to the trade unions' cause of justice at work if it is based on reason, not force; persuasion, not violence; partnership, not confrontation.

And the TUC? Well, the TUC is living in the past and is not fulfilling a vital function. Any organization which doesn't have a significant role might keep going for a while with a certain momentum, carrying out old rituals like having a Congress every year. Habit and ritual have a place in many union leaders' lives, but these echoes from the past do not help the TUC advance. It's just a nostalgic nod to an era of influence which never really existed.

I see a number of amalgamations taking place. We will probably merge with the AEU and maybe Roy Lynk's UDM. The cause of skilled and qualified people is not being best served by the fragmentation of the voices speaking on their behalf. Organizations like the EETPU, the AEU, UDM, MSF (the former ASTMS and TASS merged unions) plus others like the Electrical Power Engineers' Association could be far more effective if we spoke with a more certain and unified voice.

Not long after I took over as General Secretary, I had the idea for an organization which I dubbed Union 2000. Even now, I can still see it happening. The first expression of it was a meeting I had early in 1985 with Clive Jenkins of ASTMS and Gavin Laird, the AEU General Secretary, at the Goring Hotel in London's Victoria. Clive's response was very cautious. He asked, 'Couldn't we first develop some joint purchasing arrangements?' Not very diplomatically, I said, 'Clive, I think the problems of the future shape of the British trade union movement demand more of us than that we buy our pencils together.'

I reported to our 1985 Conference about my ideas:

ASTMS has recently decided to institute a postal balloting system for their Executive. It would seem to me that if we three could get together, the AUEW, ASTMS and EETPU, then the possibilities of a real advance in trade union organization would open for us. We could sit down and devise a new union, a union for the twenty-first century, a union representative of and designed to serve the interests of all its members, and we would truly have used our time and experience to good purpose.

Our union and the ASTMS would balance the AUEW in numbers and one of the three potential partners could not really afford the other two coming together without them. If we could get it right, there would be a real move forward in the interests of all

195

trade-unionists, but that, I stress, is a personal view, although you will understand if I seek to press it upon you or upon my colleagues both inside and outside our own union. We need to lift up our eyes from present difficulties and plan something better for those who come after us.

But whatever ideas that leaderships come up with, no matter how convinced general secretaries are of the desirability of changes, the last word, the decisive word is with the members. Any major proposals for joining up would have to be approved by the membership of the organizations concerned, and we would not have it any other way.

I was questioned by journalists. Clive immediately got into a tizzwazz. He wanted to qualify how he had been at this meeting. His own people were getting at him. He finally took a complaint to the Press Council over an article which appeared in *The Times*. He lost.

Clive couldn't do anything politically speaking. He was then too bound by the future merger with the Communist-dominated TASS union, led by Ken Gill. But the AEU and ourselves developed the idea and we staged a meeting at the Trades Union Congress with like-minded general secretaries. They included Gavin Laird, Albert Williams of the UCATT building workers, and Bill McCall of the Institution of Professional Civil Servants. We decided to return to our Executives to get the go-ahead.

Although my lads saw their futures inextricably linked to the EETPU, they immediately saw the attraction of this revolutionary idea: that the main unions handling skilled and qualified people should come together. My Executive backed it – I was never so proud of them. So did the AEU. UCATT divided and was unable to make a clear response. IPCS said, 'Not just now.' An opportunity was lost.

In 1987, we were pressed over our differences with the TUC, particularly our single-union, strike-free agreements. Our opponents tabled motions attacking them. We tabled a counter motion warning that, as long as we competed for membership, these problems would continue. The only way forward, we told the TUC, was for us all to virtually become one union. The TUC would be one big union and we would operate as departments within that great union. There would be common services for our members. Many small unions exist purely to send a delegate to the Congress. They don't provide any modern services like research or financial advice for their members. If we brought everybody together, the individual member could be assured of a much higher level of service. It would cut out an expensive tier, supply everyone with the same benefits and create a much more effective negotiating structure – instead of a dozen union officials going along to an employer and filling seats for the day while the group's Chairman and Secretary do all the work.

My opponents in other unions thought it was a ploy to avoid criticism levelled against us over single-union agreements. There was such an element of tactical planning in our proposal. But I challenged them to call my bluff and offered to start talking about my 'Grand Design'. Of course, they wouldn't pick up the gauntlet. Instead, they set up the Special Review Body that made our agreements their first target.

It seems at the time of writing that there is a good chance of the AEU and ourselves coming together. That probability is one I have worked hard to shape. In 1989, the joint efforts of the leaders of both unions were frustrated by a narrowly adverse vote (sixty-one to fifty-eight) of the AEU's National Committee. Notwithstanding that rebuff, the EETPU Conference decided to pursue discussions to secure closer working with other representative groups. In carrying out that decision, I reported to our '91 Conference that I had had a series of General Secretary to General Secretary discussions with Gavin Laird of the AEU. But, as I told him in a letter of 12 April:

> It would be foolish not to recognize that the high point we reached in 1989, prior to your National Committee, has receded within the EETPU. Certainly, where support for amalgamation was at its strongest – on the Executive Council – it has diminished.
>
> You may gather from the enclosed copy of our amalgamation debate (Jersey, May 1989) that we had considerable opposition and scepticism from delegates. You will understand that my words were sharper than usual – stimulated by the disappointment of your National Committee veto.
>
> It may be that one could say of 1989: 'There is a tide in the affairs of men'. We had built between us an expectation with our members and with industry, and we were perceived to have been knocked back. I think we both agree that it is more difficult now in 1991. Time has changed components in the scene.
>
> My retirement, though not imminent, does diminish my influence. A new EETPU General Secretary could hardly see as his first duty the securing of amalgamation.

I told our delegates:

Despite that different situation we now face, we both feel that a wider discussion could be of advantage to both our unions. Those discussions will begin in July.

I know, colleagues, the apprehensions and, indeed, in some cases, hostility that a number of you feel about amalgamation. Rest assured that it is your vote and that of your fellow members that will decide the matter. That is – if the Executive can agree on a proposal to put to you. I will do all I can to secure such an agreed proposal.

Colleagues, when you only have limited time left to influence events, it is not exactly like waiting to be hanged, but it does concentrate the mind wonderfully. One's words may be more faltering, but at least a conference like this will know that the speaker has no personal axe to grind – no personal interest to serve. To my colleagues and officials who have linked their careers – their lives – to this union – and indeed to AEU officials – I say fear not an amalgamation.

Competent and experienced officers will have a greater role to play – a larger canvas to paint upon – than is available in our separate unions. Your abilities will bring you to the fore.

Even more important – we could together attract many other skilled and qualified elements in society. Fragmentation would be behind us and together we would be a powerful influence and voice for skill, responsibility and reason.

I urge Conference to see this matter of amalgamation, not in the light of the difficulties you have experienced with the AEU, still less by the prejudice of little EETPU-ers. Rather, I ask you to consider the world of twenty and thirty years' time – the world of our children and grandchildren.

Can one really believe that the precisely defined roles of the craftsmen of today will survive? They are already blurring – instruments are absorbed into electrical; plumbing into mechanical – the future is already taking shape and, more threateningly, operation and production workers intrude into maintenance.

To have an influence on that future we need – those that come after us need – an effective union to serve skilled and qualified people. I will do all I can in my time left to secure such an organization.

Soon after our Conference, a small working party from both unions met at our historic Esher college. We gathered around a table upon which the Treaty of Versailles had been drafted. In opening, I told my colleagues that we hardly had a less difficult task than the author of that treaty!

It was a task that many others had failed to complete – reaching right back to those who began our union in 1889, through names forgotten in the between-war years and up through the post-war years and the efforts of such notables as Lord Carron, Sir Leslie Cannon, Lord Chapple and Lord Scanlon. Could we succeed where they had all failed? I thought we could. It might seem that our non-TUC status made it more difficult, but there were other more positive circumstances pertaining for us.

The hard Left, hostile to both leaderships, were at an all-time low as a blocking force. Their gods in Russia and Eastern Europe had tumbled – their temples were in ruins, their confidence in tatters. The political struggle was not daunting. A little acidly, I said we only had the easy job of adjusting individual and collective needs, ambitions and expectations. I would not say it was the last chance we had of coming together, but if we failed now, then it would be some time before we could consider amalgamation again. I urged that we did not address ourselves to every matter of detail and difference because that only maximized the constituency of opposition, but rather sought a decision from the members to amalgamate and to sort out problems when we had come together.

We made great progress. By September 1991, the presidents and general secretaries were able to write to members of both unions as follows:

> You will probably have seen press reports about our amalgamation discussions. However, we want to ensure that you, the members, are kept as well informed and up to date as possible.
>
> Although we have had a number of discussions in the past, these current talks have been the most positive ever.
>
> We believe that a combined union with over one million members, £100-million worth of assets and 30,000 shop stewards would be able to deliver a service to the members unmatched in the trade union movement. It would also be a major force in industry and society, not only in this country, but also in the developing European scene. In a rapidly changing world, we would be able to ensure that the needs and wishes of all our members are properly met.

The programme towards amalgamation will be as follows:

1 Consultation with members, committees and full-time officials.

2 Initial ballot to create the new union.

3 A ballot within one year on affiliation to the TUC.

4 A ballot within four years to adopt a final Rule Book.

The date of the first ballot has yet to be determined, given the need for the fullest prior consultation.

As you will understand, we still have some way to go on detail and we will keep you informed. Then YOU, the members, will have the final say.

However, we regard this as the most exciting development in the history of our two organizations and a major advance for our joint membership.

I feel now that the momentum towards merger is irresistible and I am pleased to have played a major part in securing it. I feel certain, too, that the UDM, who quite rightly consider themselves as skilled men, will not be attracted to following Arthur Scargill's NUM into the TGWU. This will be a political move if it ever happens – if the TGWU can swallow Arthur Scargill sideways. It may be that elements of the NUM itself, because of their antipathy to going into an unskilled union, will be more attracted by our grouping of skilled and qualified people. We would welcome them with open arms to join us along with the UDM, the engineers and our growing number of skilled construction workers.

My grand design is coming about, albeit belatedly and slowly. It will lead to a skilled professional union attractive to a number of other small groups. I cannot see organizations like the Electrical Power Engineers' Association standing outside such a gathering. Each addition to it will increase the attraction to others. So I am confident of a future which will have that effective voice for skill and responsibility in society. It is certain to have its effect on other groupings, particularly unskilled and service unions like the GMB, the TGWU, plus public service unions like NUPE and NALGO who are already talking.

I can see there will be maybe one, but probably two or three unions emerging from that sort of pressure. By the end of the century, the seventy-odd unions operating at present could be concentrated into four or five unions.

The big question mark then is whither the TUC? Many see the need for some liaison, but it would be a much-slimmed-down body, almost along the lines of an employers' confederation. It will certainly not have the power, influence and disciplinary procedures it has wielded in the past. I anticipate a very loose, thin grouping rather than a full-blown TUC. Not that I wish the TUC ill, even though it did kick us out. It has outlived its purpose, if it ever had one. It was of some use when unions were unable to speak on their own behalf, and felt the need to group together and speak with a powerful voice for the whole movement and with a facility to discipline affiliates.

Unions themselves will become so large and potentially powerful that they will not need the TUC and will certainly not accept discipline from competitors. Even so, these new super-unions – virtually mini-TUCs in their own right – must be wary of being distant from the ordinary members' needs, views and desires. In their own interests, the union giants of the twenty-first century must allow devolvement so that, as with many of our single-union agreements, practically the whole of the negotiating action, the interface between union and employer, takes place at the local factory. Effective members' boards or works councils – elected by the shopfloor regardless of whether they are trade-unionists (though that is what I prefer) – meet the manager and his team. They discuss the problems, not just of how much money they are going to get, but the whole running of the plant.

The national union acts as a long-stop in case any problems cannot be settled there. It can be called in by the workers for information and research, training and education, and to provide access for their representatives to conferences in order to give local members the best possible representation in society. The effect is to give real people at the grassroots a chance to grab hold of their futures and fashion the way their jobs and their workplace develops. This is far more preferable than district and national committees saying, 'Let's have an overtime ban, or a work-to-rule. Let's go on strike.' That's all for the birds. That's all in the past.

The way forward is a members' union in action. It will have more resources and be more efficient in backing up the front-line representatives. That's the way I see the trade union movement developing. And I can't see anything stopping it.

Matters like minimum conditions and hours of work are increasingly going to be the subject of trans-national negotiations. The multinationals want worldwide deals to ensure efficiency, so we will

201

have to find union partners in France, Germany, America and Japan. Some have already begun this process. Indeed, a factor which has prompted me to want an early merger with the AEU is the knowledge that we could develop a much better relationship with Germany's IG Metall, Europe's most powerful union. This is Germany's single manufacturing union. It was formed on British advice in 1947. We planned the German trade union movement rather than have it grow haphazardly like ours. Consequently, they have a rational trade union structure. IG Metall is a very rich and powerful group which the employers respect.

A merged AEU and EETPU attracting all sorts of other skilled groups could partner IG Metall. Such a partnership would have a powerful attraction to other European unions. That would provide the sort of negotiating set-up which employers will need to make deals in Europe's new companies and the existing multinational firms operating within the European Community.

I am sure that the way the Labour Party has developed since the last general election, and certainly since Neil Kinnock became Leader, gives it the best chance of surviving and being an alternative government. If Labour had continued along the élitist path and a small minority of political know-alls had continued to determine the direction and leadership of the Party, it would have melted away without support. It was clear that in the elections of 1979 and 1983, and to a lesser extent in 1987, Labour suffered from unrepresentative policies which ordinary voters rejected. They were dear to the hearts of those who knew, those who were informed and didn't read the *Sun* and the *Mirror*, but kept to the safety of the minority *New Statesman* and *Tribune*. Labour suffered for that.

Kinnock has led the Party away to a more central position, which ordinary people can identify with. He is probably handicapped by the experience people had in those years. Some can't quite yet believe that Labour has changed. They concede that they have put on different clothes, but they're not yet convinced the person within them is different from the one they rejected in the past. A body of experience and trust has to develop. The bad, unrepresentative years of Labour linger on in people's minds and have not yet disappeared. That's the big hurdle Kinnock and the Labour Party have to get over before they secure a majority amongst the wider electorate.

It's the general view that the British people are not very political and that they don't trust any party too long. I think there is some truth in this. Maybe it wasn't so much that Mrs Thatcher won in 1987 as Labour lost. Certainly, people would not trust Labour on defence in 1987. The only alternative was to vote for Maggie and the Conservatives, whom they disliked, but less than Labour's unilateralism.

If the economy continued in a downward slide and failed to revive in the way John Major hopes, then that negative attitude of the British voter could work in Kinnock's favour. It's doubtful the result would enable him to form a majority government, but he may share power with Paddy Ashdown and the Liberal Democrats. If the economy perks up, Major will lead the Tories to yet another victory.

Will Kinnock be given the push if he fails to win? It would be most unfair if having achieved all he has – more than any other single person could have done in the Labour Party – Kinnock does not continue as Leader. I know there are a lot of voices in the Party saying Neil should move over for the very formidable figure of John Smith, the Shadow Chancellor. I have great regard for John, and he would certainly make an excellent Labour Leader. Politics is cruel and unfair, so it may well be Kinnock himself may not want to continue.

Underneath the hard shell I have built up, I do feel for individuals and, personally, I would not like to see Kinnock being removed unless Labour had a disaster by doing worse than in 1987, then, no matter what, he would have to go. But if he made, as I think he will, advances short of an overall victory, I think it would be unfair to sack him. However, politics is not a fair game, and he may have to go anyway. I am certain that if John Smith was Leader, the following election would see a Labour victory. It would be a victory based on the Tories' failure to control the economy.

The exposure to the single European market is both an opportunity and a danger. In the immediate future, it will express itself more in terms of the danger. I don't think British industry is geared to take those opportunities. We have fallen behind on training so much that we have little chance of competing with the Germans. They have twice as many people being trained as us. Throughout Germany's industrial structure, there are double the number of skilled people – trained to at least craft apprenticeship level. Against our main competitors like Germany, Japan and the United States, plant for plant and product for product, we can't compete. When you look at it objectively, it isn't that British workers are innately idle. It's because they haven't had the opportunities to become skilled.

We usually have too many people involved in a process which, again, is expensive. If you have more people, you cannot pay them high wages. They are not encouraged to move on to skills by their own efforts. Britain is handicapped because it does not have a high enough immediate level of skill and productivity at the sharp end. Inevitably, this results in higher prices and poorer quality. If you fail on quality, you don't sell. So, a series of deficiencies in British industry act as a vicious circle conspiring against success. That is why the new European market contains so many man-traps for us.

It will be made even worse if Labour goes ahead with its plans for a National Minimum Wage. It sounds a very nice, cosy liberal move to help those poor people who are not getting £3.40 an hour. But life isn't about picking up sweets and saying, 'This is a nice one. I'll have that.' It's much harder than that, particularly when you have competitors out there trying to take away what business you have left.

We have to address ourselves to what will make us a more effective and wealthier country. That way, we can start dealing with some of the problems that exist in our society, including poverty and deprivation. The Minimum Wage, by raising the level of people who earn below £3.40 an hour, means that in some industries they would actually tread very closely on the existing skilled wage. For instance, in an industry which we are currently making our concern – building and construction – the skilled rate is little more than £3.40. If you bring up the rate of the newest entrant to within a few pence of the skilled man, that's going to cause an explosion. It would engender inflationary claims and make our products uncompetitive. More importantly, it certainly wouldn't encourage any of those unskilled people to acquire skills and responsibility. That, in turn, is harmful to the whole performance of our country. Put that way, nobody can disagree. But offered the simple question, 'Are you for a minimum wage?', everybody is for something nice.

We cannot run the British economy like a waiting room at the Department of Social Security – expecting handouts we have not earned. Nobody owes Britain, or anybody operating within Britain, anything at all. Out there in the real competitive world you have to win by your own efforts, and if you're not doing that, you have to identify your deficiencies and bring them up to scratch. It means increasing skills, less employees at some factories, lower wages at others. The choices about how jolly it would be in an ideal world to pay ourselves more and work less efficiently are not available to us.

It has taken me a lifetime to come to these views, but I cannot see any other opinions being expressed within the trade union movement which are either tenable or honest.

Admittedly, it does make it hard for me and my union colleagues to persuade workers to take less when they see the massive salary increases awarded to senior managers following on from the privatization of electricity and other industries, but I do not rush to condemn these rises. In fact, measured against their contemporaries in private industry, their pay was low. In principle, I would accept that there had to be some upward movement. However, I find it politically inept that it should have been done in such great jumps, particularly at a time when the economy was in difficulty and restraint was the watchword for the workers. It could be argued that a considerable part of the bosses' pay windfall will come back to the general coffers through taxation. But the underlying effect will be to feed the 'them and us' attitude which militates against a proper togetherness, a partnership to deal with problems in industry.

If trade unions have any mission in the next century, it will be to establish the best deal for all, to put the collective, the country's interest first, not just their own factory or section. It should become a factor in their members' minds when decisions are made. Unions can have that unifying, indeed, moderating effect and should be the voice of the member overall, so they can bring some influence to bear when the scales need to be evened up.

They will have to do it without me. I will have thrown away my rule books, my conference agendas and handed over to my successor, the EETPU President, Paul Gallagher. It was not an easy decision to go early. But the one thing I will take into my retirement is the comradeship of the EETPU – and by that I mean the friendship of every single one of the members and officials I have been proud to serve. Even though I have worked for the members with all my ability and I have been their man, they haven't agreed with me every time. But they know I have done my best. I've had a very fulfilling career with the union. It would be easy to get into my sixties, be centre stage and think I am indispensable, that things would be far worse without me.

I think Frank Chapple had second thoughts about going a year or two early, and for a while after his retirement, he lingered on, popping back to the office at Bromley, somehow seeking a role which was no longer there. My phone would ring with the message, 'Mr Chapple is on his way up.'

No matter how hectic the situation, I would see him. We were under tremendous pressure over the miners' dispute. It was all coming to our door, and I was having to make appearances here, there and everywhere to explain our view. I would be sitting in my shirtsleeves, but would immediately put on my coat, sit down, pick up the *Financial Times* and say, 'Oh, hello, Frank. Come and sit down.' We'd have a chat and I would resume the turmoil when he'd gone.

I wasn't ever going to ask, 'Frank, what should I do?' This wasn't out of disrespect to him, but I knew that with the power of his personality and the presence he had in the union I would never develop my own influence if I leaned on him and sought his counsel. That may have appeared very hard to him as the prospect of it now appears very hard to me, but there is no other way of doing it. There has to be a clean cut and the new lad has to be thrown in to the deep end.

I used to tease my colleagues about when I might go by saying that my hero was George Meany, head of the United States TUC, the American Federation of Labor and Congress of Industrial Organizations. George was a former plumber, who died in bed at eighty-four, still in the job. My people became worried that I was serious about a Meany rerun. When all the valves are going at full stretch, you feel great and wonder if you should stay. But I have seen colleagues, who seem to be fitter and more effective than me suddenly go. My dear colleague and friend, Fred Franks, the electricity supply national officer, died suddenly from illness caused through exposure to asbestos many years ago. It was a very daunting experience to see such a fine strapping man die like that. Fred's death was a sad warning to us all of our mortality, and helped push me into accepting I had done enough.

This trade union business takes its toll, not just on those of us who have chosen the life – we can have no proper complaint – but on families. I have made only passing references in these pages to my own – indeed, I have done my best throughout the years to protect their privacy. But I unreservedly acknowledge that without that family area – that haven – of calm and love in my life I would never have made it through these difficult years. Brenda, my wife for thirty-eight years, has been both my closest support and when necessary a candid friend. Her judgement about people is better than mine. Our two fine sons, Ivan and Shaun, are now well advanced in their careers, married to Linda and Carol. Life has been more than good to me for Ivan and Linda have three sons. Brenda and I share the joy of all grandparents in Darren Craig – aged two and a half years – and his twin brothers of seven months, Duncan Craig and Ryan Craig. I think I owe to them all a little more time, a little more of myself, than I was able to give in earlier years.

In any case, I thought it best to go when people were saying, 'What's he going for?' rather than 'When's the old bastard leaving?' I think I've managed to get it right.

But I'm not going to be idle and retire to my allotment. I shall carry out what tasks society feels I am capable of doing. I have recently been made a member of the Lord Chancellor's Advisory Committee for Legal Education and Conduct. It's been a fascinating experience for me in a quite different world, but one which has always had my interest. In my early days in Canada, that would probably have been my career choice had I finished my education there.

I have regarded the legal profession with some awe and respect. Whenever we have been in difficulties and ended up in the High Court with some external challenge or interpretation of rules, I have never ceased to be amazed at the way judges can use their incisive minds to unravel complex rule books which have taken a hundred years to tangle up.

My successor, Paul Gallagher, has been a very able and hard-working President. My only advice to him is keep cool, listen to everyone, but make your own decisions and know when to take a rest. I'm due a longer one.

I was lucky to inherit a union in a good financial state. I leave it even richer. If valued with its investments and its property, the EETPU is worth more than £50 million. We have an impressive headquarters, a training school at Cudham in Kent, a college at Esher, plus our Buxted country estate in Sussex where members and private groups can enjoy a life of luxury at a realistic price.

For those first few pioneers who gathered in 1889 and had to have a whip-round to buy a minute book, the union has come a long way. Apart from the cul-de-sac of the Communist years, we have all added to the reputation and stability of the union.

The most distinctive thing about the years I have been General Secretary is that we developed what some would say were antagonistic, but I say were different, positions to the rest of the trade union movement. In Frank Chapple's day, it never got to the point of really hurting and separation from the trade union tribe. Harsh words were exchanged when Frank spoke up on behalf of reason at the Isle of Grain, but, as I have indicated earlier, it never reached breaking point. The issue was subjected to a classic TUC fudge, served up with a coating of sugary compromise.

I have been sharper in standing by those positions of principle, which in the end caused our unprecedented expulsion for defending the rights and choices of individual members. We stood for their right to join a union of their choice and make the deals they want with their workmates, and employers. The law is now catching up with us and members of other unions will soon enjoy the same freedoms. If we had backed off, the cause of individual freedom would have been dented.

Through those years we have made our stand on the international stage. We have been foremost in championing Polish Solidarity and for standing up for the dissidents in the Soviet Union. If we hadn't, by our actions and the stands we took in the British trade union movement, stood by our principles, then we would have diminished our voice on the international scene. You can't be in favour of Soviet workers belonging to independent unions free of external influences and, at the same time, give in to unrepresentative leaderships in other unions at home. That simply won't wash with the members or the voting public.

I had to stand my ground on those long-held beliefs at a time when it meant putting up or shutting up. And I would not shut up. I may not have been popular with everyone, but I was the members' choice and the members' voice. That was my big comfort all through the difficult times – that I immediately got overwhelming support by any measure of opinion wider than the activists of the trade union movement gathered at the Congress.

I was both humble and proud to be re-elected as General Secretary in 1987 and to receive the highest vote ever accorded a trade union leader or candidate for political office in Great Britain.

I have lost count of the number of people who have told me after meetings and conferences, 'I'm glad you said that. You said what I wanted to say.' But they never say it themselves. Nor do they support you openly. In this movement, as in every other walk of life, there need to be some who will take on the role of gladiator; to fight on behalf of people who will not or cannot fight for themselves. I have been proud to be a warrior on their behalf. What is even better, I enjoyed it.

Index

209